THE GILT EDGE OF AMBITION

Bird's-eye view of Sacramento, looking northeast from the Sacramento River. Late nineteenth century.

The Gilt Edge of Ambition

A Sportsman's Gamble for Power and Baseball

L. Jonsson

2026
Solvent Press
Santa Monica, California

Published by Solvent Press, Santa Monica, California

Library of Congress Control Number: 2026905203

ISBN: 979-8-9948426-1-4 (paperback)

giltedgeofambition.com
contact: info@giltedgeofambition.com

First Edition, 2026

10 9 8 7 6 5 4 3 2 1

Printed in the United States of America

IN LOVING MEMORY OF

Carol Ann Kripp Olson

1926 – 2020

My grandmother
and the granddaughter of Ed Kripp

ACKNOWLEDGMENTS

My deepest thanks go to my late grandmother Carol, my late Aunt Nancy, and my mother Jan, who made sure I knew who Ed Kripp was. Because of them, this story was not lost.

To my sister, Michele, for carrying the sometimes complicated Kripp legacy with me.

To Roberta Kripp Prazak for her stewardship with the city and for helping to preserve Ed Kripp's memory.

To Michael VanDuyn, who listened to countless drafts and offered ideas and insight. Thank you for your genuine interest in who Ed Kripp was and for matching my enthusiasm as the history unfolded.

To Alan O'Connor, author of *Gold on the Diamond*, for his careful review of the manuscript, for helping keep Ed Kripp's name alive in Sacramento's baseball history, and for generously providing many images for this book.

To R. E. Graswich, journalist, author, and historian of Sacramento, for reading an early manuscript and offering insight that sharpened both the narrative and its questions.

To Pär Sånglöf, for his boundless creative ideas.

Finally, to my late father, Bengt Stellan Jönsson. This project reflects the habits he instilled—curiosity, self-reliance, and a willingness to step into unfamiliar territory and figure things out along the way. Those lessons helped me more than he ever knew.

FOREWORD

By Alan O'Connor

Author of *Gold on the Diamond*

I'VE LONG BEEN a student of the history of baseball in Sacramento with an emphasis on professional baseball from 1886 through 1976. In my research I encountered Ed Kripp when he was with the 1890s Gilt Edge ball club and when he opened Buffalo Park in the 1910s. However, I knew next to nothing about his history before the Gilt Edge, between the time of the Gilt Edge and Buffalo Park and between 1920 and his death in 1942. Lisa Jonsson does a terrific job of filling those gaps and recreating Kripp's entire history.

Ed Kripp emerged during the formative period of baseball in California. The Gilt Edge club competed at a time when the structure of professional baseball in California remained fluid. Players and club officials often occupied overlapping roles, and the distinction between athlete, promoter, and businessman was not always clear. Teams were sustained not only by talent on the field but by the ability to secure grounds, attract spectators, and generate financial backing. Baseball was both sport and enterprise, and its fortunes reflected the broader energy and volatility of turn-of-the-century California. This book adds greatly to our knowledge of Gilt Edge baseball, Buffalo Park and Sacramento history.

Kripp was among those figures whose activities extended beyond the diamond. He operated within a public sphere where sport, commerce, and reputation were closely intertwined. Contemporary accounts indicate that his life included episodes of conflict, legal difficulty, and association with Sacramento's more turbulent elements. Disputes, confrontations, and business controversies formed part of his public record. Such circumstances were not uncommon in an era when municipal regulation was limited and civic development often advanced through informal networks of influence. Kripp was not a simple or untroubled figure. However, his story is very compelling.

In *The Gilt Edge of Ambition*, Lisa Jonsson returns to contemporary newspapers and archival materials to reconstruct both the man and his times. By grounding her narrative in primary sources, she situates Kripp within the broader framework of Sacramento's early baseball development and the city's social landscape. Her careful research provides readers with a fuller understanding of how individual ambition, public reputation, and the growth of organized sport intersected.

This book adds a thoughtful and well-documented chapter to the story of Sacramento and its enduring connection to the national game.

—Alan O'Connor

TABLE OF CONTENTS

INTRODUCTION

WHEN MY GRANDMOTHER Carol was a little girl, she traveled with her parents on the *Delta Queen* steamboat overnight from San Francisco to Sacramento to visit her grandfather, Ed. These visits were treasured moments: the whistle at departure, the way he made her feel important when he turned his attention toward her, the sense of visiting someone remarkable. Carol carried those memories her entire life and passed them down to me. But when I began researching his life, the man in those stories did not quite match the newspaper articles.

I have walked Kripp's geographic footprint. I was raised in the San Francisco Bay Area where he spent much of his time, and I later lived in Sacramento, the city he helped transform. I have stood at his grave in the Sacramento City Cemetery, directly across from the ground where his ballpark once was. I have watched the Sacramento River Cats play at Sutter Health Park, a direct lineage of the team he built more than a century ago.

And long before I understood any of this history, I learned to play piano on the baby grand that once stood inside his Dreamland Dance Hall. These encounters made his world tangible; this was no longer just a story preserved in old newspapers.

Ed Kripp was a builder. He led the Sacramento Gilt Edge baseball club to four consecutive championships, a first in California history. He built Buffalo Park in 1910 on a former garbage dump and opened Dreamland Dance Hall in 1923.

His path, however, was unconventional. He moved easily between respectability and the city's underworld, and the newspapers of his era could not agree on who he was.

What emerges from archival records and family stories is a man who understood something essential about Sacramento. The city needed gathering places, spectacle, and moments when people from every walk of life could come together and feel proud of where they lived. Kripp gave them that—and in doing so helped shape a shared civic identity.

What interested me most as the research deepened was not just what Kripp did, but the systems that made his success possible—and later made it untenable.

This book is not just the story of Ed Kripp. It is about how power actually worked in early California—not in speeches or statutes, but in saloons, ballparks, courtrooms, and boardrooms. Through his life, the book traces how that authority was built, contested, and ultimately formalized in a city still inventing itself, revealing how modern professional sports and civic power took shape on the West Coast long before the major leagues arrived.

My grandmother's stories began this journey. The newspapers complicated them. The years of research reconciled them. From that, Ed's story emerged.

Now, I'm honored to tell it.

PROLOGUE

The Wager

ED KRIPP did not look like a man building a ballpark. By the winter of 1909, his name appeared more often in police ledgers than on the sports pages. He ran illegal gambling rooms. He took bets on horse races relayed by wire from Emeryville. He operated at the edge of legality and sometimes beyond it. Negotiation was not his only instrument; violence, at times, enforced his order.

Respectable Sacramento knew who he was—and pretended not to. But baseball knew him too.

A decade earlier, before he ever poured concrete or commissioned grandstands, Kripp had already reshaped professional baseball in California. His Gilt Edge club of the late 1890s dominated the state, winning consecutive championships no other club had matched. They traveled well, played hard, and drew crowds wherever they went. Kripp understood baseball not as a pastime but as an enterprise—one that required discipline, spectacle, and capital.

At the turn of the twentieth century, baseball on the West Coast mirrored the cities that hosted it—improvised, temporary, easily undone. Teams rented land they did not own. Parks rose and vanished with little notice. Championships brought pride but not stability. When things failed, owners blamed markets, leagues blamed cities, and cities blamed one another. Kripp was among the few who recognized this not as a seasonal problem but a structural one. He helped organize and incorporate the California League, formalizing schedules, rules, and territorial agreements in an era when most West Coast baseball still ran on handshake deals.

The league itself was short-lived, but the model endured. It established precedents—central oversight, enforceable commitments, coordinated competition—that would later underpin the Pacific Coast League and, eventually, the West's integration into major-league baseball.

That system required capital. And that capital came from places polite society preferred not to examine too closely.

So when Sacramento began talking about professional baseball played in a permanent park—rather than borrowed fields and collapsing grandstands—it was not a banker or a reformer who stepped forward. It was Ed Kripp.

He chose a garbage dump.

Just outside the city limits, at Eleventh and Y Streets, the land sagged under years of refuse. Part wetland, part dumping ground, it was a place where water pooled and rot lingered even in winter. No one imagined a future there. No one thought of baseball.

No one except Kripp.

Standing in the cold mud, he saw something else: control. Space. Permanence. A site cheap because it was foul, unwanted because it was wet—and crucially, just beyond the city's regulatory reach. Where others saw waste, Kripp saw a foundation. Where the city had thrown things away, he would build something that demanded recognition.

Buffalo Park would rise from that ground.

And with it, Kripp would attempt something harder than winning championships: to convert power built at the margins, through gambling rooms and tolerated illegality, into something that would endure. Something visible. Something the city could not easily dismiss.

Buffalo Park was only part of the wager.

What Kripp was testing went beyond sport. He was asking whether California, still improvising its cities and institutions, was willing to accept lasting authority from a man it had long tolerated but never fully embraced.

Once that possibility took hold, it could not be unseen.

To understand how a gambler came to build a ballpark—and why Sacramento accepted it—we have to go back to where Kripp's ambition first took shape.

PART ONE

THE MAKING OF A MAGNATE

1861–1900

Downtown Sacramento, 1890.
Photograph by Frank Appleton. Sacramento Public Library.

China Slough, near historic Chinese quarter, 1878.
Central Pacific Railroad photograph.

Sacramento flood, 1862, K Street.
Sacramento Public Library, Sacramento Room.

Washington Hotel, Washington Township.
Photograph by Ralph H. Shaw. Center for Sacramento History.

CHAPTER 1

The Turnstile

1861–1894

SACRAMENTO had not yet decided what it wanted to be. It was California's capital, the seat of law and order, where politicians in frock coats debated the future of the West. But, beneath the raised streets and the veneer of Victorian respectability, the city's heart still beat to the rhythm of the mining camp it had been just a decade before.

The state capital sat on dangerous ground. The Sacramento River moved wide through the valley, slow and deceptive. For decades it threatened to swallow the city. The worst came in the winter of 1861–1862, when Sacramento nearly disappeared underwater.

Sacramentans made a desperate choice: they would not abandon their city. Instead, they would rebuild it higher. The project was uneven and expensive. In the commercial core, streets were filled and raised, and some buildings were jacked upward to meet the new grade. Others were not. Wooden sidewalks were nailed above the packed earth, bridging the gaps.

Beneath those raised boards, original floors, entrances, and brick façades lay entombed in shadow. When boots crossed the sidewalks, the sound traveled downward, echoing faintly against the buried walls. The city had risen, but it had not erased what lay beneath.[1]

Beyond that elevated district, the city remained at its original, flood-prone elevation. Here, residents lifted their sidewalks to escape the muck, while the roadbeds themselves remained unchanged, turning to canals of mud each winter.[2]

Ninety miles away, San Francisco was rising under different terms—more capitalized, more visible, already learning how to turn spectacle into credibility.

Sacramento worked in the opposite direction. It was governed by offices, not markets; by committees, not crowds. The city looked orderly, but its arrangements remained provisional. Vice was tolerated, but expected to remain discreet—contained in back rooms or shifted across jurisdictional lines. The city was comfortable with understandings it could quietly undo and uneasy with anything that made informal power permanent. It did not reward display. It rewarded control. In practice, the law functioned less as a barrier than as a turnstile—regulating movement rather than stopping it outright.

The capital was still young, still uncertain of what it would become—and in that uncertainty, a clever man could find opportunity.

Into this world of quiet arrangements, Edward Lukens Kripp, the fourth of six children, was born on April 15, 1869.[3] He was one of only three children who survived childhood: his older brother Fred Conrad and his younger brother Newton.[4] In the Kripp household, two very different versions of the American Dream sat at the dinner table.

Ed's father, Frederick Kripp, born in Bavaria and raised in the United States, belonged to an immigrant generation that trusted labor more than speculation. In Sacramento, he lived by his hands—first as a barber, later as a rancher. What Frederick modeled was endurance: show up and work steadily, and accept what was allowed to you.[5]

Ed's mother, Margaret Ann Kripp, née Conrad, married Frederick Kripp in 1861 and represented Sacramento's more respectable lineage. Her father, Samuel Conrad, a Pennsylvania carpenter and devout Mormon, crossed west in 1849 with his wife, Mary Rinker Lukens Conrad, and their growing family as part of an eighty-wagon train. They raised ten children, many born in different states along the way, before settling in Washington Township across the Sacramento River.[6]

In 1850, Conrad built the Eagle Hotel at Eighth and J Streets, then turned to farming and landholding as Sacramento stabilized. The Conrads were builders and stayers—people who accumulated respectability through continuity, ownership, and restraint. Their authority rested on being known, visible, and acceptable.[7]

But there was a volatility in the Kripp blood, a restless streak that seemed to skip the father and settle with concentrated force in the sons. Ed would spend the next years of his life moving through vice, not as a bystander but as someone determined to impose order on what he saw others handle haphazardly.

By the time Ed came of age, the city had become a narrow band of development between the river and orchards. Horse-drawn streetcars ran down J and K Streets. Storefronts lined the elevated sidewalks. In summer, dust hung over the roadbeds; in winter, the river pressed against the levees.

Gas lamps hissed above the roads, their mantles throwing a steady amber glow that pooled at intersections and thinned between them. Electric lines were being strung across a city still built for gas. Gas and electricity burned side by side.[8]

J Street was the city's center of gravity. By day it held cigar shops, clothiers, restaurants, and theaters. By night, behind partitioned doors, card rooms and small gambling parlors operated quietly, and saloons stayed open long after respectable businesses closed. Newspapers spoke of civic progress, but everyone knew where the back rooms were.

Nearby, Japanese, Mexican, and African American communities clustered along the river and the industrial margins of the city, supplying the labor that kept its commerce, railroads, and river traffic moving.[9]

Just south of Sacramento's commercial spine lay I Street and the city's Chinese quarter, known locally as Yee Fow—the "Second City." It was a compact district of shops, boardinghouses, and theaters pressed along the slough, edged by warehouses and rail spurs.

Men worked as cooks, fishermen, and laborers, often sleeping above their shops or in narrow rear rooms; many also labored on the railroad lines radiating from Sacramento.[10] Women were fewer but also worked as cooks, seamstresses, and caretakers. Some were drawn into sex work through debt and coercion, while city officials often treated Chinese women as presumptive prostitutes, even when evidence suggested otherwise.[11]

Newspapers and police referred to the men who guarded gambling houses and collected debts as "highbinders." The word suggested menace; the reality was more structured. Municipal statutes existed, but order in Yee Fow was maintained largely through economic ties and—when necessary—intimidation.[12]

Elsewhere in Sacramento, the law asserted itself publicly. In Yee Fow, it arrived as negotiation. By the time Kripp reached adulthood, Yee Fow was not an abstraction but a place he would encounter repeatedly—and soon enough in an official capacity.

It is one of the great ironies of Ed Kripp's life that his education in vice began on the city payroll. In September 1890, the City Trustees appointed the twenty-one-year-old Ed as a deputy constable. His mandate was specific and almost comically ambitious: he was to patrol the city during the State Fair and "prevent all gambling within the limits of Sacramento city."[13]

For a young man with sharp eyes, it was an ideal assignment—though not for the reasons the Trustees intended. Charged with stopping the games, Kripp spent his days embedded in them, watching how faro banks rotated dealers to avoid patterns, how lookouts signaled the approach of police, how money that should have flowed to the city treasury instead moved quietly upward through the ranks of the force. He learned the mechanics of concealment, the price structure of silence.

Those who carried the statutes were rarely the ones who controlled the gate. Police officers, city trustees, ward politicians, judges, and business owners all shared quiet discretion over when it spun and when it locked. The currency that moved it was not singular. Sometimes it was cash passed hand to hand. Sometimes it was tolerance—an understanding that certain doors would remain unexamined so long as disorder stayed contained. Often it was silence: names not spoken, reports not filed, and questions not asked. Enforcement did not fail in Sacramento; it adjusted. It calibrated itself, expanding or contracting depending on who was watching.[14]

Kripp also discovered a capacity for physical dominance. He was not a large man. What he possessed instead was speed and certainty, a violence that did not hesitate once it began. As constable, his arrests carried a kind of athleticism—quick pursuit, sudden contact, and control taken in motion rather than after it.[15]

In April of 1891, while assigned to collect poll tax, Ed Kripp encountered a Chinese man named Ah Lee who refused to pay. Kripp demanded his name and the tax. Ah Lee did not argue. He turned and walked away.

Kripp pursued him. When he reached Ah Lee, he seized the queue—the long braid worn down the back—and yanked him to a stop. Startled, Ah Lee swung instinctively. The blow missed. Kripp stepped forward and struck him, knocking him to the ground. When Ah Lee tried to rise, Kripp struck him again, then dragged him to the edge of the street and threw him into the gutter.

The violence unfolded in public view, a visible demonstration of power. Chinese merchants watching from nearby storefronts, other officers within sight, and the city's informal networks that transmitted news more efficiently than any police report were given the same lesson:

resistance to Kripp's will would be answered not with legal process, but with force—immediate, visible, and unchallenged.

Only then did Kripp make the arrest.

When Ah Lee appeared in Police Court the following day, he was battered and swollen, his eye blackened, his cheek injured. The charge was not assault but disturbing the peace. The man who had been beaten stood as the defendant; the man who had beaten him stood as the accuser. Ah Lee was fined twenty-five dollars.[16]

The episode offered an education in the city's unspoken rules. Authority in Sacramento did not always flow from the statute book. It also flowed from the selective use of force, applied to those the law ignored—and later ratified by the courts. Ah Lee was Chinese. He was poor. He had no recourse. Kripp acted not outside the law but through it, turning street violence into a legal judgment.[17]

By 1891, Sacramento was accustomed to seeing how quickly disorder could turn violent—particularly in places where official presence was thin and restraint thinner still. Ed witnessed these lessons not only in his own patrols but at home, where his older brother, Fred Conrad, tested the limits of self-restraint and circumstance.

Fred's adventures took him a short distance from the city, to Brighton Junction, a rugged outpost about five miles away where county roads and railroad tracks blurred together in sand and dust. Tanneries, small variety stores, and saloons stood amid the rough edges of settlement, in a place where Sacramento's streets gave way to open lots, work yards, and the less orderly country beyond town.[18]

That October, Fred walked into a saloon at the Junction and fell under the influence of the proprietress, Mrs. Kirn. The papers noted that he was charmed by her "smiles and beer," and when the hour grew late, Fred refused to go. When the barkeeper, identified only as Jaggi, stepped in to eject him, Fred drew a pistol and declared that he would "stay all night." In the scuffle that followed, a shot rang out, and the bullet tore through Fred's thigh, leaving him wounded and publicly disgraced in a place where such incidents rarely went unnoticed.[19]

The sight of his brother limping away from the scandal suggested a cold logic: success would mean being the one who held the gun, not the one who took the bullet.

From Sacramento's riverfront, one could look directly across the river to the town of Washington in Yolo County. First platted in 1849, the settlement answered to more than one name by the turn of the century—Washington and Broderick used side by side in newspapers, records, and even the mail.[20] Broderick entered civic and legal use, but the name Washington never quite disappeared, lingering in records, print, and habit.[21]

The river was not merely a line on a map. For decades it functioned as a structural boundary—shaping where industry clustered, where oversight thinned, and where speculative ventures took root.[22] In Washington, businesses also operated under looser oversight than within city limits. Sacramento police had no jurisdiction there, and its gambling houses and saloons were well known to anyone who dealt in cash or risk. Just a short ferry ride from the city, it felt like a different jurisdiction entirely. This was where Ed Kripp was born, into a family that prized steadiness, labor, and reputation—and the means to maintain them.

By 1893, at twenty-four, Ed was managing the West End Saloon inside the Washington Hotel. Whatever pretense of Victorian respectability the building once carried did not survive long. This was not simply a place to drink. It was a place designed to forget.

The *Bee* sent reporters to investigate and returned with breathless accounts of "Wild and Drunken Orgies" that lasted until dawn, calling the hotel a "public scandal" and "the most notoriously disreputable place in Washington."[23]

In the language of the day, this meant nights of unchecked drinking, gambling, and noise that spilled well past closing hours and into public view. Yet the public record may not fully account for what took place behind its doors.

Years later, Kripp's granddaughter Carol would recall family visits to the old hotel. Her mother insisted on bringing fresh sheets. Large mirrors, once bolted to the ceilings, lingered in memory—fixtures whose purpose Carol did not understand as a child, but which spoke quietly to the kind of business the hotel had been built to serve.[24]

At home, Kripp had already assembled the outward shape of legitimacy. He married Emma Waldren in 1891. Within a few years, they had two children, Florence and Orlin.[25]

But Ed Kripp did not want to be a barber. He did not want to be a farmer. He wanted to be a player. And in 1890s Sacramento, the surest way for a young man without a fortune to get close to the action was to pin on a badge.

In another city, the revelations surrounding the Washington Hotel might have ended a man's public future. In Sacramento, they did not. Among families like the Conrads and the Kripps, scandal was less a moral verdict than a calculation. It was something to be managed, absorbed, or quietly ignored. Ed knew Sacramento. Moral outrage here was often ceremonial.

Proof came just two months later. On April 11, 1893, fully aware of his reputation, the City of Sacramento swore Ed Kripp in as a regular police officer.[26]

It was the kind of arrangement that made such cities function. To the department, Kripp's experience was not a liability but a credential. While enforcing the law he gained something more durable than a badge: an intimate understanding of how influence was actually brokered. Nowhere was that lesson more practical than in Yee Fow.

Ed Kripp's relationship with Sacramento's Chinese community was neither distant nor accidental. As a constable and later as a police officer, Kripp encountered Chinese merchants and laborers not sporadically but daily, in spaces where enforcement was personal rather than procedural. He learned names, faces, and routines. Familiarity bred neither trust nor sympathy so much as predictability, and predictability had value on both sides.

To Chinese merchants, Kripp represented someone who could be negotiated with rather than appealed to. He was not a distant city institution but a man who could be found, spoken to, and understood. He enforced the law with a heavy hand, but he did so consistently, and in a district where policing was often selective or performative, consistency itself became a kind of currency. Kripp did not dismantle gambling operations or highbinder influence; he managed their boundaries.

On the streets of Chinatown, Kripp was rarely called "Officer." He was known as "Ah Jack," a Cantonese term that marked him as a daily fixture of the district's social fabric. He knew which alleys held the highbinders and their long-barreled revolvers.

On January 16, 1894, tensions spilled into the street. Newspapers reported that a Chinese highbinder had attempted to shoot Officer Kripp, an incident that underscored how volatile the standing arrangement in Chinatown had become.[27]

Violence on the street soon gave way to scrutiny in the courtroom. The pressure around Ed Kripp had narrowed as attention centered on the police officers accused of profiting from vice. The grand jury was in session, investigating corruption inside the Sacramento Police Department. A dense crowd of Chinese residents from all levels of society packed the courthouse; the grand jury's probe into Officers Alter and

Kripp had seemingly 'struck Chinatown to its depths.'

Witnesses moved in and out of the courtroom in steady succession. Chinese merchants. Interpreters. Officers. City officials. The proceedings stretched late into the evenings.

Attorney W. H. S. Scott had set the inquiry in motion. He told reporters that Officers Henry Alter and Edward Kripp had accepted bribes from Chinese merchants and highbinders. He stated plainly that he could prove it. The charges were printed widely, repeated often, and spoken aloud.. Scott understood the consequences. He had accused sitting officers of corruption and named names in public.[28]

On the evening of January 17, the grand jury reached its conclusion. After calling dozens of witnesses—including the Chief of Police and the Mayor—it decided there was nothing in the accusations and declined to proceed. The investigation ended without indictments.[29]

Officially, the matter was closed. The city returned to its routines. But in Sacramento, closure did not always mean resolution.

The next night, January 18, Scott was walking home near Seventh Street, between J and K. It was a familiar route. The street was quiet, lit intermittently by gas lamps that hummed against the cold. Between them lay pockets of shadow deep enough to disappear into. Footsteps echoed longer than usual in the frigid air.

Someone stepped out of the darkness.

The first blow landed hard enough to drop Scott to the packed street, the dull impact echoing between the buildings. He did not rise. The attacker continued, kicking him while he was down. The assault was brief, concentrated, and decisive. When it ended, the figure withdrew into the same darkness from which he had emerged.

It was Edward Kripp.

Passersby found Scott unconscious in the street. He was taken for medical attention, arriving with a fractured jaw and internal injuries.

Kripp was arrested and charged with battery.

In Police Court the following morning, he entered a plea of guilty, and Judge Devine postponed sentencing for one week. When the sentence was handed down, Kripp reached into his pocket and produced a twenty-dollar gold piece—a shining double eagle—to pay his fine. It was a flash of wealth that felt out of place for a common beat cop. As he left City Hall, the title of "Officer" was gone, replaced by one that followed him far longer: Ex-Officer.[30]

The river lay only blocks away, pressing against its levees in the winter dark—pressure contained, but never absent.

Kripp did not retreat. Power belonged to the man who could control the turnstile.

CHAPTER 2

Order, of a Sort

1894–1895

THE BEATING of W. H. S. Scott did not provoke the crisis some expected. The city did not erupt. There were no riots, no mass demonstrations. Sacramento absorbed the event the way it absorbed so many others—quietly, with calculation. The courts had ratified the exchange.

Kripp was not the author of this violence; he was its student. In gambling rooms where he spent much of his time, enforcement was selective and reputation traveled faster than law, and standing came from action rather than restraint.

The attack on Scott followed that logic. It was not spontaneous fury but a display meant to settle a dispute publicly and permanently. Within the Kripp family, such confrontations were neither shocking nor disqualifying. Over time, these lessons hardened into habit, turning situational enforcement into personal method: an approach to power that relied less on institutions than on the certainty that resistance would be costly.

By 1894, Sacramento's political climate had hardened. Sheriff O'Neil moved aggressively against the gambling dens along J and K Streets, asserting his power against a city administration that had long preferred to regulate vice rather than eliminate it.

Mayor Steinman's administration continued to treat vice as a source of revenue, relying on licensing fees and so-called "high legal authorization." O'Neil took the opposite approach. To demonstrate that the city's licenses were meaningless under state law, he needed a visible target—and he chose a former officer.[31]

By then, gambling had become Kripp's most profitable enterprise. He had opened a cigar shop on J Street, its shelves neatly stacked with boxes bearing imported labels, everything in plain view and carefully ordered. The real business operated behind a heavy door, where Chinese lottery tickets were sold and dice rattled on green felt.

The raid came on the afternoon of April 12.

Deputy Sheriff Ross had infiltrated the establishment, posing as a gambler for a week to gather evidence. At 5:00 p.m., he arrested the dealer, Ah Fong, and blew a sharp whistle—a signal that marked the transition from surveillance to enforcement. Sheriff O'Neil and his deputies poured in. Kripp was behind the counter. He bolted for the rear, trying to slam the door to the lottery annex. He was a split second too slow. O'Neil met him at the threshold, his hand clamping around Kripp's throat in a "vise-like squeeze," pinning him against the brick of the alleyway. Even Deputy Thomas Johnson, described as "giant in size and strength," had to "take a hand in the fray" to help the sheriff subdue Kripp.

The arrest turned into a brawl. Dragged onto the sidewalk, choking and humiliated, Kripp snapped. To the surprise of the officers, he wrenched an arm free and drove a "hot and heavy" volley of punches before they swarmed him. Order was restored not by restraint but by numbers. The press later characterized him as "lively as a cricket" and "about as plucky a man as there is in the country."

It took the entire squad to control him.[32]

While Kripp was carted to jail, the deputies began hauling away evidence of the lottery, including green cloth-covered tables and gambling boards. Sheriff O'Neil was confident in his victory, boasting that he would bring fifty witnesses for the prosecution.

Released on $200 bail that evening, Kripp claimed that during the chaos, his store was left unguarded and a sack of $170 was stolen. He did not back down; he sued the sheriff and his eighteen bondsmen for $10,260, alleging he was beaten and imprisoned without a warrant.[33]

By naming the bondsmen in his suit, Kripp targeted the wealthy private citizens who financially guaranteed the sheriff's conduct. This savvy maneuver ensured that any judgment won would be paid by "deep pockets" while placing immense social and political pressure on the sheriff from his own influential backers.

The fight did not remain a street matter for long. Just five days after the brawl, the scene shifted from the sidewalk to the Police Court.

The courtroom was crowded. The spectators leaned forward, hungry for "racy testimony" about the inner workings of the gambling den. But Ed Kripp had bet on the cynicism of his neighbors.

As the jury selection began, the process revealed the true sentiment of the city; it became painstakingly difficult to find twelve men who viewed the "Chinese lottery" as a crime worthy of punishment. One prospective juror, H. Gribble, was excused after admitting his feelings leaned "very far toward the defendant." Another, C. Megerle, was even more blunt, stating he "would not convict a man for selling a nickel watch lottery ticket." Juror Upson admitted he hated lotteries, but then tied himself in knots explaining that he would require more evidence to convict a gambler than a burglar.

By 11:00 a.m., the initial jury pool was exhausted. The court was forced to recess so Bailiff Hardy could go out into the city and "hustle up twenty more talesmen" to fill the box.[34]

The trial ended quickly. The jury had deliberated and reached a decision before 6:00 p.m. Acquitted.

Ed Kripp walked out of the courthouse a free man before dinner. The sheriff's warfare had lost its first battle—not on a legal technicality, but because the city simply did not care.[35]

Order, of a sort, was restored.

What Kripp learned early was not how to break rules, but how selectively they were applied—and where the boundaries actually mattered.

But triumph in Sacramento was rarely permanent. The victory came at a cost. Embarrassed, the authorities tightened the screws. Raids increased. In November 1895, officers returned to Kripp's cigar stand and arrested his father-in-law, Thomas Waldren, for running a dice game.[36] Despite the "vigorous warfare" proclaimed by officials, City Attorney Brown publicly criticized the police for their improper arrest methods. Instead of traditional enforcement, Brown noted, officers allowed proprietors to send men to the station house in their place, where they paid the customary fines and returned to business as usual.[37]

At the same time, the Central California Savings Bank had secured a massive $2,500 jury verdict against Kripp over an outstanding promissory note. By December 1895, the bank moved to foreclose, securing the right to seize and sell his pledged collateral.[38] Yet his establishments kept operating, and he continued to attract a steady clientele. His "sporting house" was contributing over $5,000 in gambler fines to city coffers—money it was apparently willing to accept even as the sheriff pursued him.[39]

The verdict had not ended the conflict; it had merely mapped the minefield. Sacramento did not care about the morality of his business, only that he did not make a scene in the street. Open warfare was loud, and the city preferred to sleep. The lines were already drawn; he just had to make sure he was the one holding the pen.

CHAPTER 3

The Sporting Man

1894–1896

A SCRAMBLE FOR CAPITAL defined the following years. Kripp's ambitions already exceeded Sacramento's tolerance, and every step forward brought legal pressure or financial constraint. He needed time: to accumulate resources and to let attention shift elsewhere.

In June of 1895, Ed and his wife Emma left the Sacramento heat for the mineral springs at Bartlett. The *Bee* noted their presence among the "following-named Sacramentans" taking the waters.[40] It was a performance of normalcy, calculated for public view, from a man whose J Street gambling rooms had recently been raided—spaces deliberately designed to resist police entry.

When Kripp returned to Sacramento, his strategy had sharpened. He was still deeply involved in gambling, but he had begun to understand the value of appearances. Respectability did not require abandoning vice—it required ensuring that vice was not the only thing the public saw.

For Kripp, that meant the racetrack.

By the mid-1890s, racing had become a constant in his life. Each reform campaign brought scrutiny; scrutiny required adjustment. The circuit offered a solution: he could evade pressure without ever looking like he was running from it. Kripp owned several thoroughbreds that traveled by rail from meet to meet in narrow cars, tended by grooms who managed feed, water, and injuries accumulated along the way. Kripp traveled with them. His name surfaced briefly in racing columns—from

Montana to Denver to the Midwest—then vanished when the meet ended.[41]

In these places, he had no standing and no protection. Each track meant new officials, new rules, new fees to be paid before a horse could even enter the gate. When pressure came, he could leave. That, too, had its advantages. Watching his best animals break down on unfamiliar tracks, Kripp learned what neither gambling rooms nor racetracks could offer: power without place was temporary. What he had not yet learned was how to stay in one place without drawing attention.

Racing would continue, but in April 1896, he took a different step. He opened Kripp & Co. in the Capital Hotel building at 1196 Seventh Street. This was not a smoky backroom, but a professional bureau that treated information as a commodity. Capitalizing on Sacramento's obsession with horse racing—particularly the contests at Ingleside—Kripp sold speed and certainty. Advertisements promised full descriptions of each race and results "almost as soon as at the track." The slogan was blunt: *It's our business!*

By controlling the flow of information, he built both capital and a network of influential sporting men. In the rigid social hierarchy of the 1890s, the "sporting man" and the "sportsman" rarely occupied the same room. The former was a creature of the gambling underworld—of poolrooms, prize rings, and back-alley wagers—while the latter was a gentleman of leisure, aligned with respectability, fair play, and the public face of sport.

Kripp, however, moved comfortably between both worlds. He possessed the grit to navigate the network of saloons and gambling rooms and the polish to sit among the city's respectable investors. Poolrooms—gambling parlors where bets were placed on horse races via telegraphed results—formed part of the former, operating largely out of public view. Baseball, however, offered a rare convergence of those spheres in the open—a public game sustained by private appetites.[42]

The man who had managed the Washington Hotel and operated the Sacramento gambling syndicates seemed to have found respectability, or at least, to have found a form of ambition that could be pursued in the sunlight. Ed Kripp was in his mid-twenties and on the verge of becoming the owner and manager of the most successful baseball team on the West Coast. The team played at Oak Park Recreation Grounds, at Thirty-third Street and Fifth Avenue.

Ed Kripp, detail from team photo, ca. late 1890s.
Courtesy of Alan O'Connor. Private Collection.

In California, professional baseball lagged behind its reputation. It remained a rough, improvised affair—clubs assembled and dissolved with little warning, leagues held together by personal authority rather than durable rules. The game inspired loyalty, but it did not yet command trust. Kripp would later recognize this as the sport's central weakness: enthusiasm without structure. Teams appeared, vanished, and returned under new names. Promises were made, then quietly withdrawn. What the city remembered most clearly was not victory, but betrayal.

Sacramento baseball had already produced its own cautionary tale. In 1891, the Sacramento Altas—once the pride of the capital—collapsed in a scandal that revealed how fragile the sport's institutions truly were.

By the start of the California League season that year, the club was already unstable, its management changing hands amid accusations of dissension and "hippodroming," or game-fixing.

In mid-August, two of the team's own players purchased the club's "alleged franchise" for $2,000, persuading a local investor, Mrs. Laura Vice, to supply $1,500 of the funds. By providing the capital that kept the organization afloat, Vice effectively became what was likely baseball's first woman owner.

The arrangement lasted barely a month. The new management collapsed, and the league's "grand moguls" simply disregarded Vice's claim and parceled the Sacramento franchise elsewhere. In 1892, the city was removed from the California League altogether to make room for Los Angeles. There was no appeal, no compensation, and no assurance that Sacramento's investment had ever meant anything at all.

Determined to recover her money, Vice hired the law firm of Hart & Burnham in 1893 to sue the men who had sold her the franchise. Her attorney exposed the sport's central weakness: the California Baseball League had never been formally incorporated. Without legal standing, the franchise she had purchased was little more than an informal claim—nothing beyond a few uniforms, bats, and baseballs, even as league positions continued to be reassigned elsewhere.[43]

By the time another league was proposed in 1894, Sacramento's merchants and fans had learned to read such promises skeptically. The city did not lack interest in baseball. It lacked any reason to trust the men who claimed to run it.[44]

Mrs. Vice was left with nothing to show for her money. Her lawsuit revealed what many already suspected: in a game governed by custom rather than law, ownership itself could vanish overnight.[45]

Kripp paid attention. Reputation alone could not protect an investment. Without incorporation, ownership was theater.

This was the era of the club boss, dominated by figures like Henry "Hank" Harris. Known universally as "Uncle" Harris, he embodied nineteenth-century baseball authority—recruiting players through reputation and pressure, imposing order through personal confrontation, and treating rules as inconveniences rather than foundations. He argued decisions from the field itself, challenging umpires directly and settling disputes in real time.[46] His power was real—but personal: portable, informal, and rooted more in individual force than durable institutional structure. Clubs were identified with the man as much as the city—"Uncle's team"—and even their fortunes were attributed to him, winning streaks and sudden reversals alike.[47] He was perpetually "on the move," assembling San Jose and San Francisco teams to face rivals from Stockton and Los Angeles.[48]

To insiders, his energy impressed. To the public, the product he helped create felt chaotic, unstable, and increasingly untrustworthy.

Kripp recognized the type. He had built a reputation this way himself—and knew how easily it unraveled.

In the early 1890s, games could turn on a call and end in chaos. The most notorious example occurred on June 29, 1893, in a game between Oakland and San Francisco's "Uncle" team that the press headlined as "Ten Innings and a Riot." The match was a tumultuous affair that exploded in the tenth inning with an uprising led by Oakland catcher Hank Spies. Players and spectators poured onto the field in protest of the officiating, and what had begun as a league game ended as a street-level brawl. Baseball had once again slipped beyond control.[49]

These were the scenes Sacramento remembered.

By April 1894, that memory surfaced plainly, when the paper warned that Uncle Harris and other old-time magnates were attempting to "boom" yet another six-club league involving Sacramento. The city, it noted, would offer no encouragement. Having been "bilked so much by baseball fakirs," merchants and fans alike refused to risk any more of their "good money."[50]

At the same time, another collapse was unfolding.

As baseball struggled with its own instability, the Panic of 1893 tore through the American economy. National unemployment surged to between 17 and 20 percent.[51] The worst of the crisis lingered for four years. For many Sacramentans, the price of a baseball ticket became an impossible luxury—another reminder that the sport, as it was then organized, offered no margin for survival.

What failed was not interest in baseball. It was faith. After 1893, spectators did not stop loving baseball—they stopped trusting it. A ticket competed with rent, coal, and groceries. Fans became suspicious of clubs that might vanish before payday, of leagues that promised stability and delivered excuses. Baseball had to prove it could endure lean years. Until it did, enthusiasm alone would not fill the stands.

Kripp did not treat The Panic as an aberration. He treated it as a warning about how quickly informal systems could disappear.

The era of the club boss had revealed its limits. Without capital, without incorporation, without infrastructure, baseball could not withstand either scandal or shock.

Even as Ed Kripp studied why baseball collapsed, he was building a second kind of security—one that did not depend on gate receipts or league votes. After the death of his grandmother, Mary, the Conrad ranch in Yolo County—370 acres located south of Washington and about a mile and a half downriver from the old Yolo Bridge—went to auction in September 1895. Kripp purchased the property for $14,200.[52]

The following year, he quietly acquired additional river parcels behind the levee, paying ten dollars apiece for low, exposed, unpromising lots; the exact sort of ground respectable investors avoided.[53]

Kripp was no longer thinking in wagers. He was thinking in durability—calculating what the future would require and positioning himself for the long game.

Gilt Edge Baseball Club and manager Ed Kripp.
Courtesy of Alan O'Connor. Private collection.

Frank Ruhstaller, ca. 1885.
Center for California History.

Baldwin Hotel, 1879.
San Francisco Public Library.

CHAPTER 4

The Gilt Edge

1895–1897

THE AMERICAN CIVIL WAR was an unlikely incubator for the game of baseball, transforming it from a regional curiosity into a national obsession. As regiments from different states mixed in camps and prisons, the "New York game" traveled with them. Soldiers played to escape the boredom of camp life and the horrors of battle.[54] In December 1862, a baseball game at Hilton Head, South Carolina, between New York regiments reportedly drew a staggering crowd of up to 40,000 spectators, including troops and Confederate prisoners of war.[55] When the armies disbanded, returning soldiers carried the standardized rules into every corner of the reunited nation.

By the mid-1890s, baseball had become a common language. Newspapers tracked games with the same scrutiny as grain prices or railroad stocks, and crowds gathered with a speed that revealed how quickly the sport was becoming more than recreation. In California, however, the game's popularity had outpaced its institutions. Clubs formed and vanished, leagues reorganized, contracts shifted, and control often belonged to whoever could supply money, grounds, and nerve.

For Ed Kripp, that instability looked familiar. He understood volatile systems better than most. He had spent the previous several years navigating gambling rooms, racetracks, and speculative ventures where fortunes could disappear overnight.

Baseball, however, offered something those worlds could not:

visibility. It carried enough of the risk, spectacle, and uncertainty that appealed to his instincts, but it was public enough to build lasting influence.

The Gilt Edge club—often referred to in the sporting pages as the Gilt Edges or the Sacramentos—did not materialize out of thin air. By New Year's Day of 1895, the club was already grinding out victories on the valley's outlying diamonds.[56]

Kripp did not simply want a winning nine. He wanted a brand that could be leveraged. The Gilt Edges were not merely ballplayers; they were the frontline of Kripp's expanding empire.

As Ed Kripp assembled what would become Sacramento's dominant professional baseball team, he briefly operated a second non-league club known as the X-Rays.[57] The team functioned as both proving ground and insurance policy in a sport where rosters shifted constantly and clubs disappeared overnight. Kripp owned the club, managed it, and took the field himself—appearing at both center field and third base. It was a revealing image: the future baseball magnate moving between executive decisions and the dirt of the diamond. The club often appeared as a preliminary attraction for stronger teams, including the Gilt Edge, placing Kripp in both worlds at once.[58]

The X-Rays played fast, high-scoring baseball and, for a time, overwhelmed local competition. It was a style built on aggression rather than caution, and it worked.[59] However, they were temporary by design. As the Gilt Edges began drawing larger crowds and stronger competition, Kripp folded his attention into the club that offered something the X-Rays never could: scale. The X-Rays disappeared as quickly as they had formed.

Long before the crowds arrived to fill the wooden bleachers, Kripp was already assembling the machinery of a dynasty. Major League Baseball existed—but it remained concentrated in eastern cities thousands of miles away. In California, clubs like Gilt Edge represented the highest level of professional baseball available, drawing top regional talent and intense public attention in a state large enough to sustain its own baseball economy.

Gilt Edge was a team built for dominance from the start, capable of traveling to Lodi to secure a decisive 15-to-0 win and descending upon Auburn to dismantle the locals with another staggering score of 35 to 13, as the "battery work of Hughes and Devine" was already drawing notice. Early lineups included Shanahan and Henesey, reliable local players who helped stabilize the club in its formative years.[60]

There were also seasoned local fixtures like James Denny, a veteran third baseman who, as early as 1892, had been a mainstay for the Altas, playing high-stakes matches for $50 a side at Snowflake Park, where the winning team took all.[61]

The game itself still favored toughness and improvisation. The home club furnished only two balls, and as they were driven into the dirt or lost to the fences, replacements were scarce. By the middle innings, the ball in play was often scuffed, darkened, and softened, its movement less predictable than designed. Pitchers worked not with a fixed instrument, but with one that changed character as the game progressed.[62]

Only a decade earlier, pitchers had been restricted to underhand delivery; now, throwing overhand, they were learning to generate movement and deception in ways the earlier game had not allowed.[63] At the center of Kripp's roster stood Charles "Demon" Doyle, a pitcher who threw with controlled violence—owning the inside of the plate, challenging hitters without apology, and using every advantage the rules allowed. Doyle had mastered the new overhand style, and when he took the mound, opponents knew they were in for a fight. He embodied the identity Kripp wanted for the Gilt Edges: aggressive, unapologetic, and unwilling to concede an inch.[64]

But aggression alone was not enough. It required a counterweight, and that counterweight was Ervin Harvey. He wore a red sweater and possessed a shock of blonde hair that made him instantly recognizable.

He arrived from the Minneapolis Millers with an unusual quality for a rising pitcher: he drew no attention to himself. In a sport loud with bravado, "Silent" Harvey worked without display. He did not boast, did not argue, and in critical moments he dismantled opposing lineups with precision. For Kripp, that reliability made him more valuable than flash ever could.[65]

And then there was Jay Hughes.

Portrait of Jay Hughes.
Author's collection.

Born in Sacramento, he would grow into one of the finest pitchers of the turn-of-the-century game. He had an arm destined for bigger stages and the rare ability to dominate from the mound and drive in runs at the plate.

His value was already becoming visible beyond Sacramento. Kripp could showcase him and try to protect his contract, but in a game of porous contracts and fluid rosters, no player was ever fully fixed in place.[66]

In a roster increasingly filled with "mercenaries" recruited from across the state, Tim Shanahan was a rare and vital link to the city itself.[67] Along with Hughes, he was one of the few Sacramento boys—familiar enough to the local crowd that his absence from the lineup was noted in the papers. His value lay in steadiness rather than spectacle. He covered ground efficiently in center, and contributed at the plate without drama.[68]

These players formed the foundation of Kripp's ambitions. They demonstrated that Sacramento could attract and develop talent worthy of the professional game's highest standards, and they set the stage for the Gilt Edge's emergence as a genuine power in California baseball.

Even officiating reflected the new professionalism. A dual umpire system paired McDonald, a National League umpire, with Captain Fisher, representing civic authority. Police presence signaled legitimacy. Where vice once required discretion, baseball now invited visibility—and law enforcement lent its weight to the game's endorsement.[69]

The Gilt Edges' name was not ornamental. "Gilt Edge" was a premium beer brand produced by Sacramento's Buffalo Brewing Company, and the team was sometimes referred to as the Brewers. In a league where most clubs took their names from neighborhoods or civic pride, Sacramento's team carried its sponsor in its identity.

Buffalo Brewing, founded in 1888 and later consolidated under the influence of Captain Frank Ruhstaller, operated at a scale unmatched by most local enterprises. Its distribution extended well beyond the city limits, and its capital reserves were substantial enough to sustain advertising campaigns, production expansion, and market competition. When the brewery's interests merged more tightly in the late 1890's, the Gilt Edge name signaled not just local pride but commercial backing with real depth.

Other teams relied on gate receipts, sporadic patronage, or unstable investor pools. The team's alignment was deliberate. Winning did not merely entertain; it extended the brand. Each victory reinforced the association between the team and the product it represented. Success on the field translated into market presence beyond it. Kripp's advantage was simple: he turned baseball into a durable asset.

By late summer of 1897, the appetite for the game had outgrown the architecture. The Gilt Edges did not just win; they ignited a spectacle. In June, the Oak Park Recreation Grounds were packed with the largest crowd of the season, fully 1,500 fans who did not just sit—they became a force of their own.[70]

On the field, the dominance was undeniable. Fielders moved with a precision that left visiting clubs helpless. The "rooters" filled the bleachers and "yelled for them throughout the game with increasing zeal," their noise rising as the home team battered Lodi 15 to 6.[71]

But the crowd was more than a spectacle. It was counted.

Men passed through the gates one by one, coins exchanged for admission, tickets torn and dropped into boxes that would later be opened and tallied. A packed fence might suggest popularity, but a recorded gate was something else entirely. Numbers could be written down, carried into offices, and laid on desks as proof.

Visiting clubs expected their share of the receipts. Grounds managers deducted expenses. Promoters debated what percentage belonged to whom and who had authority to verify the figures.

Baseball in Sacramento was no longer an exhibition sustained by enthusiasm alone. Kripp recognized that Sacramento needed a park that matched its appetite—a permanent structure worthy of a city finding its voice in the roar of the "cranks," a collective that would soon number two thousand strong, lining the fences and shivering in the cold just to witness a victory.[72]

At the beginning of the 1897 season, Ed secured a four-year lease on Snowflake Park, located between 28th and 30th Streets and R and S

Streets. The site was chosen deliberately: the train station sat directly at the park's corner. It was a flat expanse of dirt and grass near the railroad tracks, but Ed poured $3,000 into it—a small fortune at the time. Newspapers described it as one of the finest grounds in the state.[73] Lumber, grading, seating, and fencing locked his money into the ground.

Snowflake Park marked a decisive escalation. Unlike earlier grounds that could be abandoned or repurposed, this was a fixed commitment. The park stood in full view of the city, converting ambition into exposure.

The city's steam roller leveled the ground, and the grandstand, with a seating capacity of 3,000, offered an excellent view of the entire field. The park's name, "Snowflake," was not about weather but branding, taken from a bourbon label marketed by Sacramento grocer and whiskey dealer Thomas B. Hall.[74]

On Sunday afternoon, August 15, the refurbished Snowflake Park reopened to the public. To mark the occasion, the Gilt Edge faced the California Markets of San Francisco. Mayor Hubard was invited to throw out the first pitch, and other city officials joined him in the stands. The afternoon was more than the reopening of a ballpark. It was a public demonstration that Sacramento's premier baseball club now possessed a permanent home worthy of civic ceremony.

At Snowflake Park, the gate no longer simply recorded demand—it enforced it. Admission flowed through fixed entrances, ringed by fencing that defined where spectators could stand and where they could not.

The park itself imposed order, converting open enthusiasm into regulated access. Where earlier crowds pressed against ropes or railings, Snowflake's gates established a boundary that made every entrance countable and every exclusion deliberate. The same gates that controlled entry could also direct purpose.

When the Gilt Edges traveled to San Francisco in September, Kripp turned Snowflake Park over for a charity contest, "generously tendering" the grounds to the rival clubs. After expenses, the receipts were divided among the Protestant Orphan Asylum, the Sisters' Hospital, and the Foundlings' Home.[75]

But civic usefulness did not shield Snowflake Park from attack. Almost immediately, he faced resistance from political rivals and competitors who saw the Gilt Edge's success as a threat. In October 1897, a "BASEBALL PARK WAR" erupted when rivals attempted to "kill off Snowflake Park" by asking the City Trustees to open Twenty-ninth Street right through the park. Kripp reminded them how much he had already spent, including the use of the city's own steamroller to level the field.[76]

By the spring of 1897, Sacramento's air was ripe with possibility. Almond blossoms scented the orchards, and Ed Kripp's Gilt Edges were becoming something more enduring than any gambling room or lottery ticket. Ed Kripp was constructing a dynasty in a league that was still fluid and chaotic.

Yet in that disorder, Ed saw his opportunity. By late August, Sacramento was 5-1, the best record in a crowded field that included Los Angeles, Riverside, Santa Clara, and Stockton.[77] The games drew crowds of merchants and railroad workers, miners still carrying the dust of the Sierras on their boots, and women in Sunday dresses cheering alongside men in work clothes. Sacramento was finding its civic pride not in gold or politics, but in the crack of the bat and the roar of the crowd.

By late summer 1897, the Gilt Edges were commanding attention well beyond the capital, traveling to face clubs from California's largest cities and doing so on hostile ground. In San Francisco, newspapers framed these games as measuring sticks—tests of whether Sacramento's success could hold outside its home park. One such contest brought the Gilt Edges into direct competition with Los Angeles on a city diamond before what papers described as an immense crowd. The game was billed as one of the best of the season, and the turnout reflected it.[78]

In a tightly contested game defined by pitching and control, Sacramento prevailed by a single run, securing a narrow victory over Los Angeles that drew loud approval from the stands and quiet notice from rival clubs.[79] It was not an isolated result. Earlier that month, Sacramento had also defeated Oakland in tournament play, reinforcing the sense that its rise was not confined to a single matchup or opponent.[80]

When the club returned from these victories on the road, including a decisive win over Oakland's Reliance in San Francisco, the reception carried into the city itself. At the depot, Kripp stood at the center of a gathered crowd—accompanied by a brass band—that met the players and formed a procession through the streets, the Gilt Edges were cheered as they passed.[81]

If those wins established credibility, another game removed any remaining doubt. Against San Francisco opposition, the Gilt Edges delivered one of the most lopsided results of the season—a 23–1 dismantling at Snowflake Park that newspapers described as shocking even to local fans.[82] Sacramento, once treated as an upstart, had now beaten Los Angeles, Oakland, and San Francisco clubs decisively. The victories did not arrive as a single fluke or favorable stretch; they accumulated, week after week, in different cities, against different opponents, until they became difficult to dismiss.

But what had begun as a successful club was now becoming a problem. Sacramento's rise unsettled the informal hierarchy that had long governed California baseball, where power clustered around larger cities.

The tensions soon broke into the open. Sacramento and Oakland had been operating within the Pacific States League and its associated tournament structure, but by September the arrangement collapsed. During the Examiner tournament in San Francisco, the Gilt Edges and Oakland's Reliance club—managed by J. Cal Ewing—were abruptly expelled after playing an exhibition game, a practice tolerated within the league but suddenly invoked as grounds for exclusion. The justification was procedural. The timing was not. The strongest club in the field had been removed at the moment their dominance was becoming unmistakable.[83]

When offered reinstatement on terms that placed their return in the hands of rival clubs, both Kripp and Ewing refused. Rather than submit to conditions set by competitors, they broke from the tournament entirely.[84]

The consequences followed immediately. Within days, the same figures appeared at the center of a new effort to reorganize the game. What had been a dispute over a tournament became something larger: a move to replace an unstable system with one they could control. Sacramento Gilt Edge, Oakland, Stockton, and San Francisco began aligning under a new circuit —the California League, a revival of the same league that had collapsed earlier in the decade and left investors like Laura Vice without recourse—now built on fixed agreements rather than informal understandings.[85]

San Francisco entered not out of allegiance to a fixed system, but because the league offered something the existing arrangement could not: a regular schedule, agreed divisions of gate receipts, and the promise—however fragile—of stability in a game still prone to disorder. It was in this moment that Ed saw an opportunity to shape what came next.

As the economy began to thaw from The Panic, Ed Kripp stepped out from the shadow of his earlier legal troubles and into a different kind of room. He headed to San Francisco, where ambition announced itself openly—through markets and grandiosity—where capital gathered in public view, and wealth was meant to be seen. Opulent hotels, theaters, racetracks, and restaurants were built not only to serve residents, but to impress them. Power flowed through investors. Legitimacy came from visibility: crowds, headlines, and money changing hands in plain sight.

In late September 1897, Kripp found himself participating in that arrangement, serving on the primary committee charged with formally incorporating the California League.

The meeting convened on September 28 at San Francisco's Baldwin Hotel, at the corner of Market and Powell Streets, a building designed to impress even those accustomed to power. Built two decades earlier by Elias J. "Lucky" Baldwin with wealth drawn from the Comstock silver boom, the hotel occupied an entire city block and stood as one of San Francisco's most conspicuous symbols of Gilded Age ambition.[86] Its Second Empire façade, mansard roofs, and sprawling interior were meant to signal stability, wealth, and order—qualities California baseball had long lacked.

Inside, the dining room was crowded with familiar figures. Baseball men gathered at long tables beneath gaslight and chandeliers, their conversations low and deliberate, cigar smoke hanging in the air as they discussed bylaws, guarantees, and the league's finances. The atmosphere carried a sense of return—a feeling that the good old days of the California League might be made durable at last, not through enthusiasm, but through incorporation.

This meeting was different from the league's earlier, fragmented attempts. The goal was explicit: the California League would be formally incorporated, with enforceable financial rules designed to survive the next downturn.

Kripp attended not as a spectator but as Sacramento's director.

Beside him sat Walter Henesey, one of the Gilt Edges' earliest players. Working with league officials, Kripp helped draft a framework meant to impose discipline where optimism had repeatedly failed.

The league was organized around four founding clubs: the Gilt Edges of Sacramento, the Reliance club of Oakland, the Stockton nine, and the Olympics of San Francisco.[87] Gate receipts would be divided precisely: sixty percent to the contesting teams, thirty-five percent to grounds management—a formula intended to professionalize revenue and limit the disputes that had unraveled prior seasons.

Crucially, the remaining five percent was placed in a special fund to be awarded as a cash prize for the championship trophy at season's end. The pennant now carried not only prestige but money—an incentive that anchored competition to balance sheets as well as pride.

With incorporation secured and bylaws in place, Kripp traded the notoriety of his "Ah Jack" days for a quieter legitimacy. Henry "Hank" Harris remained a prominent institutional link to the league's chaotic past, alongside figures such as Colonel Robinson, another holdover from its earlier era, while Kripp emerged as one of its architects, shaping a structure designed to last.[88] By securing championship funds and formal incorporation, Ed ensured that the "return" of the sport was a permanent, professional fixture. He was moving the game away from the vest-pocket management of the "old guard" and toward a professionalized industry where he would finally hold the "Magnate" status he had long coveted.[89]

Back on the diamond, that institutional framework found its counterpart in a different kind of consolidation. While the league increasingly relied on bylaws and formal governance, authority within the Gilt Edges moved in the opposite direction—not toward committee, but toward a single proprietor. The 1897 season had begun with a shared leadership structure, but the circle of command soon narrowed. Walter

Henesey, who had been the face of the Gilt Edges as a player with a managerial role, found his influence shifting toward the league's executive board. By August 1897, the dual burden of managing the dugout and serving as a League Director became untenable. At a public banquet, Henesey was presented with a "costly gold watch" and a diamond-studded charm—tokens of appreciation that doubled as a formal severance from his daily managerial duties.[90]

With Henesey moving into the boardroom, the transition of the Gilt Edges into a "one-man show" began in earnest. Ed Kripp recognized that to win the pennant, the team's administrative and athletic functions had to be separated. Henry Devine, the veteran catcher and original team member, briefly took the on-field managerial reins to stabilize the roster, but his true value remained on the field behind the plate..[91] Jay Hughes, the managing member whose pitching anchored the club's viability, was relieved of administrative responsibility as well. His arm was too valuable to be spent on negotiations.

As these founding figures stepped back or moved on, Ed Kripp stepped forward to fill the vacuum. The "committee" style of management was dead. Kripp assumed sole control over the team. He had become the singular magnate of Sacramento baseball. This consolidation transformed a collective of ballplayers into a private commercial empire that answered to no one but him.

With the formation of the California League, Kripp held both the Sacramento franchise and the lease to its grounds, placing the team's finances, facilities, and competitive direction under a single will. The Gilt Edges were no longer operating as a civic enterprise, but a privately controlled operation.[92]

With incorporation in place and control consolidating under Kripp, the season's last work was on the field: the race that would prove whether the new structure could hold. Late in the season, the California League pennant race came down to to its familiar axis: Sacramento and San Francisco. While clubs in Los Angeles, Riverside, and Stockton drifted in and out of contention, the standings repeatedly returned to the same calculation. If Sacramento could finish ahead of the Olympics, the pennant would come home. That outcome was not by chance, but by design: Sacramento's margin came from decisions made above the dugout—scheduling, roster discipline, and financial tolerance—that Kripp alone controlled.

Coverage treated the San Francisco Olympics as the Gilt Edges' most persistent rival. Games between the two clubs carried immediate standings consequences, and the papers tracked them closely as the season tightened. Sacramento's margin for error was thin, but it was real. The pennant was not going to be decided by reputation or geography, but by head-to-head results down the stretch.[93]

In the meantime beneath the surface, the financial pressures of this new professional era were creating fresh friction. Reports of widespread dissatisfaction erupted among tournament clubs over profit-sharing and managerial control.

For Kripp, this chaos was not a deterrent, but a classroom. Baseball in California was part sport, part business, and part street fight, and Ed was learning to dominate all three arenas simultaneously.

As autumn settled over the city, the season was not yet finished. The Trustees' plan to cut a road straight through Snowflake Park still hung over the grounds, the threat running across his diamond. Kripp fought for the field because the field made the team possible. A four-year lease and a grandstand meant nothing without men who could draw paying crowds and defend Sacramento's pride on the field.

In 1897, he had them. By waving his new Director title and the league's incorporation papers, he signaled that any attempt to pave over his diamond would be met with an expensive, statewide legal battle.

On November 14, 1897, the traditional horn blowing ceremony at Seventh and K Streets took place. In the center of the chaos stood Ed Kripp, actively taking part in the ritual as the ear-splitting, metallic blare of long tin horns drowned out the rhythmic clang of the passing streetcars.[94] For Kripp, the celebration was a loud, public declaration that the Baseball Park War was over and his investment at Snowflake Park had survived the political assault..

The noise carried for blocks, but it did not stop at the city limits. Sacramento had made its case—in public, in print, and in law. The Gilt Edges were no longer a local experiment or a civic indulgence, but a proven enterprise anchored to land, money, and authority.

What remained uncertain was how long that success could remain its own.

Sacramento Gilt Edge Baseball Club portrait.
Courtesv of Alan O'Connor. Private collection.

CHAPTER 5

The Pennant—and the Price

1897

SACRAMENTO BASEBALL had a reputation for advantages that went beyond simple skill. In November 1897, after losing to the Gilt Edges, Stockton fans searched for an explanation beyond pitching or practice. One offered this to the *Evening Mail*: "the Gilt Edges had been "training on that brand of beer for two weeks," while just a small sip left some Stockton players seriously impaired.[95]

For the moment, that explanation was enough.

But when the famous Baltimore Orioles—fresh from capturing the post-season Temple Cup and featuring future Hall of Famers like Hughie Jennings and John McGraw—traveled to California in late November 1897, the matches seemed almost predestined to be a rout.[96] They brought with them crack pitcher "Brother Joe" Corbett, a top-tier hurler whose fastball had been feared across the Eastern states. The nearest major league teams were back East, and their exploits reached California with an almost mythical quality.

Barnstorming tours were physical gambles—long rail journeys, unfamiliar grounds, hostile crowds, and no protection beyond the gate receipts. A twisted ankle in Sacramento meant no salary come spring. But the Orioles' California tour was not a courtesy. It was offseason business—barnstorming for cash in cities where every audience member paid at the gate.

Their visit made one thing clear: California could draw a crowd. The question was whether it could stand up to Eastern competition.

As the Orioles moved through the state, the champions left little doubt about the gap between Eastern major league power and most Western clubs. In Oakland, they dismantled the Reliance club at Recreation Park, overwhelming them by a score of 9–4, a contest marked less by drama than inevitability.[97] Baltimore's speed, discipline, and depth was remarkable. Oakland never truly settled into the game.

Napa fared worse. On November 23, before nearly a thousand spectators, Baltimore administered what the *San Francisco Call* described plainly as a "drubbing," beating the local nine 17–1. The Napa players appeared nervous and rattled from the outset, while the Orioles' batting and fielding drew open applause from the spectators.[98]

San Francisco followed. The Orioles again imposed their dominance, defeating the Olympics 9–4 in a game that blended power hitting with relentless pressure on the bases. The contest was treated as a major sporting event, but its outcome confirmed a growing pattern: California teams could draw crowds, but they could not yet withstand sustained Eastern precision.[99]

By the time Baltimore arrived in Sacramento, the results elsewhere had set expectations. The champions had moved through the state methodically, exposing structural weaknesses and competitive limits. Against Oakland, Napa, and San Francisco, the Orioles had not merely won—they had controlled the terms of play.

On Thanksgiving Day, November 25, the Gilt Edges faced them at their home grounds, and four thousand people gathered at Snowflake Park to witness the attempt.[100] The air was cool that afternoon, and the onlookers bundled in coats and hats. The atmosphere before the first pitch was tense. The crowd, though enthusiastic, carried an undercurrent of anxiety. The local people were nervous the first two innings, awed by the name of the winners of the Temple Cup.

The game's opening moments seemed to confirm the crowd's unease. Two runs in the second inning gave Baltimore a quick advantage, and the afternoon threatened to follow a familiar pattern—Eastern authority, Western resistance, and a slow drift toward resignation in the stands. The spectators could feel it—that slight slump of shoulders, the quiet that fell over the bleachers.

But what happened next revealed something about the character of Kripp's team. They did not crumble. The sequence of the game showed the Gilt Edges clawing their way back from the early deficit, methodically taking control of the momentum. With each home team hit, you could hear the crowd rise again.

The surprise came from the mound. Baltimore's pitcher Corbett, expected to dominate, struggled from the outset. The Eastern star instead found himself in trouble almost immediately.

"Corbett went into the box for the Baltimores, but was touched up by the Brewers so often that he retired in the fourth inning and Horton took his place." It was a shocking development: one of the Temple Cup champions, pulled from the game because Sacramento's batters had gotten to him.

Horton, his replacement, provided only limited relief. "While two runs were batted out in Horton's first inning, he pitched out the game." Even though Horton managed to complete the contest, the damage was done.

The Gilt Edges subsequently settled down and "beat out the Giants in one of the most hotly contested games of the season." For Sacramento, the day belonged entirely to Jay Hughes.

"Jay Hughes, for the Gilt Edges, pitched a great game, and his support throughout was of a high order."[101] His skill and intensity kept Baltimore's offense at bay and formed the foundation of Sacramento's victory. Hughes contributed at the plate as well, collecting three hits and earning thunderous ovations. The *Sacramento Bee* captured the moment with the headline: "Oh, We Don't Know, You're Not So Warm."[102]

The final score told the story: Sacramento 4, Baltimore 3..[103] But the score did not capture what had transpired. Sacramento had not merely defeated a major league team. After an early deficit, they took command of the game and silenced the crowd's early doubts.

As the crowd departed the park that Thanksgiving afternoon, they carried with them the knowledge that their city's baseball team could stand on the same field as the champions of the East and prevail. Eastern papers reported the tour without qualification, treating Sacramento's Gilt Edges as a legitimate opponent rather than a novelty stop.[104]

Sacramento's civic pride soared. Merchants who had bet on the outcome celebrated in the saloons along J Street. The Gilt Edges had proven their legitimacy, and Ed Kripp had proven his vision. The team he had assembled could stand toe-to-toe with the best in the nation.

Baltimore infielder Hughie Jennings immediately wired manager Ned Hanlon, and the club signed Hughes for the 1898 season, acquiring a pitcher developed under Ed Kripp's control and paid from the Gilt Edges' payroll..

Hughes's contract revealed the limits of California baseball's success. Sacramento could develop a pitcher like Jay Hughes, but it could not keep him. Eastern clubs had deeper pockets and clearer authority, and when Baltimore moved to sign him, there was little Sacramento could do. Hughes had won games for the Gilt Edges. The next season, he would be winning them for Baltimore.

His move to the major leagues was formalized with the headline "Baltimore Now Claims Him - 'Jay' Hughes Is a Full-Fledged Oriole." The article revealed the business behind the sport: "The Gilt Edges' Star Pitcher Has Entered the National League and Next Season Will Wear a

Baltimore Uniform—Contract Signed To-day." Hughes's reputation as a phenomenal pitcher had spread beyond California, and Baltimore "lost no time in endeavoring to enlist his services." The contract terms showed Hughes's value—he had dictated his own terms with Baltimore and would receive $1800 for the season, demonstrating the leverage a talented West Coast player could exercise even with Eastern teams.[105]

With the ink dry on the contract, the wire carried the news east and back again. Hughes would soon leave Sacramento's diamond for an Eastern railroad schedule and a Baltimore uniform.

Yet life on the field did not pause for sentiment. The Gilt Edges still had a season to finish—clawing their way through California's competitive landscape, game after grueling game, town after town.

The season came down to exactly the matchup the league had anticipated. On November 28, 1897, Sacramento faced the San Francisco Olympics with the championship still unresolved. There was no mathematical ambiguity left. A victory would settle the race.

The next day's headlines left no doubt about what had happened.

"GILT EDGES WINNERS OF THE BASEBALL TROPHY," the *Union* announced, reporting that Sacramento had "wound up the season" by defeating the Olympics.[106]

The *Bee* echoed the conclusion, confirming that the pennant was secured only after San Francisco had been put away in the final contest.[107]

This was not an upset. It was a resolution. The club finished the race by defeating its closest rival and secured the pennant on the field.

The championship had not been foreseen at the season's start, but it did not arrive by chance. "Silent" Harvey delivered when the pressure was greatest, his arm steady and his control intact in the closing weeks. His curveball had frustrated opponents all season, and in the final stretch he took the mound repeatedly and won, not with power alone, but with precision and command.[108]

Harvey's pitching carried Sacramento through the last games, but the pennant rested on decisions made long before the standings tightened. The roster had been assembled deliberately. Roles were defined. Investment replaced improvisation. When the final out was recorded, the result reflected design, not fortune.

The season closed with ceremony. On the evening of November 29, 1897, the Gilt Edges gathered in Sacramento for a championship banquet that unfolded less like a casual celebration than a civic occasion. The tables were set, the players seated together, and the evening stretched on for hours—marked by speeches, songs, and repeated toasts to the season just concluded. Beer magnate Captain Ruhstaller presided at the head of the table, while figures familiar to Sacramento baseball circulated through the room, offering remarks that treated the pennant as something earned, displayed, and publicly affirmed. This was not a hastily arranged supper at the end of a lucky run; it was a formal closing ritual, staged with confidence and meant to be seen as such. When the speeches ended, the gathering did not immediately dissolve. The players lingered, conversation carried late, and the night closed with the easy assumption that the enterprise they had just celebrated would continue.[109]

For a brief moment, everything aligned. Kripp had achieved something rarer than victory: legitimacy. The Gilt Edges were no longer an improvisation or a civic gamble; they were an institution, supported by contracts, capital, and counted crowds. For a man accustomed to reversals and constant negotiation, the season ended not in dispute but in confirmation. The park had held. The crowds had come. The pennant was his.

Yet Kripp was learning that credibility required rules—and rules created losers. Authority in his hands was authority taken from others, and the limits of that control were already visible on the diamond. Jay

Hughes's contract carried him east to Baltimore. The season ended in triumph; the roster did not.

As the 1897 pennant banner hung through the quiet of winter, it served as a target as much as a trophy. Come spring, the arguments would no longer be settled in boardrooms but at home plate, in front of two thousand eyes, each certain they were right.

CROWD ENTERED THE DIAMOND.

Lively Time at Yesterday's Baseball Game.

SANTA CRUZAN ON BASE TALKED TOO MUCH.

"Crowd Entered the Diamond,"
Sacramento Bee, April 25, 1898.

HUGHEY FEARS FOR HIS LIFE.

Umpire Smith Asks Police Protection at Sacramento.

The Crowd Did Not Like His Decisions and Called Him Names.

"Hughey Fears for His Life,"
San Francisco Examiner, October 24, 1898

CHAPTER 6

The Diamond Came Alive

1898

BEFORE THE BASEBALL SEASON of 1898, Kripp tested Sacramento's standing in public. During San Francisco's Golden Jubilee and Mining Fair, he brought the Gilt Edges to the city to measure their quality against Bay Area competition. Organized by Mayor James D. Phelan and San Francisco's commercial elite, the Jubilee marked the semi-centennial of the Gold Rush—an anniversary staged as proof of endurance, prosperity, and civic order.

Kripp understood that these were not ordinary games. The Gilt Edges—hailed by the press as the "local cracks"—traveled to San Francisco to appear at Recreation Park at Eighth and Harrison, a few blocks from the fair's pageantry and its self-congratulation. They were pitted against the winners of the Jubilee's charity tournament, using the event as a high-profile platform to demonstrate Sacramento's baseball strength. The games were less about standings than reputation—an opportunity to measure Sacramento's legitimacy against San Francisco's stature under the approving gaze of the state's commercial elite.[110]

When the team returned to Sacramento, spring brought a different energy. Baseball was no longer contained within the diamond. The city did not merely observe the game; it pressed toward it—cranks and rooters gathering at the fences, their voices carrying across the field.

On April 24, the *Bee* described what had occurred the previous day with a headline that left little to interpretation: "Crowd Entered the

Diamond—Lively Time at Yesterday's Baseball Game." The disturbance began with what the paper called a "dirty ball." Santa Cruz third baseman Devereaux tripped Gilt Edge runner Stanley as he came for the plate, sending him sprawling before he could score. The play ignited immediate protest. Voices rose from the stands. Fans surged forward. Within moments, the boundary between field and stands collapsed.[111] Men in work clothes stood in foul territory, shouting at base runners. Women gestured from behind the pitcher's mound. The umpire was forced to move people back from the lines simply to keep the game going.

Kripp watched the crowd blur into the diamond. The spectacle of their devotion was unmistakable—a living measure of Sacramento's appetite for the game.

Yet success did not mean the Gilt Edges paid the highest wages in California baseball. By 1898, rival clubs were closely watching Sacramento's dominance and responding with competitive offers of their own. Newspapers reported that other teams were offering "tempting baits for baseballists" in an effort to lure Gilt Edge players away as their reputations grew.[112] Winning made the roster desirable. It also made it vulnerable.

Kripp's authority extended beyond contracts into personal finance. During the April 1898 wage dispute, several players—including Shanahan, Peebles, and Borland—were indebted to him in amounts ranging from fifty to sixty dollars, a significant sum for working ballplayers. Kripp held the purse strings—and with them, control.

In April 1898, that tension surfaced publicly. Newspapers reported that seven members of the Gilt Edge team had gone on strike, demanding higher wages. Kripp responded immediately, ordering the men to turn in their uniforms and remarked that he could replace them "in an hour and a half." He added that the players were unlikely to "break their contract with me for the dubious chances of making a living in the other league," and noted that even if some chose to leave, "every one knows that the Gilt Edges, with their present backing will readily fill the places with as good or better material."[113]

When accusations followed, Kripp carried the dispute into the press. He deposited $100 in gold with the *Sacramento Bee,* pledging the sum to the city's orphan asylums if claims of mistreatment could be proven.[114] The gesture reframed the conflict as a matter of public credibility rather than wages.

James Denny emerged as the central figure in the confrontation. Kripp announced publicly, "Denny has been released from the team, and is lucky that he got to play ball with the team at all this year."[115]

Yet Denny continued to appear in subsequent game reports and remained with the team well beyond the close of the season, suggesting the separation was less absolute than Kripp implied.[116]

Control over players gave Kripp leverage, but control over the gate was something else entirely.

The instability was not new. The previous September, California League managers had effectively "gone on a strike," demanding a share of gate receipts and threatening not to field their clubs without it. The *Bee* described the dispute as a "crisis," noting that managers argued the league "takes all the money and the managers take all the risk," while directors ordered them to "carry out their contracts." Play resumed, but the argument over who controlled the gate did not disappear. It simply moved closer to the field.[117]

Baseball could inspire devotion, but strikes by players and managers made clear that passion alone could not enforce order—a lesson that shaped the ambitions of the California League. The newly incorporated organization attempted to impose order on the instability of the previous season.

In 1898, the Pacific States League reemerged as a rival. At a meeting held in San Francisco, promoters and club representatives announced its formation as a professional circuit intended to operate alongside—and in competition with—the existing California League. To its supporters it promised expansion and opportunity. To its critics, it was simply an "outlaw league."

The league was organized quickly, assembling eight clubs across six cities and naming officers before the season had begun. Its creation was presented as progress, but it immediately complicated an already unstable landscape.

Unlike modern professional sports, late-nineteenth-century baseball recognized no exclusive territorial rights. Cities could host more than one professional club at the same time, each aligned with a different league, drawing from the same spectators and often the same pool of players. The Pacific States League did not expand the map; it overlapped it. By proposing teams in cities already claimed by the California League—including San Francisco, Oakland, Santa Cruz, and Sacramento—it introduced direct competition not just between clubs, but between governing bodies themselves. Jurisdiction was no longer singular. It was contested.[118]

As meetings for the California League increasingly centered in San Francisco, Kripp grew suspicious of how consensus was being manufactured. He later claimed that he was often the only representative present from outside San Francisco, aside from Colonel Thomas P. Robinson. Yet San Francisco newspapers routinely reported broad attendance, naming men who were not there and presenting decisions as the product of consensus rather than convenience. Kripp remarked, "the San Francisco papers would come out next day and name over a lot of men said to be representing outside cities as present, although they were never there, except in the fertile imagination of Colonel Robinson."[119]

Robinson, one of the league's most visible figures, embodied the problem. Robinson's reputation had been built in an earlier era of California baseball, when clubs were often tied as much to their sponsors and backers as to any formal league structure. He had managed the Oakland club associated with clothing store Greenhood & Moran, a team rooted in the looser, commercially driven environment of 1880s Bay Area baseball, where promotion, patronage, and spectacle frequently outweighed consistency on the field.[120]

Oakland's Greenhood & Moran Team,
Colonel Robinson, top left, ca. 1880's.
Always on Sunday: The California Baseball League 1886–1915.

The longtime baseball manager and promoter was known less for steady team success than for showmanship. While managing the Oakland club Greenhood and Moran, his promotional stunts frequently overshadowed play on the field. Among the most notorious was his decision to burn a championship pennant in an attempt to rid his team of a supposed "hex," an act that did nothing to alter their fortunes.[121] Robinson also hired the volatile Norris "Tip" O'Neill and publicly announced plans to install him as manager, despite O'Neill's reputation for combative behavior and a quick temper.[122]

His management extended this theatricality into the operation of the club itself. In 1891, even newly engaged players failed to report, forcing him to secure replacements, and Robinson was known for repeatedly releasing several team members at a time to do full reorganizations. Such constant reshaping drew criticism, with one account remarking that he had already "signed enough bum players," reflecting a perception that his continual changes were both excessive and ineffective.[123]

For Kripp, Robinson's brand of showmanship was corrosive rather than harmless. He described it as 'gush,' a kind of manufactured enthusiasm designed to overwhelm scrutiny and mask self-interest. Inflated attendance figures, theatrical gestures, and newspaper-friendly declarations created the appearance of a healthy, unified league while obscuring its internal fractures.[124]

This instability was not unique to the California League. Across the West Coast, teams often lacked even fixed identities—cycling through nicknames tied to managers, sponsors, or passing whims—an indication that professional baseball had yet to fully separate itself from its improvised, personality-driven origins.

By March 1898, Kripp openly threatened to withdraw Sacramento from the California League altogether, announcing his intention to place the Gilt Edges in the newly organized Pacific States Baseball League, the rival circuit that presented itself as an alternative grounded in civic administration rather than promotion.[125]

Unlike Robinson's circle, the Pacific States League was led by men whose stature derived from public office: State Senator Eugene Bert served as president, and Jack Bonnet—San Francisco's License Collector and a former newspaperman—was named treasurer.[126] The maneuver was both strategic and symbolic. Kripp was signaling that legitimacy mattered more than allegiance, and that Sacramento would not be bound to a league whose authority rested on illusion.

That challenge did not result in a clean break. Financial instability forced negotiations instead. On April 26, 1898, Kripp and Walter Henesey traveled to San Francisco as representatives of the Pacific States League to attend a joint conference with California League officials, where consolidation was openly proposed as a remedy for a California League circuit acknowledged to be losing money.[127]

The result was a temporary merger, and on May 2 the Gilt Edges appeared under the banner of the so-called "Consolidated" league, defeating Oakland in San Francisco in the first game played under the arrangement.[128]

The consolidation was short-lived. Within weeks, the merged structure dissolved, the Pacific States League faded from prominence, and organized play reverted once again to the California League name and framework.[129]

The Gilt Edges remained within that structure, even as newspapers continued to question whether any governing body truly controlled the game—or whether oversight itself had become a performance sustained by press releases and ceremony rather than enforcement.[130] Incorporation had made California baseball real. It had not yet made it coherent.

The question of control would be answered not in private meetings, but in public—on a stage designed to celebrate order and success.

When spring arrived, Kripp understood the reality of defending a championship. Rivals studied their weaknesses. Repeating success required change. By March, the *Sacramento Union* announced that every vulnerability had been addressed: "New Material for the Gilt Edges, and All the Weak Spots Made Strong." While the core remained intact, new players were recruited and the roster reshaped.

By 1898, the "sporting" map of California had expanded to meet the growing demand for professional play. The original core of the league grew to include the vacation sands of Santa Cruz and the orchards of San Jose, a strategic move to ensure the circuit could survive the financial volatility of the era. The new competition was fierce, but the Gilt Edges remained the team to beat.[131]

Opening day was set for March 27, and Kripp wanted it to impress. The *Union* promised a diamond 'one of the greatest in the state,' filled with 'scrapers, hot grounders, base hits and home runs'—an event expected to 'set the record for all such occasions.[132]

The schedule was demanding, requiring travel by rail and ferry to San Francisco, Oakland, Santa Cruz, and San Jose.[133] Supporters followed the club by train, filling excursion cars that carried Sacramento's presence into rival grounds and returned it again at day's end.[134]

Kripp did not avoid strong opponents. He sought them. The season opened with force, and by April, Sacramento dismantled Oakland 25–2, prompting the *San Francisco Chronicle* to call it "the yellowest variety of baseball seen here since the Boston bloomer girls waddled around the bags."[135] Nearly half the crowd left before the game ended.

By August, Sacramento controlled the standings. At 12–5, they led the San Jose Prune Pickers (12–6), the Santa Cruz Sand Crabs (10–8), Oakland Reliance (9–9) and the San Francisco Athletics (10–8), while Stockton struggled at 4–11. The expansion had turned the league into a grueling tour of Northern California, but the Gilt Edges maintained their pace. Two weeks later, Sacramento improved to 13–5 as Stockton's season continued to unravel, the club falling further to 4–13.[136]

Victory did not bring calm; it sharpened emotion while stripping away whatever restraint had previously held. The pressure finally broke on a Sunday afternoon in late May.

What began as a contentious game dissolved into disorder that spread outward from the diamond itself. The arguments on the field escalated until spectators pressed in from the edges, filling foul territory and crowding close enough to shout directly at the players. Men leaned forward from the stands and drifted onto the grass, their voices joining the dispute rather than observing it. The boundary between audience and action collapsed. Officials struggled to maintain separation as shouting multiplied and bodies moved without restraint. The paper warned that the scene "almost ended in bloodshed."

Notably, the *Bee* did not attribute the disturbance to a specific bad decision or controversial ruling. The danger came from accumulation rather than injustice—from a game already thick with argument, where emotion spread faster than anyone could contain it. Order was restored only through direct intervention by umpire Mike Fisher, who stepped onto the field to push the crowd back and prevent the confrontation from turning violent. The law had not withdrawn from the game; it was already present, and even that proved barely sufficient to keep the diamond from becoming a battleground.[137]

On August 14, Sacramento crushed the Santa Cruz Sand Crabs, but the game was marked by unruly fan behavior.[138] Later that fall, a game against the Athletics ended with umpires fearing for their safety. After a 5–2 Sacramento win, umpire Smith required police protection on his streetcar ride home as the crowd continued its harassment.[139]

While the public hurled abuse at umpires, the men who owned the teams were beginning to turn on one another.

By the summer of 1898, disagreements that had once been absorbed by league meetings and newspaper columns were no longer staying there. They were breaking into daylight, carried onto the field by money, suspicion, and men who no longer trusted the count at the gate.

The league strained under constant financial suspicion. The roots of this distrust reached back into the previous season, when the *Daily Sentinel* reported a growing 'dissatisfaction' among the clubs. Regulations were being 'juggled,' and teams like the Gilt Edges and Reliance were no longer asking, but demanding, a fair division of the gate.[140] Owners convinced themselves that "tournament rules have been set aside ever since the contest started," and that gate receipts were being quietly skimmed.

That simmering paranoia finally turned physical.

On July 24, the dispute moved out of back rooms and onto the diamond. Campbell, Stockton's manager, had apparently "looked too long on the bowl that cheers," and arrived at the grounds believing his club was being shorted on receipts. He demanded that both teams place representatives at the turnstiles to count tickets as they were sold, an accusation of theft framed as a procedural safeguard. Kripp objected to the implication but agreed in principle to station a man at the gate.

The disagreement lingered.

Dust rose from the infield and hung in the stagnant air. At the gate, men counted each admission as it passed through their hands—every ticket an affirmation or a threat, depending on who was listening.

Tempers shortened under the pressure of money and pride. Finally, Campbell snapped. The newspapers relayed with evident satisfaction that he had invited Kripp to settle the accounting dispute not with auditors, but with fists—"a la Fitzsimmons and Corbett," the celebrated boxers of the day.[141]

Kripp hesitated only briefly. He was a businessman now, a manager of capital rather than a street fighter. But when Campbell pressed the challenge, the posture of respectability gave way. The former policeman stepped forward.

Kripp struck first, landing a blow to Campbell's eye that, as the *Union* reported with pointed specificity, "painted that object a beautiful blue."[142] Kripp did not fight alone, but was joined by two other Sacramento men who jumped the visiting manager.

Campbell went down, but the confrontation did not end there. The fight was broken up, coats dusted off, and tempers temporarily cooled. Disheartened and sporting a blackened eye, Campbell initially ordered his players to "take off their suits" and leave. They lingered only after bystanders pressed them to secure their guaranteed pay. The game that followed was described as a "listless exhibition," played under a sky that offered no relief from the resentment beneath it.[143]

Newspapers noted the damage done to Sacramento's sporting reputation. A public brawl over gate receipts revealed too much. It exposed the uncomfortable truth beneath professional baseball's civic pretensions: once expenses and percentages were carved away, ownership and management were still fighting over scraps.

The fallout was swift. The word moved quickly—faster than the dust had settled at the ballpark. By the time the Board convened, the story had already crossed county lines.

On August 1, the Board of Managers met at the Baldwin Hotel and "sat down heavily" on Kripp. Sacramento's July 24 victory was stripped from the standings, erased as if it had never occurred.

The league had begun to harden. What had once been a loose association of clubs now acted with something like a spine. A formal apology was demanded. Kripp refused. "I have nothing to apologize for," he told reporters. "The trouble is that the other teams in the State are jealous."[144]

Despite the disorder, Sacramento continued to win. By early November, the Gilt Edges stood at 22–10, ahead of Santa Cruz, Oakland, and the San Francisco Athletics.[145]

Final standings published in December confirmed Sacramento's dominance. The Gilt Edges finished 24–14, the league's best record.

The *San Francisco Call* announced the result without hesitation: "GILT EDGES ARE CHAMPIONS," the pennant won "beyond all possible doubt."[146]

Sacramento had captured the 1898 California League pennant.

The title did not bring calm. The 1898 season had been shaped by crowds that pressed onto the field, umpires who required police protection, owners who fought publicly over gate receipts, and disputes that ended in fists.

Sacramento had proven it could win under pressure. What it had not proven was whether success could be sustained. The gates were crowded. The receipts contested. Authority—on paper and on the field—was increasingly forced to defend itself in public view.

The championship confirmed Sacramento's dominance. It also ensured that the next season would begin under a different condition: the Gilt Edges would enter not as challengers, but as champions to be brought down.

SHEEHAN STULZ MCLAUGHLIN O'CONNOR SHANAHAN EGAN STANLEY
DENNY
HARPER HARVEY DOYLE

Gilt Edge Baseball Team with third baseman Denny at center.
San Francisco Call, December 3, 1899.

Oak Park, with streetcars, ca. early 1900s.
Sacramento Library.

CHAPTER 7

Defending the Crown

1899

THE DISORDER of 1898 had not been a failure of baseball so much as a failure of containment. In 1899, Ed Kripp set out to prove that stability could be built. Sacramento had already proven what it could do on the field. The Gilt Edges were champions yet again, their dominance no longer in doubt. But titles carried consequences. Victories sharpened rivalries. Crowds grew larger and more volatile. Every gate was contested, every call disputed. Sacramento would not enter the new season as a contender, but as a target.

The question facing Kripp in 1899 was no longer whether his club could win. It was whether it could survive success.

The hunger that had driven the 1898 team was now replaced with something more complex: the pressure of expectation. The players knew what winning felt like. The fans demanded victory as their birthright. And every other team in the California League was preparing specifically, obsessively, to dethrone the Gilt Edges.

The spring air carried a different quality that year. When crowds gathered for the opening games, there was already an assumption of excellence, a confidence born from the previous season's dominance. These were not spectators hoping their club might win. The "cranks and rooters" came expecting it.

By 1899, Sacramento's professional baseball had effectively settled—after years of instability—at Oak Park Recreation Grounds on Thirty-third Street between Fifth and Sixth Avenues. The shift was driven less by sentiment than by access, and by exhaustion. Kripp had already poured more than $3,000 into Snowflake Park and endured a long series of disputes over control and use, what the local press had dubbed the "park wars." The lesson was unmistakable: without secure access, investment meant little.[147]

As the season pressed forward at Oak Park, the ground beneath Sacramento baseball was being cleared away. Snowflake Park was being dismantled—Kripp having sold the stands and fixtures.[148]

Snowflake had been adequate when distance was measured in hooves. But Sacramento's electric lines were already changing the city's geography. Oak Park lay at the center of the city's expanding electric streetcar network, directly linked to downtown and increasingly marketed as both suburb and pleasure ground. Kripp understood what that meant. A ballpark no longer needed merely a field and a fence. It needed a current of bodies moving reliably toward its gates.[149]

He secured a ten-year lease on Oak Park.[150] The park had been developed by Edwin K. Alsip, who also owned the Central Street Railway Company. The line functioned as a ready-made funnel for Sacramento's sporting life, carrying paying customers from the city center to the very edge of the grounds. Like similar ventures elsewhere in urban America, the arrangement linked transportation and leisure into a single business model: extend the rails, build amusement at the terminus, and profit at both ends of the ride.[151] The crowd did not merely attend the game. It was delivered.

Before the league season opened, the Gilt Edges tuned up with exhibition play. One early contest drew particular notice when Seattle came south for a Sunday game at Oak Park, giving Sacramento fans a glimpse of outside competition and offering Kripp an early chance to test his club in public view.[152]

The regular season itself began in early April, and Sacramento opened sharply, edging San Francisco 4 to 3 in the first game played.[153] The start seemed to confirm what many in Sacramento already believed: the champions remained the class of the circuit.

Yet the opening weeks did not unfold cleanly. Sacramento dropped a game to Santa Cruz in mid-April after carrying the lead well into the contest, a reminder that the league would not submit itself out of respect for last season's pennant.[154] One early concern centered on pitching. The *Sacramento Union*, in a fretful April report headlined "Didn't Have Them," addressed claims that Sacramento's losses exposed weakness on the mound following Jay Hughes's departure.[155] The implication was plain. However formidable the Gilt Edges had looked in reputation, the roster still contained points of vulnerability.

Kripp had little patience for such panic. He knew what the pitching staff could become over a long season. Early standings published in the *Santa Cruz Surf* b riefly seemed to vindicate him, showing Sacramento atop the league at 3–1.[156] By May 1, the *Bee* could announce that the Gilt Edges "own the banner," a snapshot of a club that had moved quickly to the top of the table.[157]

A week later, the *Union* declared that the "hoodoo had been lifted."[158] Whatever doubts had greeted the opening of the season had not disappeared so much as been postponed.

Because the early advantage did not last.

By mid-May, the standings had turned sharply against Sacramento. A table published on May 22 that showed San Francisco leading at 12–7, Santa Cruz close behind at 10–6, and Sacramento down near the bottom at 6–10, tied with San Jose.[159] The shift was sobering. The champions had not collapsed, but neither had they imposed themselves. The 1899 pennant would not be won on memory. If Sacramento meant to defend the crown, it would have to climb back into the race.

That uncertainty on the field unfolded alongside a different instability off it. Even as Sacramento tried to steady its place in the standings, the league itself remained weakly governed, its authority dependent less on formal rulings than on who was willing to enforce them. That instability surfaced again around Charles Eugene "Truck" Eagan.

California League president Moran issued a ruling assigning Eagan to the San Jose club. Kripp refused to comply. He did so openly and without apology, treating Moran's order less as a binding decision than as a suggestion to be negotiated around. The dispute quickly grew larger than one player. It became a public test of whether the California League president possessed any real power at all. When no meaningful punishment followed, the answer became hard to miss. Kripp eventually resolved the matter the way the papers predicted he would: not through principle or appeal, but through purchase. He simply bought Eagan's rights outright, demonstrating once again that in the California League the reach of a manager's wallet often extended further than the league rulebook.[160]

The season, meanwhile, refused to settle. Through June and July, the standings compressed into a genuine scramble. By July 17, Santa Cruz had seized first place at 22–15, San Francisco sat just behind, San Jose hovered, and Sacramento—at 19–18—had fought its way back into the middle of the pack..[161] The Gilt Edges were still dangerous, but no longer looked inevitable. The race had become crowded, unstable, and real.

What changed the trajectory of the year was the very thing that had seemed uncertain in April: pitching.

As summer deepened, Sacramento began to win with increasing consistency, and the mound was the reason. By late August the Gilt Edges had surged back into first place at 29–20, ahead of Santa Cruz and San Francisco in a pennant race that had tightened into a grind.[162] By

September 19, Sacramento still led the league at 34–24, but San Francisco was pressing close behind, with Santa Cruz lingering within sight.[163] By late October, even hostile or reluctant observers in Santa Cruz described the situation plainly: the race for the pennant had narrowed to Sacramento and San Francisco.[164] A week later, Sacramento still held first.[165]

The season's emotional center came on a hot August afternoon at Oak Park.

On August 13, the largest crowd of the year packed the grounds to watch Sacramento face "Uncle Harris's" club in San Francisco—"Frisco."[166] The day felt combustible from the start. Sacramento's pitcher Iberg was hit hard early. San Francisco's bats cracked sharply through the dusty air, and the crowd answered with groans. Then Truck Eagan, usually secure in the field, muffed a straight fly. The grandstand turned on the club with a hiss that the *Record-Union* rendered cold, public, and humiliating. For a stretch, defeat looked certain.

Then Charles "Demon" Doyle entered and changed the day.

Doyle did not merely relieve Iberg; he reversed the atmosphere. He checked San Francisco's offense, steadied the defense behind him, and gave Sacramento the chance to breathe. Muller, pitching for San Francisco, had controlled the game, but Sacramento finally began, as the paper put it, to "give Muller baseball." The rally came hard and late. By the time it was over, what had looked like a promised defeat had become one of the season's great escapes. Oak Park's spectators, which had been hissing only innings earlier, roared.[167]

Games like that did more than preserve a place in the standings. They revealed the architecture of the pennant.

By season's end, even the *Santa Cruz Daily Sentinel*—no natural organ of Sacramento triumph—admitted the point in a blunt "Baseball Prediction": "Sacramento deserves the pennant, superior pitching with

Harvey and Doyle."[168] The sentence was simple, but it named the truth of the season. Sacramento's success rested on its pitching. With different approaches, they gave the club what no rival could fully match: the ability to withstand pressure and then turn it back.

By late autumn the outcome was no longer in doubt. Sacramento had secured the 1899 California League pennant, completing the season with a record of forty-six wins against thirty-one defeats and holding off a determined challenge from San Francisco in the closing weeks of play. Newspapers across the state acknowledged what the standings had already made clear: the Gilt Edges had successfully defended their title.

The *San Francisco Chronicle*, reviewing the closing stretch of the race, conceded that Sacramento had effectively settled the championship question before the season's final games were completed. The remaining contests, it suggested, offered "little hope for the locals," as Sacramento's lead had become too secure to overcome,[169] and had "settled all possibility of doubt about the league pennant" in a decisive late-season series against San Francisco.[170]

Two days later the *Bee* confirmed the result under the headline "THE PENNANT REMAINS WITH SACRAMENTO." The final standings left no ambiguity. Sacramento had defended the crown.[171]

Celebration in Sacramento followed quickly. Local supporters publicly honored the players who had carried the club through the long campaign. During a late-season gathering at Oak Park, Charles "Demon" Doyle—whose pitching had anchored the club's decisive victories—was presented with a gold watch and diamond-studded locket in recognition of his role in bringing the pennant to Sacramento.[172]

Even rival papers accepted the verdict of the standings. The *San Francisco Examiner* referred to Sacramento plainly as the league's pennant winners, while sports pages across California treated the Gilt Edges not as temporary leaders but as the confirmed champions of the circuit.[173]

The championship did not end the season's games—exhibition contests and all-star matches continued into December—but those contests only reinforced the point. Sacramento entered them already recognized as the California League champions, the club that had weathered the season's early instability and emerged once again at the top of the state's professional baseball hierarchy.[174]

The crown had been defended.

But championship baseball in California continued to carry a built-in penalty. The better Kripp's club became, the more visible its players were to recruiters from stronger eastern leagues. Sacramento had seen the pattern before. Now the process began again. As one report in *The Sporting News* observed with bleak candor, if a manager truly wished to keep his nine together, it did not pay to win championships.[175]

Harvey's performances had attracted attention first. By October the *Sacramento Union* was already bracing for the inevitable under the headline "And Next We Lose Harvey!" Chicago had laid claim to the quiet ace, and his departure was treated not as rumor, but as fate.[176] Harvey had become too valuable to remain hidden in California. He was no longer a local curiosity. He was a finished product, shaped under the pressure of a pennant race.

Near the close of the season, the *Santa Cruz Surf* reported that Harvey's final appearance would be marked with a presentation: a diamond shirt stud, given by his fellow Gilt Edge players and Captain Frank Ruhstaller.[177] The gift was small enough to fit in the palm of a hand, but it carried weight beyond its size. It signified fellowship, esteem, and the city's claim upon a player who had helped carry its ambitions.

Baseball in Sacramento had become more than recreation. It had become civic attachment. The men who delivered pennants had become local heroes.

The dismantling did not end with Harvey. Charles "Demon" Doyle, too, drew eastern notice. In late October the *Surf* reported that Doyle was headed to Louisville, observing that the Gilt Edges continued to furnish "national league timber." Harvey, it added, was already slated for Chicago.[178] Other Sacramento players were drawn into the same current. Truck Eagan was linked to outside offers, and reports soon suggested that Ban Johnson's expanding American League had entered the California talent market aggressively.[179] By early 1900 the list of claimed or pursued Sacramento men had grown long enough to threaten the core of the club itself.[180] The Gilt Edges were not merely being admired. They were being stripped.

For a moment it appeared that the championship team would be broken apart almost beyond recognition. George Harper was brought in as one possible answer, a practical attempt to fill the gap left by Harvey's looming exit.[181] But no replacement could wholly solve the larger problem. The club was losing not only players, but continuity—its accumulated chemistry, hierarchy, and confidence.

And yet the eastern raid did not conclude as neatly as it had begun.

Louisville, the club that had first claimed Doyle, was one of the National League franchises marked for elimination in the contraction crisis that followed the 1899 season. Along with Baltimore, Cleveland, and Washington, the Colonels disappeared as the league reduced itself from twelve clubs to eight.[182] Doyle's rights were later shifted to Pittsburgh, but the eastern deal failed when the advance money required under league rules did not materialize.[183] In the end, the fiercest arm in Sacramento's rotation remained where he was—not because baseball's larger machinery had spared the Gilt Edges, but because one transaction collapsed before it could fully close. That failure mattered. The exodus had threatened to leave Sacramento in ruins. Doyle's return did not erase the losses around him, but it preserved something essential: the mound presence that had made the Gilt Edges feared and had anchored their defense of the crown.

By the turn of the century, Ed Kripp stood at the height of his public influence. He had built a champion and bent larger systems to his advantage. To the public, his power was measurable—in pennants, in crowds, in control. But success had altered the conditions under which he operated. Scouts counted his players. Leagues scrutinized his contracts. Newspapers traced his movements. What had once passed unnoticed now accumulated on paper. Baseball had taught Kripp how to work inside systems of control.

He did not yet know how closely those systems were beginning to look back.

CHAPTER 8

Under Observation

1899–1900

THE SACRAMENTO SUMMER came in stages. First the dust, lifting from the unpaved ground. Then the heat itself, pressing flat across the valley and refusing to lift even at night. The city smelled of horses and hay in a place that had not seen rain since spring.

Ed Kripp was at the height of his powers.

The baseball seasons had made him visible in a new way. His name appeared in the papers, in accounts of civic spectacle. He moved between worlds with practiced ease—the ballpark and the J Street rooms and the racing circuits south—and he had learned the particular skill such movement required: the ability to be present enough in each place to maintain authority, and absent enough to avoid accounting.

That skill had served him everywhere except at home.

At home, the system began to fail.

He was in San Francisco managing racing affairs. He followed the circuit to other towns. He remained late in his offices above a J Street establishment settling accounts. The business he presented publicly as a café and saloon that did its real work upstairs.[184]

The marriage had first broken into the open in November 1897, when Emma filed for divorce in Superior Court.

She had attempted reconciliation afterward, hoping the union might still hold. It was an early signal, though—a crack that widened quietly through the seasons that followed, even as Kripp's public reputation expanded and his name grew larger in the papers.[185] Emma meticulously clipped the newspaper reports of his poolroom troubles and kept them in her scrapbook.[186]

At some point, she stopped waiting for explanations from Ed and began collecting evidence.

She wrote to a contact in Los Angeles—a friend who, the papers later noted, held a prominent public position—and asked him to have her husband watched. The instructions were simple: observe Kripp when he believed himself unobserved. Record what he does. Report back.

The man hired for the job was F.H. Auble.

Auble's assignment led him to Southern California. As he went to work, Los Angeles was in the middle of transforming itself. The city had embarked on a large project to extend electric streetlighting through its districts, running new lines down boulevards that had burned gas for decades, pushing light into corners that had never known it. The change was visible at night in a way few civic projects ever were—the darkness itself retreating, block by block, as the new lamps came on. It was in this lit city that Auble followed Kripp. He did not need to guess where he went. He could simply look.[187]

Auble worked methodically, the way a careful man works in a city that rewards patience. He tracked Kripp through hotels and streets, noted arrivals and departures, recorded the names used and the company kept.

Over the course of his commission, he assembled four depositions—three from Bakersfield, one from Los Angeles—each one dense with detail.

Emma soon learned something she would rather not have known. Her name was Clara Glenn. She worked in Kripp's gambling rooms and traveled with him when he followed the racing circuit south. Kripp and Clara Glenn had gone to Los Angeles together, registered at a hotel, and lived there for many days. Bakersfield testimony told the same story:

when Kripp instructed staff to deliver his wife's baggage to his room, they understood the order to refer to Clara Glenn's belongings.[188]

On May 15, Emma's attorneys obtained an order from Superior Judge Hughes that reached directly into Kripp's operations. He was restrained from selling, mortgaging, or disposing of any property without court approval. Sheriff Johnson was appointed receiver and took charge of his assets. The court named Kripp's parents in the order as well—the plaintiff alleging that they held property belonging to her husband, that the shelter of family would offer no protection.

The charge was adultery.[189]

For a man who had spent nearly a decade working in the space between what the law formally prohibited and what it would actually enforce, this was a different kind of pressure. The court was not looking the other way. It was appointing receivers and serving his parents.

Depositions were scheduled to be taken in Los Angeles, where much of the documented conduct had occurred, and among the witnesses: F.H. Auble.

The deposition was scheduled at one of the most prestigious addresses in Los Angeles: the Bryson-Bonebrake Block, a six-story Romanesque edifice on the northwest corner of Second and Spring Streets. Its rusticated stone façade, pyramidal turrets, and ornamental ironwork made it one of the most imposing buildings in the city.[190]

It was held on a Thursday afternoon in Room 64, on the fourth floor. July heat filled the corridor outside. The proceedings ran long. Inside the room sat Kripp's attorney A.M. Seymour; Commissioner Ling, retained as associate counsel; Emma's attorney A.H. Elliott; court commissioner H.S. Rollins; and Auble on the witness stand, testifying with the flat precision of a man who had kept good records. He described hotels, streets, dates. He placed Kripp in specific rooms with a specific woman in a specific city. He named Clara Glenn. The lawyers argued and the deposition stretched through the afternoon heat and into the evening.

Kripp was not inside the room.

He had quietly taken a position in the corridor outside the door at the start of proceedings and remained there while Auble testified on the other side of the frosted glass. He stood in the hallway while his own history was read aloud into the court record—hotel to hotel, city to city, the sworn testimony assembling itself into something that could no longer be privately managed.

Two days earlier, it was later alleged, he had attempted the same thing in Bakersfield, where another detective's deposition was being taken in the same case. The attorneys there had intervened. No one had been warned about Thursday in Los Angeles.

When Auble asked to be excused from the stand to get a drink of water and stepped out into the hallway, Kripp seized him immediately—by the back of the neck, driving him toward the floor. In the scuffle a pane of glass in the door shattered. Auble, nearly doubled over under the force of the grip, reached for the gun at his hip pocket. He worked it free. In a moment he had the muzzle against Kripp's body, close enough that there was nothing between the barrel and the man it was pressed against.

The attorneys ran from Room 64 and reached the hallway to find both men locked in a struggle. Commissioner Ling—Kripp's own counsel—did not hesitate. He grabbed Auble's right wrist with his left hand and in an instant had the gun clear of both of them, his hand cut in the scuffle on the jagged edge of the broken glass. Hats were knocked aside. Some bystanders in the corridor turned and fled. When it was over, the gun was in Ling's hand and Kripp was gone—sprinted away with friends, who had apparently been present on the fourth floor.[191]

Commissioner Ling, Seymour, and Auble walked to the police station and explained to the Chief what had occurred. No warrants were issued. No arrests were made. Things remained, as they often did in such cases, very close to the status quo.

Two weeks later the divorce case returned to Sacramento.

On the morning of July 6, the motion was heard before Judge Hughes at Seventh and I Streets and continued until the following morning. Kripp came down the stone courthouse steps into the Sacramento summer and found Emma there on the sidewalk—both of them arriving, finally, at the place their marriage had been moving toward for years without either saying so plainly.

Kripp asked Emma if he could take their son for the afternoon.

She told him she was going away, and refused.

Her father, Thomas Waldren, stepped toward Kripp and spoke to him in what the *Bee* described as a threatening manner—the old man moving on the younger, stronger one in front of the courthouse where his daughter's marriage was being dissolved. Waldren's hand went to his hip pocket. Kripp knocked him down and took the revolver before it could be drawn.[192]

One week later he stood in City Justice's Court on charges of battery, his attorney stating that Kripp was prepared to proceed. The prosecution was not. The City Attorney asked for a continuance on the grounds that an important witness was absent, but Judge Anderson declined, noting the case had been pending long enough. When the continuance was denied, the City Attorney moved for dismissal instead. The court granted it, and the battery charge evaporated.[193]

On November 27, 1900, the divorce came before Judge Hughes for the last time. Kripp's attorneys moved through the proceedings with efficient precision, waiving the reading of any papers that might throw additional light on matters already established. Emma took the stand and testified to their marriage, two children—one seven, one five—and sat down. The defense introduced no testimony and consented to a decree. The depositions that Auble and the others had assembled—three from

Bakersfield, one from Los Angeles, each placing Kripp in a room with a woman he had introduced as his wife—were submitted without objection. The settlement terms had already been arranged that morning by Emma's attorneys: $7,000 for relinquishing all claim to community property, with $1,000 paid in cash immediately and a mortgage on the Yolo County ranch securing the remaining $6,000 at $1,000 a year. She received custody of both children and the household furniture. Kripp would pay the deposition costs. She would pay her own attorneys.[194]

For most of Kripp's career, the law had been something he operated alongside rather than under—a set of pressures he could read and manage and, when necessary, move around. It had functioned as a turnstile, not a wall. Now it had become something else: a mechanism that had turned on the man who thought he understood its workings. Private conduct had become public record.

Emma carried forward a quieter life as Kripp moved on with his enterprises intact.

The balance had shifted, even if the momentum had not.

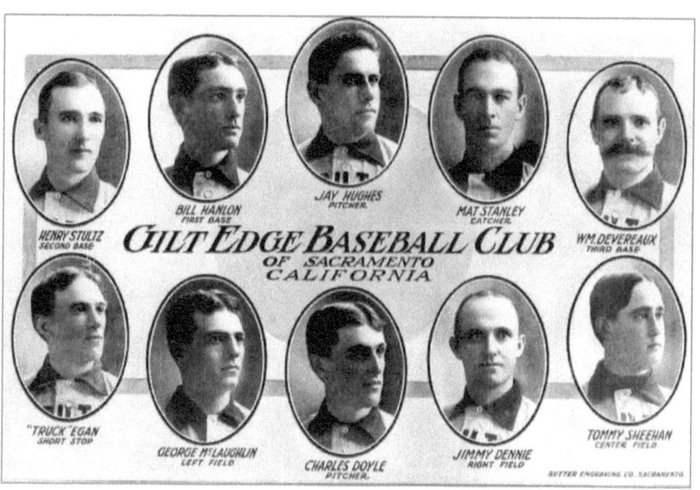

Gilt Edge Baseball Club.
Sacramento Public Library, Sacramento Room.

Gilt Edge Baseball Club with manager Kripp, 1900.
Courtesy of Alan O'Connor. Private collection.

CHAPTER 9

The Last Uncontested Season

1900

ED KRIPP made a striking public announcement on January 22, 1900, at the height of his baseball dominance. The *Sacramento Bee* ran the headline with blunt simplicity: "Ed Kripp Says He Has Had Enough—Someone Else Must Manage the 'Gilts.'"

For three years Kripp had delivered Sacramento the strongest professional club the city had ever seen, and the results were beyond dispute. A decision was reached after experience. "I have for three years given Sacramento the best team it ever had," he told the *Bee*, adding that someone else could now "take up the burden."

What followed was not a lament about competition or public indifference. The problem, as Kripp described it, was structural. Baseball consumed money but rarely produced it. "There is nothing in it financially," he explained, observing that players were among the most difficult labor forces a proprietor could manage: when the club lost money they resisted reductions, and when it prospered, they demanded the surplus. His own affairs in Sacramento already required his attention, and he reminded readers that he still held a ten-year lease on both ball grounds. Anyone willing to assume the rental could take the club. "I am out of it."[195]

By 1900 he had already discovered what baseball could and could not do. It could generate crowds, civic pride, and intense loyalty. What it could not reliably produce was margin. The enterprise demanded constant arbitration between players, investors, schedules, and rival clubs. Under Kripp's direct supervision the system held; without it, it threatened to unravel.

The timing made the announcement more dramatic. Kripp's Gilt Edges had just completed three consecutive pennant-winning seasons and become the dominant club in California baseball. No other baseball man in the state had assembled such a record, and yet the architect of that success publicly declared that he was finished.

At the same moment, the composition of the club was once again shifting. One of Sacramento's most prominent figures, Tommy Sheehan, had already been taken east by St. Louis, removing a familiar presence just as the new season approached.[196] His departure was treated less like a routine contract transfer than a civic farewell. On March 1, a banquet was held in his honor at Grangers' Hall, where local leaders and baseball supporters gathered to mark his engagement with the National League.[197]

Meanwhile the practical question of who would run the Gilt Edges remained unresolved. In early February the *Bee* described the club's management as "still unsettled," even as the 1900 circuit began to organize. Names circulated—Captain Frank Ruhstaller and James Dennie among them—but no successor emerged with clear authority. The roster remained formidable; the leadership did not.[198]

By March a possible solution appeared in the form of Jimmie Butler, a former cigar merchant who held some financial interest in the club. Butler undertook the practical work necessary to keep the organization functioning. Players were signed, the grounds prepared, and improvements made to Oak Park, including a new roof for the grandstand. Yet his position was framed consistently as managerial rather than proprietary. He appeared less as a new owner than as a caretaker maintaining a machine.

The arrangement lasted only weeks. In April, Arthur H. Beebe, a Sacramento businessman, bought out Butler's interest and announced that he had assumed complete control of the franchise under an agreement with Kripp. Beebe publicly dismissed rumors of internal disagreement and declared himself the "sole owner," responsible for payroll and personnel decisions. The assertion carried an unmistakable tone of authority. If Kripp had imagined control might remain loosely delegated, Beebe's posture suggested a more permanent transfer.[199]

Ownership did not immediately produce stability. Beebe openly questioned whether expensive players—among them the formidable "Demon" Doyle—would remain on the payroll, raising doubts just as the season opened. To the public the turbulence seemed sudden. To Kripp it confirmed what he had already concluded: the enterprise demanded constant presence. Remove the central authority and the system drifted toward noise.[200]

If ownership appeared fragile, loyalty within the game seemed more durable, though it too had limits.

For two seasons Sacramento had watched from afar as its former pitching star Jay Hughes built a national reputation in the East. After leaving Sacramento for Ned Hanlon's Baltimore Orioles in 1898, Hughes followed Hanlon to Brooklyn when much of Baltimore's talent was shifted to the Superbas the following season. By 1899, he had become one of the most formidable pitchers in the National League, helping drive Brooklyn to a pennant and establishing himself as one of the era's most valuable arms.

His decision in 1900 therefore stunned the baseball world. Hughes announced that he would leave the Major Leagues and return to Sacramento. The *San Francisco Call* reported the development with evident surprise, noting that the fact he had recently married a Sacramento woman partially explained the move. The pitcher who had conquered the East was returning to California.

Mr. and Mrs. Jay Hughes.
Sacramento Bee, April 14, 1900.

The story behind the decision quickly became part of local lore. In late 1899 Hughes rushed west after learning that his family's Sacramento homestead faced foreclosure. According to reports, he arrived in the city on the very day the property was scheduled for auction and halted the sale by paying the mortgage before the hammer could fall.[201] Newspapers treated the episode as a dramatic homecoming, and Sacramento residents responded with enthusiasm. When it appeared Brooklyn might attempt to lure him back, local supporters organized an informal fund. Led by Harry R. Blair and supported by businessmen and members of the Chamber of Commerce, admirers raised an $800 purse within days to supplement the club's salary offer and keep Hughes in Sacramento.

The arrangement was finalized soon afterward when Hughes married Mary Waters, a Sacramento native. Friends declared that in marrying her he had made the "home run of his life," while newspapers observed that he had turned away the "gold of the Eastern clubs" in favor of the city his wife preferred above any other.[202]

The celebration that followed belonged as much to Sacramento as to the ball club itself. The money that secured Hughes's return had been raised by admirers rather than guaranteed by contracts, and the gesture reflected civic affection more than organizational power.[203]

For Kripp, observing from the margins, the episode illustrated both the promise and the limitation of the system he had built. Hughes had not emerged by accident. Kripp had given him innings, visibility, and pressure—using him heavily in consequential games and providing the stage that allowed Eastern scouts to notice his talent. Sacramento could develop stars. What it could not yet do was guarantee they would stay. When Baltimore had previously claimed Hughes, it exposed the imbalance that Ed Kripp already understood: Western clubs could produce elite players, but Eastern organizations possessed deeper capital and stronger contractual authority.

Despite the winter's uncertainty and managerial upheaval, the Gilt Edges quickly reasserted their dominance once play began. By late April Sacramento was again displaying the aggressive, disciplined style that had become its signature. On April 30, the *Bee* reported that the club was "on the upgrade" after defeating Oakland in San Francisco by a score of eight to three.[204]

The roster remained formidable and center fielder, Tim Shanahan, appeared destined for the Major Leagues. He had received a letter from the manager of the Kansas City club—one of the strongest in the Western League—inquiring about his terms for the following season.[205]

While teammates such as Harvey, Doyle, and Eagan made preparations to head east, Shanahan stayed behind. He was not well enough to go. A few months earlier, as Sacramento pressed toward its fourth consecutive title, Shanahan collapsed on a San Francisco street corner at

Sixth and Howard. He had suffered a hemorrhage of the lungs and was taken unconscious to the City Receiving Hospital, where doctors diagnosed advanced tuberculosis.. Even then, he insisted on returning to his lodgings. He would recover enough to play again—but not until after the season ended.[206]

Despite everything, Sacramento dominated through the summer. By late May, the Gilt Edges were winning consistently against every opponent. The roster had depth. Positions were specialized. Players were spoken of as "prospects." California baseball was no longer informal—it was beginning to resemble the organized seriousness of the Eastern professional game.

By early August, the standings reflected what the crowds already knew.

On August 25, Jay Hughes delivered an eleven-inning performance against San Francisco that tested both teams' endurance and underscored Sacramento's pitching supremacy.[207] The contrast with other franchises only made Sacramento's achievements more striking.

By 1900, the Oakland Reliance franchise had earned the derisive nickname "The Dudes" in the San Francisco press, a nod to their perceived lack of grit on the diamond. While Kripp's Gilt Edge squad was known for "exciting exhibitions," the Dudes were criticized for playing a game so "slow and full of everything but life," that spectators compared it unfavorably to cricket. In June, when the Dudes fell to Stockton 7 to 2, they "froze and played monuments" on the base-paths—standing helpless as Stockton's pitchers twisted "hot curves" past their bats.[208] For Kripp, the aesthetic and athletic failure of the Oakland program was more than a local liability; it was a liability to the league's bottom line.

Against that backdrop, Sacramento's hold on its players remained intact. Departures to the East tested the team, but the city and the organization retained a gravitational pull. In September, Tommy

Sheehan—celebrated in the spring as Sacramento's emissary to the East—returned back home after his engagement with National League clubs.[209] The circuit pulled at its players, but it did not always keep them. Sacramento remained a point of return.

As the pennant race tightened in October, Sacramento added a familiar arm to its staff. "Brick" Devereaux, who had earlier pitched for Santa Cruz, joined the Gilt Edges and won his Sacramento debut before the home crowd, helping keep the club on course for a fourth consecutive pennant.[210]

Success on the field did little to quiet tensions away from it. Earlier that month, San Francisco manager Uncle Henry Harris had publicly branded the Gilt Edges "quitters." Sacramento's players answered in an open letter, rejecting the charge and pointing to three consecutive pennants and their current place atop the standings.[211]

Even Harris's hometown newspaper, the *San Francisco Call*, criticized his conduct beneath the headline "Uncle Henry a Very Bad Loser."[212]

But by winter the outcome was inevitable. On November 11, the *San Francisco Chronicle* declared, "GILT EDGES TOO FAR AHEAD TO BE CAUGHT—The Pennant Already Virtually Belongs to the Capital City Men."[213]

Kripp had built more than a team. He had built a culture of winning. It could survive a season. The question was whether it could survive his continued absence.

On December 3, the record became official. Sacramento finished 50–35, securing its fourth consecutive championship. The news moved faster than print ever could. Word reached the city from the grounds and spread outward—along streetcar lines, through saloons, and down the length of J Street—before night had fully settled.

Men spilled from the Columbia Café and nearby bars as the result became known, voices rising above the clatter of carriages and the metallic ring of streetcars. Cheers replaced speculation. The season was over. Sacramento had won again.

The confirmation came the following morning. The *Bee* fixed the result in ink, running the headline in bold black type: "GILT EDGES – THE FOUR TIME WINNERS." It was proof of what the city already knew, something tangible to hold—a record that, at the dawn of a new century, Sacramento stood alone at the top of California baseball.

The *Bee* marked the achievement historically: "Four times, the twenty-sixth pennant has been triumphantly carried to the roost... This year marks their fourth capture, and shows that Sacramento has had the best ball team in California for the past four seasons."[214]

Sacramento's dominance from 1897–1900 carried a consequence: visibility. Players passed through the Gilt Edges with unusual frequency, not because the club was unstable, but because it functioned as a proving ground. Jay Hughes moved from Sacramento to Baltimore, then Brooklyn and led the Superbas to a National League pennant.[215] Others followed—catchers, pitchers, infielders—drawn eastward by higher wages and larger stages. Later, Los Angeles would do the same, recruiting Sacramento players wholesale when new leagues formed.

What made Sacramento vulnerable to poaching was the same thing that made it powerful: concentration. Kripp had built rosters dense with talent, replaced weak links quickly, and demanded results. Success was not sentimental. It was transactional.

San Francisco produced stars. Oakland produced survivors. Sacramento produced systems—and it was those systems, meticulously engineered by Kripp, that drew attention long after he had stepped away. That attention was survivable only so long as the machine could function without its architect.

After 1900, the club continued to be known as the Gilt Edges, even as control moved away from Ed Kripp. Following their last uncontested season, the name still appeared regularly in the press—a lingering reminder of the dynasty he had built.[216]

Yet the Gilt Edges were no longer the team everyone chased. The following year, they finished third—good enough to compete, no longer able to dominate. The structure Kripp built still worked, but only when it was enforced. Once that enforcement faded, control gave way to balance, and seasons no longer belonged to any single club.

Soon after, league control over the franchise tightened and new ownership emerged under Michael "Mike" Fisher. With that shift the team's identity changed.[217] The change was not announced so much as absorbed, as Sacramento baseball moved from personal rule to institutional form.

Kripp's direct control of the club had ended, but the game in Sacramento had not yet seen the last of him.

Portrait of Mike Fisher.
Evening Bee, September 22, 1905.

Charley Graham, ca. 1920s.
Courtesy of Alan O'Connor.
Private collection.

CHAPTER 10

The Limits of Personal Authority

1900–1906

THE NEW CENTURY opened with Sacramento again embroiled in an escalating campaign over gambling that saw Mayor Clark positioning himself as a moral crusader. In February, he enlisted the support of local clergy, who used their pulpits to rally public sentiment against the city's poolrooms, which he claimed were "ruining the young men."

His efforts culminated on February 12, 1900, when the City Board of Trustees passed an ordinance officially suppressing bookmaking. However, the victory was marred by explosive allegations of hypocrisy. During the proceedings, Ed Kripp interrupted the board to publicly charge that, before becoming Mayor, Clark himself had held a twenty-five per cent interest in Kripp's own poolroom. Despite these threats, Clark vowed to prosecute poolroom owners "to the bitter end."[215]

Once the moral fervor of the spring had satisfied the churchgoers, the city's enforcement mechanisms were dismantled, replaced by a strategic and profitable blindness.

The arrangement had worked for years—but the city around it was changing rapidly. Sacramento was expanding unevenly at the turn of the century. Its population had grown by roughly twenty percent since the 1870 census, to just over thirty thousand—and was still climbing. By the middle of the decade observers were already describing the capital as "full to overflowing" with families boarding in hotels because houses could not be built fast enough to keep pace. Migration from the East fed the growth, and the surge only accelerated after the San Francisco earthquake of 1906 sent thousands inland in search of stability.[216]

Expansion altered the terms of tolerance. A larger city meant more strangers, more traffic, and fewer quiet understandings that could settle disputes before they reached the courts. Neighborhoods pushed beyond the old grid toward Oak Park and the developing tracts of East Sacramento, surrounding land that had once stood far enough from downtown to host ball grounds and poolrooms without scrutiny. What had been marginal space now sat within the daily movement of the city.[217]

The informal economy did not disappear as Sacramento grew, but maintaining it became more difficult. Visibility increased. Reputation still mattered, yet it could no longer settle every conflict.

Across Sacramento, enterprises that had long depended on personal authority were being forced into more formal terrain. Gambling had relied on quiet understandings. Baseball on reputation and proprietorship. Suburban development on confidence and credit. None of these arrangements vanished at once, but all were becoming harder to sustain. What had once been managed through influence and accommodation increasingly required contracts, courts, capitalization, and institutional sanction.

The shift appeared first not in arrests but in earnings.

Not long before, Kripp offered the clearest account of the change, not to a reporter but in a sworn affidavit. His gambling business, he testified, was losing money. The difficulty was not competition or mismanagement. It was a "moral wave" moving through Sacramento that had damaged receipts and disrupted operations.[218]

The same city that celebrated him as a baseball magnate was becoming less comfortable with the economy that had helped finance that success. Gambling continued, but it required greater protection and more careful negotiation. Profit narrowed as the cost of maintaining silence rose.

The contradictions surfaced openly in November when the *Sacramento Bee* published a satirical interrogation under the headline "Mayor Clark and the Chief Know Nothing About Poolrooms." The article posed a series of pointed questions to the city's leadership: Why were illegal poolrooms operating openly? Why were well-known gamblers conducting business in daylight? Why did enforcement never seem to reach the south side of J Street?

Chief Sullivan's response was a masterpiece of denial. He claimed to know nothing about any such operations. His detectives, he said, had found no evidence of gambling—even as the *Bee* noted that a sporting man had personally informed a reporter that Jim Flanagan, a well-known gambler, had been running a poolroom for over a week.[219]

The paper pressed further with another article, "Why Is Kripp for Clark?"—that examined Kripp's public support for the mayor.[220]

The question was framed bluntly. Among Clark's supporters was "Ed Kripp, the sporting man who is now and for months past has been running a number of gambling games in Washington, across the river."

Kripp's position in Sacramento rested on more than elections or ordinances. It depended on his ability to maintain arrangements long enough for them to function—ventures sustained as much by confidence as by capital.

He was not the only man discovering the limits of that system. Elsewhere in the city, similar enterprises were already beginning to collapse. Two years earlier, one of the city's most ambitious developers had already exposed the fragility of that system. Alsip's collapse made that visible.

Edwin K. Alsip was the man responsible for the railway that carried Sacramento's crowds to Oak Park. With street railway operator L. L.

Lewis, he owned and operated the electric line connecting the city to the park. Alsip had also founded the Oak Park subdivision in 1887, laying out its streets, promoting its lots, and financing the development through a web of mortgages and building-and-loan credit. The system worked as long as confidence held. Lots could be promoted, loans renewed, obligations rolled forward, and the future treated as collateral. But Alsip had stretched that future too thin. When pressure came, there was not enough solid value beneath the paper to hold him in place.

In January, the *Sacramento Bee* reported that he was missing under the headline "Where Is Edwin K. Alsip?"[221] Immediately, attachments were levied. Bondsmen were notified. Within weeks, legal notices ordered the sale of property tied to Edwin K. and Mary K. Alsip.[222] His wife and daughter publicly declared they did not know his whereabouts.[223]

Yet the disappearance refused to resolve cleanly. After the first reports that he had fled, two separate accounts claimed Alsip had been seen in the city—recognized and spoken to. The sightings clarified nothing. They only deepened the confusion: a man legally exposed, officially missing, and briefly present before vanishing again.[224]

The disappearance quickly became a public unraveling. Reports suggested that Alsip had left with surprisingly little money, a detail that only deepened uncertainty surrounding his flight.[225] Men who had worked closely with him claimed they could make little sense of his actions and insisted he had given almost no indication that collapse was imminent.[226] Rumors soon circulated that he had not gone far at all—that he remained somewhere in California, moving quietly rather than escaping entirely. As creditors pressed claims and suspicion widened, the matter escalated beyond financial embarrassment and into legal consequence. A warrant was eventually issued for his arrest.[227]

What had first appeared to be the disappearance increasingly resembled the collapse of an entire system built on confidence, credit, and the assumption that tomorrow would continue paying for today.

The courts proceeded without him. Mary Alsip remained to confront the wreckage of the enterprise he had built. Over the following years she appeared repeatedly in foreclosure proceedings as mortgages were dismantled and deeds transferred through the slow machinery of the courts. Long after her husband had vanished, the property he had promoted as Oak Park's shining future was divided, sold, and retitled piece by piece.[228]

Almost two decades later, his body was brought back quietly for burial in the City Cemetery. The *Bee* noted that there was "no stir" over his death.[229] Only a handful attended. A few years earlier, hundreds would have followed him.

Oak Park itself endured. The street railway continued to run. The cottages filled. The man who had built it did not.

Sacramento had already seen how easily personal empires could vanish. Baseball would soon provide the same lesson.

The fourth consecutive pennant did not reveal the dynasty's strength; it concealed how narrowly its dominance had been held together. Ed Kripp had built the Gilt Edges not just by arranging lineups, but by enforcing order, settling disputes, and securing obedience through reputation and the visible willingness to act. Much of what sustained the club happened beyond the box score. Agreements were informal. Discipline was immediate. Rival clubs negotiated not with a neutral competitor, but with a man whose influence stretched beyond the diamond.

That dominance was real—but it could not be transferred. It existed in Kripp, not in the structure around him. When Kripp's authority receded, no institution was prepared to replace it.

By December 1900, gossip suggested he was "anxious to reassume" control, alleging that his agreement with Arthur Beebe contained a "mutual mistake." In January 1901, Kripp filed suit seeking to reform the agreement, claiming the transfer had been intended to last only for the 1900 season. Beebe, having collected the profits of a championship defense and fortified by counsel, refused to yield.[230]

By March, the dispute had moved to Superior Court, hinging on whether Beebe's ownership was temporary or permanent. The case was heard the following month and resolved by compromise: Kripp retained a financial interest, while Beebe continued day-to-day operations. What surfaced in court was less betrayal than exposure. An arrangement that had thrived on personal control now depended on contractual language—language broad enough to sustain competing interpretations. Success had created value. Ambiguity made it contestable. What had once been settled by a man's word could now be disputed in court.[231]

By midseason, Beebe—now responsible for day-to-day control—was addressing discipline problems publicly. In June, Deveraux, Hanlon, Stricklett, and Sheehan were fined for misconduct during road games in Oakland and San Francisco. The penalties were reported openly in the press, and the players protested them.

Beebe's response, printed on June 19, 1901 under the headline "Beebe Says They Must Obey Rules," was printed publicly:

"I have held out the fines imposed from the salaries of the men fined. If they don't want to play ball, now is as good time as any to have it settled. If they do, they must obey the rules. There have been no withdrawals."[232]

Under Kripp, discipline was enforced as leverage—asserted, not explained. Under Beebe, it required justification. The standings reflected the retrenchment. A third-place finish in 1901 marked a clear retreat from the championship years. Coverage narrowed to box scores and player statistics. Civic exuberance thinned. The loss of stature registered not only in the clubhouse but in the standings. What had begun as a dispute between two men was becoming structural: the question was no longer who controlled Sacramento baseball, but what framework would govern it.

Kripp recognized the shift early. By the summer of 1901, he spoke publicly about the need for a new league. The California League, he argued, could no longer rely on informal agreements and rotating proprietors. It needed clearer authority, firmer commitments, and a structure capable of surviving individual withdrawals. The instability consuming Sacramento baseball was not a failure of effort or talent; it was a failure of organization.[233]

That instability was already visible in Sacramento. As uncertainty deepened over who controlled the franchise, newspapers reported that Beebe considered moving the club entirely, floating a conditional proposal to relocate the Gilt Edges to Honolulu if local backers failed to guarantee roughly $3,200 for transportation, salaries, and expenses.[234] Nothing came of it. The club remained in Sacramento, but the significance lay not in the unrealized removal—it lay in the fact that removal could be publicly entertained at all. A team that once anchored Sacramento's civic identity was now treated as a movable asset—something to be leveraged, relocated, or discarded. The certainty once enforced by men like Kripp had been replaced by uncertainty.[235]

By 1902, the California League itself contracted to four clubs—unusually small even by contemporary standards. Newspapers treated the reduction matter-of-factly, as an attempt to stabilize professional baseball after years of uneven attendance and ownership disputes.[236]

In Sacramento, that effort at stability became a contest over control. Beebe warned publicly that he might have to fight for the franchise, signaling a new terrain: success now meant holding recognized title, not merely winning games.

Kripp, once the unquestioned center of Sacramento baseball, now appeared in print as a destabilizing alternative—an owner without title, influence without sanction. By warning he might have to fight for the franchise, Beebe signaled an appeal to legal authority—a decisive shift away from the personal-enterprise model toward one where legitimacy would be enforced by contracts, courts, and league offices.[237]

On January 23, 1902, the *Sacramento Bee* reported that Mike Fisher, a detective and former Gilt Edge umpire, had been selected as manager. The league framed the decision bureaucratically: officers elected, dates fixed, each manager required to submit a $500 certified check to meet obligations. Franchise ownership and management were no longer settled informally—they were now matters of league authority.[238]

The crisis that had marked the end of the Beebe era was gone, replaced by routine organizational work—contracts, obligations, and a club built deliberately rather than inherited. In April, Beebe publicly claimed he would not interfere with Fisher or retain Oak Park grounds, but he also warned he might sue the league magnates in San Francisco.[239] In practice, the dispute mattered less than the change already underway: authority over the club had shifted.

Under Fisher, Sacramento's team did more than operate differently, it became something else entirely. By summer 1902, newspapers had stopped calling them the Gilt Edges, referring instead to the Sacramento Senators. This was more than a name change. The Gilt Edges had been Kripp's team—a reflection of his vision, his will, and his direct control.

The Senators carried no individual claim. The Gilt Edges had belonged to a man. The Senators belonged to a system. The new name signaled a shift from proprietorship to civic branding, from personality to institution, a deliberate effort to make the team part of Sacramento itself rather than the pocket enterprise of a "sporting man."

The Senators differed sharply from the Gilt Edges at their peak. They were procedural, civic, replaceable. Control no longer ran through a single commanding figure; it moved through contracts and league decisions. Sacramento baseball had not collapsed. It had changed form. The shift was not a contradiction—it was a public performance of order. Opening-day parades, brass bands, and ceremonial first pitches marked the city's commitment to organized baseball. Governor George Pardee threw out the first pitch in 1902 using a silver-banded ball, a keepsake afterward presented to him. Ceremony broadcast civic legitimacy.[240]

The 1902 results were bleak. Sacramento occupied the bottom position in the four-team California League, a standing noted repeatedly in published tables.

Midseason commentary placed Sacramento decisively in last place. Late-season standings showed no material change.[241] By September and October, the Senators remained fourth, finishing the year at the bottom of the league.[242]

By fall 1902, the instability reshaping Sacramento was formalized across the West. Newspapers reported the proposed Pacific Coast League, which would consolidate San Francisco, Oakland, Los Angeles, Sacramento, Portland, and Seattle into a single professional circuit.[243] Smaller cities lingered at the margins, quietly excluded, reinforcing that entry would be selective. In December, Portland and Seattle committed formally, leased grounds, and organized stock companies. Rival leagues were threatened with extinction.[244]

On December 30, 1902, the Pacific Coast League was declared fully organized. The new circuit bound its members for three years, adopted American League playing rules, and required each city to deposit a $5,000 cash forfeit as a guarantee of good faith—money due before the season could begin.[245] It would soon emerge as the dominant professional league on the West Coast.

The rules extended beyond play into conduct—profanity, disorderly behavior, managerial interference—enforced by fines, suspension, and expulsion.[246]

The *Sacramento Bee* reported that Truck Egan and Thomas Sheehan had signed contracts to play for Fisher the coming year.[247] Egan's presence carried a broader western pattern. Like many West Coast players drawn eastward during the winter of 1900–1901, he briefly entered the National League orbit, appearing in early-season Pittsburgh coverage before quietly returning west.[248] By the summer of 1902 he was again playing regularly in Sacramento, now under the Senators' name.

But organization of the new league alone could not solve practical limits. Oak Park's grandstand seated roughly 1,500—insufficient for a Class A circuit spanning the West Coast. Low fences invited freeloading; unpaid spectators climbed and watched for free. Sacramento could compete on the field, but the city could not compete at the gate, especially against San Francisco and Los Angeles.[249]

The Pacific Coast League itself opened amid instability. Rival circuits tried to collapse it by enticing players with salary increases and advance money.[250]

The "baseball war" had reached a fever pitch as the Pacific Northwest League and rival California teams began a relentless raid on rosters, dangling "considerable raises in salary" to lure players away. Mike Fisher, known for having a tongue "loose at both ends," viewed these contract jumpers as nothing short of traitors.

The tension broke at the Sacramento depot when Demon Doyle, Win Cutter, and Hildebrand attempted to slip away to join Charlie Reilly's opposition team in Los Angeles. They were carrying advance money from the Southern California club in their pockets.

Fisher, however, was a step ahead. He intercepted the trio on the platform with a police officer and warrants in hand, turning the train platform into a courtroom. He presented the players with a blunt ultimatum: submit to arrest for the money they'd taken or return to Oak Park. Under the watchful eye of the law, the players folded. They surrendered their bags, canceled their departure, and—in a final act of submission—returned the advance money to the Los Angeles manager. By the next morning, Fisher was able to triumphantly declare that his team "will be as advertised". On the platforms of 1903, the final line of defense wasn't the league office—it was the law itself.[251]

By late summer 1903, Fisher reached a clear conclusion: a Pacific Coast League club required incorporation. He proposed transferring ownership of the Senators to a formally organized company backed by local capital, with a board of directors responsible for financing operations, absorbing losses, and raising funds for injuries or travel. Maintaining a Class A club, he estimated, required roughly $3,500 per month. Fisher framed the team as a civic asset, a weekly advertisement for Sacramento across the West Coast. The Chamber of Commerce approved the plan and appointed a committee.

Nothing followed. No funds were deposited, and no corporation was formed.[252]

As the deadline approached, the question sharpened into a headline: "Shall the Nine Go or Stay?"[253]

Fisher waited—and then quickly stopped waiting. He declared Sacramento "too small" to support a Pacific Coast League club, and "no money is to be made here." The following day, he registered to vote in Tacoma, signaling his departure. Sacramento declined his offer to sell the club for $5,000. Pacific Coast League baseball was gone.[254]

At first, the gamble appeared to work. In 1904, Fisher's Tacoma Tigers captured the Pacific Coast League pennant. Newspapers later recalled the "old Tacoma Tigers," noting how members were "making good" across the Coast.[255]

But championships did not guarantee gates. By autumn 1905, Fisher was negotiating with Spokane businessmen over disposing of the franchise. Attendance wavered, and by late September discussions over the club's sale were publicly reported. In November, the franchise transferred to Fresno. Approved by the League, it reopened in April 1906 as the Fresno Raisin Eaters.[256] The name reflected agriculture; instability remained. Fisher no longer owned the club outright. He managed under directors, subject to financial oversight and league discipline.[257] The season unraveled quickly. Fresno finished last in the Coast League standings.[258]

By November 1906, the relationship between Mike Fisher and the Fresno club directors had devolved into a public "wrangle" over the settlement of their financial affairs. The dispute was so entangled that local papers predicted it would only be straightened out in the courts.[259]

On November 1, Fisher was noticeably absent from the bench, signaling the end of his tenure as manager. At the heart of the conflict was a $500 claim for Fisher's interest in the franchise—specifically the "old Tacoma team property" he had brought with him. Fisher's original contract stipulated a three-year term: if he stayed for the full duration, he would relinquish his interest to the club for free. However, because the directors had given him a ten-day notice that he was "no longer wanted," Fisher insisted on the $500 buyout.

The directors countered with a financial threat of their own. They argued that if Fisher pushed his claim for the franchise fee, he would be held liable for a proportionate part of the losses of the season, an amount they claimed would far exceed his $500 demand.[260]

As Fisher cleared his desk, his former player Charlie Doyle took over the managerial reins, leaving Fresno's future in the Pacific Coast League hanging in the balance.

A Pacific Coast League franchise could no longer survive on the instincts of a single operator—not in Sacramento, not in Tacoma, not in Fresno. Fisher's own situation showed the strain. Though he still carried the reputation of a club boss, the franchise itself was now subject to directors, financial oversight, and league discipline. The old model of personal control was fading, but the new structure had not yet found its footing. When the Raisin Eaters disappeared from the Coast League schedule after 1906, the vacancy felt less like a loss than a warning.[261]

For Sacramento, the exile solved one problem and left another. Pacific Coast League baseball had departed, but the city's informal economy had not. Ed Kripp remained—not at the center of the diamond, but still part of Sacramento sporting life. While Fisher had chased legitimacy north, gambling persisted. The physical landscape of Sacramento baseball was changing as well.

Snowflake Park had already been dismantled. The final erasure occurred in 1903. That April, the *Bee* had reported that the Board of Trustees "ordered the opening of Twenty-ninth Street, through the old Snowflake Park baseball grounds." Michael Hughes petitioned to use the land for livestock. Championship grounds reverted to pasture; chalk lines disappeared into clover.[262]

Oak Park survived, but could not pay for the baseball played there. For Kripp, the lesson was clear: without ownership of the ground beneath you, you owned nothing at all. The league had replaced the era of the "big personality" with a new world of boards, votes, and corporate oversight. It had shuffled managers across the coast, but it had not displaced the lucrative economy that actually financed the city's nightlife. That network still thrived on both sides of the river.

Baseball required negotiation. Gambling would require something else: invisibility.

PART TWO

THE EMPIRE

1901–1922

LOCAL RACE TRACK GAMBLERS ARE HAVING THEIR INNING

THE COLUMBIA CAFE, SIXTH AND J STREETS, WHERE BETS ARE BEING LAID, ALTHOUGH A POLICEMAN STANDS GUARD.

Columbia Café on Sixth and J Streets.
Sacramento Bee, December 11, 1909.

CHAPTER 11

The Poolroom Wars

1901–1906

IN EARLY 1901, Ed Kripp made his choice: he would double down on gambling and the networks of informal power that ran Sacramento's underworld. Attempts to straddle legitimacy and vice had failed. Respectability could wait; for now, profit ruled.

The failure had been recent, and visible. In the fall of 1900, creditors moved against him. The National Bank of D.O. Mills & Company initiated attachment proceedings over an unpaid note tied to his Yolo County property.[263] Within weeks, the contents of his establishment were sold at sheriff's auction—barware, liquor, even a worn billiard table, which fetched twenty dollars.[264]

In August, Kripp renewed his ambitions in public. When the State Board of Agriculture auctioned the pool privileges for the State Fair—one of the most lucrative gambling franchises in California—he entered the bidding against the most established operators. He offered $16,400 for twelve days of racing, an extraordinary sum, losing only to Caesar Young, a dominant figure in California's race-betting world.. Newspapers remarked on the magnitude of the wagers and on Kripp's confidence. "To the victor belong the spoils," he said afterward, accepting the verdict without complaint. He understood the scale of the game he had stepped into.[265]

It was not a failure so much as a declaration. Kripp was willing to put tens of thousands of dollars on the table against the best-financed men in the trade. He intended to operate on that level.

Ed himself was no stranger to being the bettor. The scale of his gambling was measured not only in money, but in duration. That same year, at the Occidental Hotel in Santa Rosa, he sat at a faro table for twenty-two hours. He began play at six in the evening, remained through the night until seven the next morning, and returned again at noon to continue. When he finally rose from the table, he had lost $1,400—reported at the time as the largest loss and longest sitting at faro on record in Sonoma County.[266]

The same appetite—and control—extended beyond his own play. Ed Kripp's poolrooms were not merely businesses. They were lines of control—defended and enforced through a shifting balance of intimidation, violence, and law.

That control had an address.

His primary vehicle for this would be those discreet betting parlors where men wagered on horse races. Kripp's poolroom above the Columbia Café did not announce what it was. Like the city that sustained it, it preferred discretion to display. At street level, on the corner of Sixth and J Streets, it presented itself as a simple saloon. Men came and went through the front door. Whiskey was poured. The sign stayed respectable, and nothing about the first floor suggested that it was anything more than another downtown drinking place.

This was the same operation Sheriff O'Neil had targeted years earlier—the enterprise that reformers once held up as evidence of the city's moral collapse. This was one of the city's most persistent points of conflict during the Poolroom Wars. Access was controlled. Reporters noted that only men who were considered "safe"—regular customers known to the operators—were admitted, while strangers required introduction. During periods of pressure, lookouts were posted, and doors at the top of the stairway were kept closed to delay police entry.[267]

Even in his gambling rooms, Kripp imposed boundaries. Boys were not admitted. Drunks were turned away. The rules were less about reform than control. Disorder invited attention. Attention invited enforcement.[268] Kripp did not drink heavily. He preferred to remain sober. He preferred control in rooms where control was easily lost.[269]

When the political climate allowed, the rooms operated openly. Pool selling formed the core of the business, but faro, roulette, and craps were also played at various times, with one *Bee* reporter describing the establishment as running "at full blast," with no legal sanction for the games."[270]

Inside, the rooms were arranged for speed and discretion. At the center of the space sat a small buzzer—referred to by players as a "dice box"—wired to the stairway below, which allowed one to sound an audible warning through the room, giving dealers and patrons time to scatter money and pocket dice.[271]

The operation was designed to collapse inward when necessary. During raids, police found green felt tables, chips, and cards pulled from closets and side rooms where they had been stowed away, only to be brought back into use once the pressure lifted.[272]

And if that understanding failed, there was a final layer of protection. As a contingency for an actual raid, the gambling room was built with two secondary exits that opened directly into the rooming house next door. Players could melt into the adjoining building and reemerge as tenants or passersby, the boundary between lawful lodging and illicit play thin enough to step through.[273]

Downstairs, the Columbia Café continued to function as it always had, serving drinks and maintaining the appearance of normalcy.[274]

When the pressure of local reform made it too hot to hold, Kripp did not retreat; he simply moved the game beyond the city's reach where Sacramento's 'moral wave' did not apply. Yolo County proceeded more cautiously than Sacramento, relying on complaint rather than patrol. By 1901, this permissiveness had become routine. Gambling houses operated openly in Washington, drawing crowds from Sacramento and beyond.

The most prominent of these establishments came to be known as the "Yolo Monte Carlo," a large, organized resort rather than a backroom poolroom. The *Bee* reported that faro and other games were "flourishing upon the turn of a card," conducted not in secrecy but in full view of the community and with little interference from county officials.[275]

Ownership of the Monte Carlo was no secret. The *Bee* and the *Daily Democrat* reported that the establishment was owned and operated jointly by Ed Kripp, as chief proprietor, along with Angus Ross, and that it was conducted "in open defiance of the statutes" governing gambling in California.[276] The article observed that despite the visibility of the operation, county officials appeared untroubled by its scale.

The partnership was uneven. Kripp was the strategist and public figure, willing to confront editors, cultivate politicians, and test the limits of publicity. Ross was a professional gambler, appearing in the record as an operator in his own right—running faro games under his own name and, at times, independently of Kripp.[277]

Inside, the Monte Carlo functioned as a system. Multiple faro banks operated simultaneously, surrounded by steady crowds. Roulette wheels turned beneath electric light, and dice games filled adjoining rooms. Chips and checks moved constantly across felt, wagers ranging from modest five-cent plays to heavier stakes. Contemporary newspapers referred to such games as "tigers," a term used in the press to describe gambling operations and the money they consumed.[278]

On the north side of the hall, keno callers worked through the night, their rhythmic cries punctuating the sound of play. Winners were expected to "set up the drinks" for their table—ten cents a glass.[279]

The tables drew a mixed crowd. Newspapers remarked on men in working clothes gambling alongside well-dressed patrons, all drawn by the same promise: the chance to double a night's pay, or to lose it just as quickly.

Operations in Washington were widely regarded as a "matter of course," less a moral problem than a sign of prosperity. One paper noted that the town had "but one vacant house," attributing its vitality to the steady flow of gamblers.[280]

Law enforcement did not dispute the Monte Carlo's existence. Sheriff Griffin of Yolo County stated publicly that gambling could be suppressed if residents demanded it, but without formal complaints there would be no warrants to serve.[281]

R.C. Gorton, editor of the *Yolo County Message*, refused to accept that arrangement. For weeks he attacked the gambling interests in print. He quoted statutes. He named operators. He described the trade as a "miserable, low-lived business," and mocked Kripp's reported vow that he would "go to hell" to protect his poolrooms.

The editorials did not fade after a day's outrage. Other papers began repeating the charges. What began as local criticism became a county-wide campaign.

On November 9, 1901, the conflict left the page. That afternoon, Gorton crossed the bridge from Washington toward Sacramento. Near the metal "chimes" that framed the span, Kripp came up behind him. He wore rubber-heeled shoes, which made little sound on the wooden planks.

He gave no warning.

Kripp struck Gorton from behind, knocking him down onto the bridge deck. The assault continued as the editor lay on the planks, the blows described by reporters as repeated and severe. During the struggle, Gorton attempted to draw a revolver from his pocket. Kripp wrenched the weapon from his hand and hurled it over the railing. The gun disappeared into the Sacramento River below.[282]

Gorton was left bloodied on the bridge. The fight was over as quickly as it had begun.

The next morning, the *Woodland Daily Democrat* ran the story under a blunt headline: "KRIPP DENIES IT." Kripp did not deny the encounter. He denied that it constituted a crime. "I guess I did him up pretty badly," he told reporters. He described himself as a philanthropist, citing hundreds of dollars given for levee repairs and fire plugs in Washington, and spoke of plans to donate a hose cart to the town.

Then he drew the line that mattered.

"I was born on this side of the river," Kripp said. "Gorton is a stranger."[283]

Later that day, the *Yolo County Message* informed its readers that its editor had been "brought home for repairs." The phrase was careful. It named no assailant. It described no crime.

Reporting on the incident, the *San Francisco Call* noted that the poolrooms in Washington reopened immediately after the assault.[284] Within days, papers across the county framed the incident not as a conclusion but as an escalation. One headline called it a "newspaper war."[285]

Gorton returned to print "still undaunted," announcing that he intended to continue the fight "to a finish."[286]

On December 3, Gorton traveled to Woodland and swore out a battery of warrants, not just against Kripp and Ross for "running faro games," but against the entire infrastructure that allowed Washington's gambling operations to flourish.[287]

He filed charges against Mary Hanson for renting her property to gamblers. He filed charges against Constable Lawrence Burns for "neglecting" to arrest the gamblers despite having evidence.[288]

It was a comprehensive assault on the network of corruption itself. Sheriff Griffin served the warrants the following morning.

Kripp was in San Francisco but returned quickly, accompanied by an attorney. They went to Judge Ruggles' office to "pay his respects to the Court." Kripp posted a $250 bond and walked free.[289]

The beating on the bridge had not ended the conflict. It had made it visible—across the river and in print.

But as 1901 drew toward its close, something extraordinary happened. On November 18, Lou B. Littlefield, the owner of the *Message's* physical plant and equipment, used "legal process" to dispossess Gorton of his lease and oust him from the paper. Littlefield, who had been Gorton's partner in the crusade against gambling, turned against him. Using the law itself as a weapon, he took control of the newspaper..

Gorton was forced out. His office was no longer his. The *Message* continued to publish, but without the editor who had created it or the campaign that had defined it. The transition was swift, with Edward Stanton immediately assuming editorial charge as Gorton was removed from the post. While the paper had previously "inveighed against the poolrooms," its sudden silence sparked immediate suspicion. It was whispered in saloons and repeated on street corners about how thoroughly the paper had been neutralized.

Rumor at the time suggested that the present actual owner of the newspaper was now none other than Edward L. Kripp himself. Having physically beaten Gorton on the bridge only days prior, the "Prince of Monaco" was now believed to have completed his victory by quietly purchasing the very voice that had denounced him.[290]

A profitable silence settled over the river, and for a moment, it seemed that Kripp's control—both on the streets and in print—was unchallenged. Yet even as the *Message* fell silent, forces beyond his personal reach were preparing to test the resilience of his empire.

Nearly three years later, by 1904, the terms had shifted. This time, it was a corporate decision that shattered the equilibrium.

The Monte Carlo was under attack again because Western Union refused to continue leased-wire service to the Washington poolrooms, cutting off the transmission of horse-race results from outside tracks. The *Daily Democrat* described the move as striking at "the life of Kripp's gambling resort," noting that while cards and dice could continue, race betting could not function without the wire. The decision was not moral rhetoric so much as corporate self-protection: by withdrawing service, Western Union avoided the appearance of openly supporting illegal operations without requiring arrests or prosecutions.[291]

Kripp and Ross attempted to adapt. Investigations followed. District Attorney Anderson was later credited with closing the games.[292]

But the rooms did not stay silent. By mid-June, word circulated in Washington that pool selling would resume at the Monte Carlo despite the boycott. The *Daily Democrat* reported that operators would rely not on leased telegraph wires but on telephone advices—race results phoned in from Sausalito—while eastern results were carried west by private messenger.

In 1904, the telephone was not an automated system but a chain of people. Calls passed through live operators, slow to connect, expensive, and dependent on discretion. When received, the results were written on a blackboard, bets taken race by race. As the paper noted pointedly, there was "no inhibition" on a private wire between Sacramento and Yolo—nothing to prevent the continued flow of information across the river.

The system had been disrupted, not destroyed. The poolrooms reopened by rebuilding the circuit through voices and informal channels rather than sanctioned wires.[293]

The pattern was familiar: warning, pause, continuation. In an August exposé on Washington betting rooms, the *Sacramento Bee* described keno, faro, and poker games operating openly, with hundreds of men crossing the bridge nightly while authorities looked on.[294] When questioned, Kripp did not deny the activity. Instead, he returned to an argument he had made before: that Sacramento's "moral wave" had merely displaced gambling rather than eliminated it. So long as juries refused to convict and officials declined consistent enforcement, he maintained, the trade would migrate across jurisdictional lines—out of the city and into Washington—remaining illegal in statute but functionally tolerated in practice. What reformers labeled vice, Kripp framed as demand; what courts called unlawful, he treated as unenforceable.

For a time, the arrangement held.

Then, in November, the law crossed into Yolo. It did not arrive by rumor or editorial. It came on foot, across the span—over water that marked the line between municipal tolerance and county law. For years, that line had shifted in practice. On that afternoon, it was no longer negotiable.

Acting on orders from Yolo County District Attorney Anderson, officers raided the poolroom owned by Ed Kripp and others in the town of Washington.

The raid took place in daylight. Games were underway. Faro layouts lay open on the tables, cards mid-turn, chips mid-count. The room did not expect interruption.

A young agent, John Winkleman, had been sent to gather evidence. Accompanied by a constable, Winkleman arrived to serve warrants on several employees. The situation turned volatile when Winkleman claimed he saw a suspect—a Chinese employee—through an open door.

Kripp called him a liar. When Winkleman returned the insult, the professional restraint gave way.

The blow sent Winkleman bolting toward the door, the scene spilling from table to threshold in seconds. The chase carried them out of the saloon and toward the bridge, suspended above the slow winter current. Behind them, the room filled with noise.

Kripp caught him near the Sacramento end of the bridge, at the place where one jurisdiction yielded to another. He knocked him down and delivered what the papers described as a "severe beating."[295]

For a moment, there was only the river below and the sound of boots against planks.

The assault resulted in a separate charge of battery. Kripp was taken into custody. Bond was posted. He was released.

The raid temporarily succeeded in its aim. The poolroom was briefly closed. But attention shifted almost immediately away from violations and toward the young man on the bridge. Newspapers questioned why a student had been placed in direct confrontation with professional gambling operators. Editorials asked why, once injured, Winkleman had been left exposed rather than shielded by the institutions that enlisted him.[296]

Kripp paid fines and continued on. Winkleman bore the public weight of the encounter. The episode mattered because it stripped reform of abstraction. Enforcement was no longer a matter of statutes and raids, but of exposure—of how little protection the system offered those it sent forward.

The bridge had carried more than warrants that afternoon. It had carried consequence. For Kripp, the confrontation marked not a beginning but an escalation. He had maneuvered around reform before and resisted authority when necessary. But this time the line was drawn in open view, on planks above the river, where retreat and pursuit ran along the same narrow path.

It did not end there.

In January 1906, he moved again, relocating his poolrooms to Riverside Road near Tenth and Y, just beyond city limits.

The *Bee* ran the headline: "Kripp Tells Why He Moved Down Riverside Road." The reason he gave was friendship. John Denny had just been named Chief of Police, a figure who moved easily in the same circles as Ed's brother Fred, himself a patrolman.[297] Kripp said he did not want to make the man's first weeks difficult. "I would not do anything to embarrass Johnny Denny, and therefore I am going out of town."[298]

The real story was simpler. Mayor Beard had decided Kripp's rooms at the Columbia Café needed to close—not because gambling was suddenly illegal, but because Kripp had backed the wrong candidate. Elkus lost, Beard won, and Angus Ross's games at the Bank Exchange kept running without interruption, having backed the right candidate. Same trade, different politics.

Before he moved, Kripp had floated one more arrangement—less a proposal than a signal. Charge fifteen cents at the door, call the race results aloud as they came over the wire, no bets taken inside. The wagering would happen on the sidewalk, through men working handbooks in the street. He laid the plan out for a *Bee* reporter with no apparent concern that it might be printed, as if the conversation itself were part of the negotiation.[299]

What that conversation also turned up, almost by accident, was the scale of what Sacramento sat at the center of. Kripp was supplying race results to poolrooms from Suisun to Reno. The Columbia Café was no longer just a local gambling house with a wire—it was the wire, with gambling arranged around it. The new rooms stood across from the city cemetery, where marble names faced the river wind in quiet rows. Inside, cards snapped against felt and coins passed from hand to hand.

When pressure crossed the river, Kripp shifted the ground beneath it. He did not abandon the trade. He relocated it—sometimes beyond city limits, sometimes back again when conditions softened. The line between enforcement and accommodation never held for long.

Like the river itself, it moved.

Ormonde, sire of Beau Ormonde.
Courtesy of Thoroughbred Heritage.

CHAPTER 12

The War Chest

1901–1907

WHILE THE CONFLICTS over gambling played out in public, Kripp was building something less visible. Kripp's capital no longer sat idle. In the early 1900s he learned to store value in forms that could move—quietly, quickly, and across jurisdictions. Racehorses were part of that strategy. With Beau Ormonde, Kripp did not just buy speed—he bought a name with global weight.

The horse was sired by Ormonde, the unbeaten champion of sixteen races, and English Triple Crown winner once hailed as the 'horse of the century,' a stallion whose value was measured not only in victories but in how fiercely his bloodline was bought and moved across borders. Ormonde himself had been sold abroad for £12,000 and later brought to California for a record price. It was proof that elite thoroughbred prestige could travel as capital—even in the age of steamships and rail.[300]

Already seasoned by a grinding early campaign, Beau Ormonde was sold to Ed Kripp, who purchased him for $4,000 from W.O.B. McDonough. Kripp treated the horse as proof that he belonged in racing's upper tier.[301] In handicap racing, the best horses were made to prove it under burden. Officials assigned extra lead weight to the fastest and most accomplished runners, forcing them to carry more in the saddle so lesser horses would have a chance. The stronger the reputation, the heavier the load.

By age three, Beau Ormonde had already established himself as that kind of horse—a "weight-carrier," regularly placed at the top of the scale and asked to concede pounds to the field. Even under those burdens, he won the High Weight Handicap in San Francisco and the Free Handicap at Tanforan, in San Bruno.[302] His performances drew notice across the country. In May 1903, a Chicago sporting column reported that "Beau Ormonde smashes record," describing one of the fastest races yet seen on the Oakland track.[303]

Under Kripp's ownership, his schedule only grew harsher. At five, Beau Ormonde was sent to the post thirty-two times, winning eight races while competing almost exclusively in handicap company.[304]

That value did not stop at the track. Reports from the Sausalito poolrooms identified Kripp as the "biggest winner among the players across the bay," cashing several successful bets on California racing. Contemporary coverage left little doubt as to the source of the advantage. Kripp's winnings were understood to have come from wagers placed on his own horse through the poolroom system he helped sustain. He stood at the intersection of ownership, information, and access—betting not as an outsider testing luck, but as a man operating inside a network he understood intimately.[305]

Kripp's strategy of treating racehorses as mobile wealth extended well beyond Beau Ormonde. In August 1904, while in Chicago to pit Beau Ormonde against elite Eastern competition, Kripp entered a bidding war for a horse named Royalty. He successfully "bid him up," winning the horse out of a selling race—a type of race where every horse is essentially up for sale—at Hawthorne Park for $2,800. This was a massive sum that highlighted how quickly Kripp could transform cash into "bloodstock," high-value horses, whenever he saw an opening to grow his inventory.[306]

However, the same Chicago trip that showed off his wealth also exposed his vulnerability. In 1904, the *Sacramento Bee* published the headline: "SACRAMENTAN IS BUNCOED." Kripp, the powerful former baseball magnate, found himself in a humiliating position— not in the familiar streets of Sacramento or Washington Township, but in a Chicago police station, dealing with swindlers who had outmaneuvered him. Kripp was there for the turf. His champion stallion, Beau Ormonde, was racing against the best horses in the country. But even in that legitimate setting, the risks of his trade remained.

In Chicago, Kripp was swindled out of $500 by a man claiming to hold a pawn ticket for $10,000 in jewelry. The ticket was bogus. Kripp tracked the couple to the Chicago Beach Hotel and had them arrested.[307] The *San Francisco Chronicle* suggested the swindle was not random. Kripp believed it was retaliation— payback for having earlier backed a gambler named Green against another operator, Harcourt, in a poolroom dispute.[308] Back home, the episode read like humiliation. A Sacramento operator fooled in a larger market. But the details told a different story. Five hundred dollars was not ruin. It was exposure—money extended in expectation of leverage.

By 1905, he added Sansonette II to his stock. Purchased for $3,000, the coal-black Percheron was a significant investment: a four-year-old "massive fellow" that had already secured a blue ribbon at the California State Fair. For Kripp, he was a bridge to the farming community of Yolo County. By keeping Sansonette II at his "big breeding farm," Kripp positioned himself as a benefactor to local farmers, offering them an "unprecedented opportunity" to improve their own draft stock.

Kripp often displayed his success with ostentation. Among his possessions, few were more treasured than his racehorse Yolo King. When the horse developed a serious dental problem—an ulcerated tooth that threatened its ability to eat—Kripp demanded the best. He commissioned a dentist to create custom gold bridgework. He reportedly declared: "This is a great horse... I want him to have a gold tooth."

The horse became a local legend: "the Big Horse with the Gold

Tooth." Kripp rode it through Sacramento's streets like a moving advertisement—wealth made visible, restraint abandoned.[309]

The ranch itself had become a "model establishment." While his thoroughbred, Beau Ormonde, continued to chase purses on the Oakland tracks, the presence of Sansonette II anchored Kripp to the soil. This was not a business of secret passages and barbed-wire fences; it was a business of wide-open pastures and public praise.[310]

But the value of the ranch was never only agricultural. It sat on the edge of Sacramento's expanding transportation corridor, where railroads and bridges were beginning to redraw the map of the valley.

When the Western Pacific Railroad scouted the Yolo side in 1905, Kripp's property suddenly became prime ground. When asked if he would sell, Kripp acted as a "Sphinx," refusing to indicate his plans while emphasizing that because "the property has water front and is near Sacramento, it was very valuable."

He played the hand perfectly, telling reporters that while he had "information from a reliable source" regarding a purchasing syndicate, "it would take a pretty good figure to induce him to sell." He openly speculated that a sale to the railroad "would mean the building of shops there, and possibly the bridging of the river" at a point just below the Southern Pacific's line, but refused to name a price.[311]

He could speculate about rail shops and bridges because the ground still held. But along the Yolo bank, the river was making its own claim. Even where the levee had held before, that stability was never absolute. But there was confidence earned in smaller storms.

Each winter the river rose and pressed against the embankments thrown up to contain it. In Washington, the streets had never been lifted out of harm's reach; the town remained close to the water, dependent on packed earth and vigilance.

In the pre-dawn darkness of February 8, 1907, the river pressed harder than usual. At first, it moved without sound, a slow accumulation against earth packed years earlier by men who believed they had measured enough.

The Kripp Ranch, formerly the Conrad Ranch, was situated just a mile and a half below the Yolo bridge, directly opposite the foot of Y Street, a prime stretch of riverfront that was now under siege. The quiet was broken by the low, rhythmic gurgle of the Sacramento River. It was a sound Ed Kripp usually found comforting—the steady pulse of the border of his land. But at 5:30 AM, the rhythm changed. It began as collapse—a section of embankment folding inward under the weight it had promised to resist.[312] Water rushed through the opening, not wild but determined, carrying silt and debris, claiming low ground first. What began as a gurgle quickly deepened into a hungry, sucking roar.

A frantic pounding at the farmhouse door shattered the stillness. A milker's face appeared in the moonlight, pale, and out of breath. He gasped as he told the news Kripp had feared: the levee was gone. Water was already in the barnyard. Kripp did not hesitate. He grabbed his canvas coat and a kerosene lantern. His boots hit not gravel, but six inches of fast-moving, ice-cold black water.

Wood floated. Crates spun and collided. The current was not yet deep, but it was moving with purpose, pulling at boots, shifting footing with each step. Men moved quickly, hauling goods to higher ground, shouting over the roar of rising water. The initial 150-yard breach widened. The Sacramento River poured through like a freight train, threatening over 700 acres of prime farmland and the southern edge of Washington.[313] Kripp stood in the yard, barking orders. Lanterns bobbed like fireflies as men waded waist-deep, fighting the surge.[314]

The rescue was brutal. Over two hundred animals needed saving. The rescue could not be done at once. The stables for his racing stock stood 300 yards from the house, already cut off by channels of moving water. Men moved in groups, wading out and back again, each trip slower than the last as the current deepened and the ground beneath them softened into mud.

Inside the stalls, the horses had already grown restless. They smelled the river. Hooves struck wood in sharp, splintering blows. When Kripp entered Beau Ormonde's stall, the water had climbed. The stallion reared, striking at the walls, the confined space amplifying the panic. Roads were gone. Land was a basin of sediment. High ground had to be found—fast.

He drove his horses through the water. Men waded ahead and alongside. Animals pressed forward, urged by voice and hand. Slow, dangerous, relentless work.[315] Progress came in pieces. A few animals at a time. Back and forth. Each trip longer, each return harder.

By then the scale of the flood was clear. Hundreds of acres lay under water, and the southern edge of Washington was already flooded, the river still pressing through the gap with no sign of slowing. Hour by hour, the yard disappeared. Fence posts shortened in the rising water. Barn doors strained against the current. The familiar boundaries of the ranch—roads, ditches, corrals, paths—lost their meaning.

Only toward morning did the work begin to hold.

At dawn, the grey light touched the Yolo side. The last of the herd—two hundred shivering horses and cattle—was safe atop the embankment at "Marty's Place." Kripp stood among them, calm, soaked, mud-caked. Not a single head was lost.[316]

"Ed Kripp by hard work saved his stock worth about $20,000," the *Davis Enterprise* later reported. The flood had done its worst, and the rush of water was finally slowing. With the herd safe and the immediate crisis behind him, Kripp's focus turned to the levee itself—and to the question of how and why it had failed.

Inspecting the damage, Kripp concluded it was deliberate sabotage. "Without a doubt the levee was cut," he told a *Sacramento Bee* reporter. Yet by the same day, addressing the press, he shifted to reassurance: "The water is going down very rapidly... the damage from the break will not be great... the levee can be faced within a short time." He had already begun calculating recovery, seeing opportunity within catastrophe. Flooded lands would be enriched with Sacramento River sediment; crops might be lost today, but the soil would be richer tomorrow.

The levee break instantly became more than a disaster; it became a public spectacle. While the water rushed through the 250-foot gap, thousands of curious Sacramento citizens flocked to the scene. The *Independent-Leader* even joked that Kripp could have funded the entire $10,000 repair himself if he had simply built a high board fence and charged a ten-cent admission fee to the throngs of onlookers.

Despite the 700 to 1,000 acres of rich pasture and orchard land now underwater, Kripp refused to act the victim. Instead, he pivoted the disaster into a sales pitch. He told reporters that the flood would actually enhance the value of his land, as the river was depositing rich silt that would "enrich" the soil and fill in low spots.

Kripp was not alone in that assessment. Engineers and surveyors—many already working for the railroads—understood what farmers had long known: floodwater did not merely destroy; it rearranged. Silt filled the lowest ground, firmed soft places, and subtly lifted land that had always sat just below usefulness. What appeared, in the moment, as ruin could just as easily become preparation—for rail beds, yards, and approaches that demanded elevation, stability, and dryness more than beauty or yield.[317]

He maintained his hold on the property, noting it was already under bond to an Oakland syndicate, and prepared to use his $20,000 in saved livestock and railroad capital to fund his next move.[318]

The livestock had been saved. Capital remained intact. The ground was altered, not surrendered.

The river had taken acreage and left value behind.

Kripp's ground had already been placed under bond to the railroad syndicate before the flood. By the time the railroads moved in force, Kripp was not among those being pressed; he was already positioned within the transaction.

On April 11, 1907, the *Bee* confirmed what had been rumored since the previous November: the Kripp Ranch had been sold—300 acres—to the Western Pacific Railway Company for $85,000.. Ed Kripp was no longer a "buncoed" gambler. He was a man with capital and leverage.[319]

The exile became liquidity. The war chest was real.

Even before the land dried, the railroads began to move more aggressively. Condemnation suits multiplied along the Yolo bank, filed in batches, aimed less at negotiation than inevitability. Property could be sold—or it could be taken. Either way, the line would run where the companies required.[320]

The repairs, when they came, followed a familiar pattern. Responsibility was divided broadly and advantage narrowly. The State agreed to contribute. The county added its share. Local landowners were assessed. The corporations whose tracks and terminals would benefit most paid comparatively little—but gained ground made safer and more valuable by public effort.[321]

For Kripp, the moment had become one of calculation rather than urgency. The capital did not move immediately. It waited.

Kripp had learned that timing mattered more than speed.

CHAPTER 13

Across the River, Back to the Park

1908–1910

ON APRIL 20, 1908, the *Sacramento Star* reported that Pacific Coast League president J. Cal Ewing had "virtually granted" Sacramento a baseball franchise to be run by Ed Kripp. Ewing, formerly of Oakland's Reliance club, had long been acquainted with Ed.[322] Newspapers across the state—from Sacramento and San Francisco to Oakland, Fresno, Los Angeles, and Stockton—carried the news.[323] Backing the bid, Kripp promised his own money, a three-season bond, and a ballpark at an "ideal" downtown site.[324]

By 1908, the PCL was no longer experimental. It was the West's top professional circuit, independent and centralized, filling the void of major league baseball. Its franchises anchored the region's largest cities, linked by rail, sustained by unusually long seasons.[325] Admission to the league meant legitimacy—a city recognized as a major baseball center.

Admission, however, depended on more than enthusiasm or money. The league had survived too many collapses and rival circuits to expand casually. Expansion therefore required agreement among the directors, and one voice in particular carried unusual weight.

Judge W. W. McCredie of Portland, the owner and guiding force behind his city's Pacific Coast League club, dominated league councils. McCredie favored a carefully balanced circuit, ideally divided between northern and southern clubs. Portland's cooperation was essential: without the Oregon franchise the California teams could not maintain a viable Class-A league. If Portland objected, expansion could stall indefinitely.[326]

That reality made Sacramento's apparent victory in the spring of 1908 seem more secure than it actually was.

Through the early summer the momentum belonged to Kripp. By June, word circulated in Sacramento that he would manage the new club and had already begun signing players. He declared he would assemble the "very best material he can," and reports spread that he had secured signatures from several members of the existing State League team. Friends confidently predicted that Brown, Enwright, and Nealon would appear in his lineup.[327]

A meeting of Coast League directors in San Francisco on July 16 seemed to confirm the outcome. The *Star* reported that Sacramento had been granted outright to Kripp, while Henry Berry secured the other new franchise for Southern California. Kripp declared he was prepared to invest $30,000 in Sacramento for the coming season, improving the park and assembling a contender. "If money can secure a pennant-winning team," the paper observed, "Kripp will doubtless have one."[328]

While the announcement circulated through Sacramento, Kripp behaved as if the matter were settled.

On marshy land stretching along Tenth Street from W to Y, he began hauling hundreds of wagonloads of earth to fill the low ground.

"I have everything fixed to begin work on the baseball park... when it is finished there will be nothing on this coast quite to equal it... I will pay good salaries... I will have no trouble organizing a club of winners."[329]

While the league debated, Kripp built.[330]

League officials watched the activity with less enthusiasm.

Kripp's greatest strength—his investments, his independence, his willingness to build first and ask later—also made him difficult to control.

To league men like McCredie, who believed stability depended on disciplined ownership and predictable governance, Kripp looked less like a partner than a problem waiting to happen.

McCredie soon made that concern explicit. Promises made in California, he warned, meant little until the directors formally approved them. Sacramento's franchise remained uncertain.

The reversal landed in the city like a thrown switch.

One week newspapers reported that Sacramento had secured its place in the league. The next, the same papers dismissed the expansion talk as "tommy rot," insisting the capital city in fact "had no franchise." On September 11, the *Star* reported that Ewing had traveled north to confer with McCredie in Portland. Kripp, still convinced the decision would favor him, continued preparing his grounds, insisting the matter was "as good as settled." McCredie disagreed. Expansion, he said bluntly, was "not practically settled at all."[331]

Kripp responded the only way he knew.

On September 16, he boarded a train for San Francisco to confront the directors directly, leaving behind a headline that captured the city's anticipation: "KRIPP'S GONE TO GET HIS FRANCHISE."[332]

While the league debated his worthiness, the evidence of his intentions continued to accumulate in Sacramento—wagon after wagon of earth filling the lowlands he intended to transform into a professional park.

Three days later the uncertainty returned.

The *San Francisco Bulletin* reported that McCredie still stood "like old Gibraltar" behind his preferred league structure, leaving Kripp "in the air."[333]

Before risking more of his own "bank roll," Kripp halted work on the grounds and waited for the directors to clarify their position.

The clarification came slowly.

On October 10, President Cal Ewing finally announced what Sacramento had begun to suspect: "Kripp won't get a franchise next year." The same man who had encouraged his plans now delivered the blunt conclusion. The decision was less a judgment on Sacramento than a calculation about control. Portland held the "whip hand" in league councils. Granting Sacramento to a powerful and autonomous operator risked creating another center of influence.[334]

Kripp did not rush to make a statement publicly. "At the proper time I will make a full explanation and everything will be settled," he said.[335]

While the league maneuvered, he prepared an alternative. The objective was direct: a park owned outright, free from city boards, or league landlords. Whatever the league decided, whatever franchise it chose to award or withhold, the ground would belong to Kripp.

The decisive settlement came in January 1909, when Coast League managers met in San Francisco to finalize the coming season.

By then, the question was no longer whether Sacramento deserved a place in the league, but under what conditions it could be admitted without reopening the conflicts the directors had spent months suppressing.

When the *Bee* asked Kripp directly about his plans, he said: "I have no definite plans ahead in regard to the grounds. I did not purchase them with the idea of making a ballpark of them, though I considered that at one time. Several have spoken to me about handling an outlaw team in Sacramento, but I have not given the matter much consideration. As a matter of fact, I am going to refuse to talk baseball for the next month or so, sort of lay low and watch the others fight."[336]

By early 1909, the league's priorities had shifted. The question was no longer whether Sacramento could support Pacific Coast League baseball, but whether it could be brought in without strengthening Kripp. At the same time, Cy Moreing's State League had emerged as a more immediate threat. Sacramento remained that rival circuit's strongest market—its largest gate, its most established baseball city, and the source of much of its legitimacy. By placing a Pacific Coast League club there under league-approved ownership, the magnates could solve both problems at once: expand into a desirable market while crippling a competing league at its center. Without Sacramento's gate receipts and prestige, the remaining towns in the "outlaw" circuit—Stockton, Fresno, and the smaller interior clubs—would struggle to survive. What appeared publicly as expansion was also a calculated consolidation of power. One Sacramento paper warned that "the baseball war in this State next year will be the most severe ever fought," as the Coast League moved to break the rising State League while both sides competed openly for players.[337]

Sacramento did indeed get a franchise, but it went instead to Charley Graham, a longtime Sacramento baseball manager, and Bill Curtin, a local investor—men the league considered safer partners. In January 1909, the *Star* reported the decision under the understated headline "Are Handing it to Graham and Curtin." Men, they said, "stand well with the Sacramento public." Sacramento would enter the Pacific Coast League after all, but not under the man who had prepared the ground for it.[338]

Choosing the Curtin-Graham partnership solved several problems at once. It allowed the Pacific Coast League to expand to six clubs, satisfied Los Angeles owners who wanted a balanced schedule, and stripped Cy Moreing of his strongest base in the rival State League.

The local press mocked the new arrangement as the "Fizz Water League," a derisive nod to the high-living Ewing and Henry Berry, who were seen as consuming too much "fizzy stuff" while making backroom deals. Kripp, despite his significant investment, was viewed as too powerful to be part of this delicate peace. He was left sidelined with a recommendation from Ewing that he be reimbursed for expenses, while the new team prepared to take the field on the very terms Kripp had fought to establish.

On January 23, the *Star* announced Sacramento's formal admission to the league. The paper presented the move as a clean expansion rather than the resolution of a prolonged political struggle. A committee to consider the schedule was appointed that same afternoon and met immediately. Sacramento was in. Ed Kripp was not.[339]

Sacramento returned to the Pacific Coast League in March 1909—but as a managed entry, not a revival, and not on Kripp's ground. The Senators opened their season at Oak Park, and the limitations of that arrangement were immediately apparent. The *Star* observed on the eve of opening day that the street railway company, owners of the diamond and grounds at Oak Park, had "not been so reckless with its money as to repair the grandstand or in covering the great holes in the roof." As for the grandstand itself, the paper added with dry resignation: fans had "given up hope."[340]

Yet the crowds came. The *Bee*'s opening day account described Sacramento and Vernon as members of "the nursery department of the Coast League," two newcomer clubs allowed to open the season on Sacramento's home field so they could get acquainted with the circuit on equal terms. The opening had started with a procession from Seventh and K Streets, in which a brass band, tallyhos, and several automobiles figured conspicuously. City, county, and state officials rode in state. The grandstand was "taxed to its utmost."[341]

Manager Graham was optimistic. "You can say for me that the Sacramento Club is out for the pennant," he told the paper. "We have been four years in the game, and each year raised the standard of the National game. I think this year will be no exception," referring to the seasons he had kept Sacramento baseball alive outside the PCL.

By August the *Star* was reporting that those closest to him said Kripp had no intention of acquiring the local State League club—which was already in debt and looking for someone to absorb it, the league itself beginning to fail—but that "anyway, Kripp wants to land the Senators on his ball field for next season." The field at Tenth and Y, where he had planted alfalfa all summer, was now "in fine shape to be made into a ball ground." The location was not new to him. Two years earlier, he had shifted his poolrooms there during a period of pressure. If he could land the contract, he would build suitable grandstands and bleachers and make a first-class place for the sport.[342]

Kripp looked one block west, to the garbage dump at Eleventh and Y that nobody else wanted, and began calculating on a different scale entirely. He had spent two years learning the precise dimensions of what the league would and would not permit. That knowledge was not wasted. It had clarified, with a precision that no amount of goodwill could have supplied, the one thing Sacramento baseball had never possessed and the league could never provide: a permanent home on ground that belonged to no one but the man who built on it.

The answer would not come from league councils. It would come from land.

By 1910, the wilderness across the river was no longer exile. After the levee break, Kripp sold much of his ranch land, and the Northern Electric Railway chose the site for its western terminus across the river.[343]

Embankments cut through orchards; the dredger, *Jupiter,* placed 20,000 yards of sand to prepare the route. Progress was not abstract. It was steel, dirt, and right-of-way.

As Kripp had anticipated, a bridge followed. Before the Tower Bridge became the city's icon, there was its predecessor: the M Street Bridge—a $400,000 steel swing span, carrying a single electric rail line flanked by wagon ways and foot passageways.[344]

The air then filled with the hum of the "Big Green Interurbans," electric intercity trains that did more than move passengers—they reorganized access to the city itself.

Before the first train crossed those new tracks, Kripp had already stopped waiting for permission. He was building.

CHAPTER 14

The Vision Emerges

1909–1910

SACRAMENTO BASEBALL returned to the Pacific Coast League in 1909—but nothing essential had changed. The city had regained its place in organized baseball without regaining control of the conditions that had undermined it before. The club still played on borrowed grounds. Authority remained divided between baseball and the street railway company that owned Oak Park. Improvements were still promised rather than built. If Sacramento intended to stand on equal footing with the rest of the Coast, it needed more than a franchise. It needed a permanent home.

Ed Kripp had reached that conclusion before the league had. While Pacific Coast League officials debated Sacramento's admission, he quietly began preparing property he owned south of the city at Tenth and Y Streets, hauling fill and planting alfalfa to stabilize the low ground. The work began months before any public announcement, suggesting that Kripp was planning for a future that Sacramento baseball had not yet secured.

For the 1909 season, however, those plans remained just that. The street railway company retained the Senators at Oak Park, leaving Kripp's prepared ground without a tenant and Sacramento once again dependent upon facilities it did not control.

Oak Park soon demonstrated why that arrangement could not last. From the stands, Kripp looked over a park that no longer matched the league it served. Thousands of fans packed Opening Day, willing to overlook splintered benches, a gray, leaking roof, worn shingles, narrow aisles, and makeshift seating simply because Coast League baseball had returned to Sacramento. But the promised improvements never truly materialized. Another season began with little more than repairs and assurances. Oak Park had been good enough to bring the league back. Whether it was good enough to keep it was another matter.

Manager Charley Graham did not believe Sacramento could afford another disappointing season. The club, he warned, had to make a better showing than it had the year before or risk losing its franchise altogether.[345] Better grounds were no longer a luxury but a necessity. If Graham was right, Kripp was preparing to risk a fortune on a club that might not survive long enough to justify the investment.

At that same moment, Sacramento itself was expanding rapidly. Between 1900 and 1910 the city's population had increased by nearly fifty percent, while development steadily pushed southward beyond its older neighborhoods. [346] If professional baseball intended to remain part of that future, it would need a permanent place within it.

Kripp responded by enlarging the scope of the project.

In December 1909 he purchased the adjoining 9.9-acre garbage dump at the corner of Eleventh and Y Streets for $3,000. Combined with his earlier holdings at Tenth and Y, the acquisition assembled what contemporary accounts described as eighteen acres—the broad tract of land that would become Buffalo Park.[347]

The site hardly resembled the home of a first-class ball club. The ground was a low, swampy stretch on Sacramento's southern edge where wagons unloaded the city's refuse and few residents had reason to linger. Yet its very condition offered an advantage no previous Sacramento ballpark had possessed: independence. The land lay beyond the control of railway companies, and the city's municipal boards.

By October the question was no longer whether Sacramento could support higher-class baseball. The crowds had already answered that. The question was whether anyone was willing to commit the capital required to build for it.

Twenty-five thousand dollars represented an extraordinary commitment in 1909. It was an investment large enough that failure would be impossible to ignore. Sacramento had already watched professional baseball collapse, and no one could say with confidence that the city's newest franchise would fare any better.

That understanding had been reinforced the year before when the *Sacramento Bee* ran a blistering assessment of Coast League operations based on testimony from Mike Mitchell, an outfielder who had escaped west-coast chaos for the Cincinnati Reds. Mitchell dismissed the circuit as "Class Z," blaming owners who cut salaries midseason, shifted travel costs to players, and ran the league on corner-cutting instead of capital. Under the National Commission, Mitchell argued, the Pacific Coast League should be the object of investigation—not the players who had jumped their contracts, but the organization that had driven them to it. "When the National Commission comes to investigate the so-called 'outlaw' league on the coast," he told a Cincinnati paper, "they will do well to inquire into the reason of this league harboring contract-jumpers."[348]

Mitchell's criticism suggested that the Coast League's problems were structural rather than temporary.

However, Kripp had wagered before. Cards, racehorses, saloons, and baseball clubs all carried uncertainty. But each shared one advantage: they could be abandoned when circumstances changed. A ballpark demanded something different. Once timber, steel, and concrete met eighteen acres of Sacramento soil, there would be no quiet exit. Success or failure would stand in plain view, fixed to the landscape for everyone to see.

On December 22, the *Sacramento Bee* announced what few would have imagined. The headline was bold and confident: "ED KRIPP READY TO CONSTRUCT $25,000 BASEBALL PARK HERE." The subheading promised even more: "Deal Pending by Which Sacramento Teams Will Be Established in New Home—Plant to Be Finest on Coast." The article laid out Kripp's plan with remarkable specificity. A deal was being arranged with the Sacramento Baseball Club; once finalized, it would mean a plant at Kripp's grounds at Eleventh and Y Streets, ready for the opening of the following spring.

The park's name carried its own message. "Buffalo Park" was more than a flourish. It publicly linked the project to Frank Ruhstaller's Buffalo Brewing Company, whose financial and political influence had become a recurring presence in Sacramento baseball. The name announced that Kripp's venture rested not merely on one man's ambition, but on the backing of one of the city's most powerful commercial interests.

Six days later, on the morning of December 28, Kripp, Charley Graham and a contractor went out to the grounds in the December cold to walk the property.[349] The reality of the project became unmistakable.

The site was a swamp. Years of the city's discarded refuse had been dumped at the edge of town, mixing with the natural wetland until the place became something worse than either. Not solid ground. Not open water. The land had nowhere to drain. Each step produced a soft, squelching sound as the mud gave way beneath a man's boot. Even in December, with cold slowing decay, the smell still rose: rotting waste and old scraps of a city's throwaways accumulated over decades.

The *Bee* highlighted the visit under the headline "Go Over Site for Proposed Ball Park"—reporting that the three men were "getting a line on the proposed plant to be erected there"—and adding a detail that mattered: Kripp had petitioned the City Trustees for permission to tap a city water main at Twelfth and Y Streets to supply the park.

It was the first proof this wasn't just a headline. The project had already moved to permits, mains, and access. The grandstands would come later. First came the things no one would ever see.

What looked like a small detail was anything but. A modern ballpark did not begin with grandstands or scoreboards. It began with water, permits, and men who knew how to turn mud into something that would hold.

Getting spectators to Buffalo Park posed its own engineering problem. A park was only useful if the city's residents could reach it. Kripp negotiated with the California Traction Company for an extension of service to the grounds. The new transit line would be "in operation by the time the season starts," the papers promised, delivering fans "within a block of the grounds or to Eleventh and X Streets," while the site would also remain "accessible by Tenth Street line of the street car company." These arrangements mattered as much as the grandstand itself. The park Kripp was building was not merely a physical structure but a machine for moving the city toward a fixed point—one that required rails as surely as it required concrete.[350]

The plan was falling into place.

Then he filed for a saloon license, and the fault lines appeared. Kripp had quietly filed an application with the Sacramento County Board of Supervisors seeking permission to operate a saloon in connection with the proposed ballpark. Locating the establishment just outside the city limits freed Kripp from Sacramento's municipal ordinances and police authority, but it did not place him beyond regulation altogether. County and state liquor laws still applied. A license did not restrain his operation; it stabilized it. What began as tolerated activity became, through paperwork and fees, a recognized enterprise—one that could be fined, regulated, and quietly left alone rather than publicly shut down.

In practical terms, the request was routine. Concessions were an established source of revenue at professional ballparks across the country, and saloons operated openly throughout Sacramento. Without liquor revenue, the margins of professional baseball were thin; with it, a club could more reliably meet its operating costs and service debt. Kripp's application framed the bar as an accessory to the park rather than its purpose—a concession intended to support a $25,000 investment. To reinforce that point, he posted a $1,000 bond backed by guarantors including F.J. Ruhstaller of Buffalo Brewing, one of Sacramento's most influential businessmen.

The reaction, however, was immediate and pointed. The *Sacramento Star* devoted a front-page story to the proposal beneath the satirical headline "BOOZE AND BASEBALL," treating Kripp's application not as a routine licensing matter but as a public provocation. The article mocked the idea that alcohol should serve as the "hand-maiden of baseball" and portrayed the proposed saloon as an attempt to blend sport, drink, and profit just beyond the city's regulatory reach. Chairman Donnelly of the Board of Supervisors confirmed the application would soon come before the Board, though, for the moment, no formal protest had yet appeared.[351]

Even within the Board of Supervisors there was no clear agreement. Supervisor Dave Ahern maintained that a long-standing understanding existed against granting new liquor licenses immediately outside the city limits, while other supervisors questioned whether any such agreement carried legal force.

What had begun as an ordinary licensing request was becoming something larger. The argument was no longer simply about a saloon license. It was about what kind of city Sacramento intended to become—and who should profit from the gathering of its citizens.

Three days later, the *Star* escalated the controversy under a more ominous headline: "May Object to Kripp Saloon." The paper warned that nearby residents might soon organize a formal protest, emphasizing once again that the proposed saloon would stand "just across the road from the city cemetery."

Public opposition quickly coalesced around the park's location. On January 4, 1910, the *Star* reported "intense opposition" from neighboring property owners and holders of cemetery plots. Approximately sixty signatures had been gathered, and both the liquor-license application and the protest were laid over for ten days. The opponents framed their objections carefully. They insisted they were "heartily in favor of athletics," but opposed placing a saloon beside a burial ground, warning that cheering crowds could disrupt funeral services.[352]

The *Sacramento Bee*'s coverage on January 6 captured the full pressure the Sacramento club was now under. Manager Graham told the paper plainly that the situation was this: "The Sacramento Club has to make a better showing this coming season than last or the franchise will be taken away." He had been told it would be advisable to secure ball grounds closer to town. The offer of Kripp's grounds was the most favorable available, and two other sites that had been considered both had significant drawbacks—chiefly that the club would be "forced to erect our stands and fix the grounds, necessitating a big outlay."

The Club's secretary, J.J. Inman, was even more direct. He was, he said, "very strongly in favor" of granting Kripp the license. Without it, the club could not have the grounds. Without the grounds, they would not play that season. "A saloon in this case is a necessary evil," Inman told the *Bee*.[353]

Kripp now faced a choice: abandon the saloon plan and build the park without it, or fight for the license despite the mounting resistance. By January 9, he chose a third course.

The *Independent-Leader* reported a new phase in the controversy:

Kripp would forgo the bar privilege he sought if a subscription of $100 per month were paid to him instead. Graham explained the logic plainly in conversation with the paper's reporter. Kripp had committed to building the baseball grounds at a cost of $25,000. He had figured on the saloon to pay the interest on his investment. If there was to be no saloon, Kripp was willing to proceed—but only if he could be "assured a reasonable return on the money he spends." Nothing had yet come of the proposal, Graham acknowledged, but something might develop that would "solve the problem of a new ball park."[354]

Graham also worked to narrow the moral target. The license in question, he insisted, was not for a "road house" but "merely for a bar for the patrons of the ball game." It would open around ten o'clock in the morning and close about six in the evening. It would be "decently conducted" throughout. Graham understood the distinction mattered. He was trying to separate a ballpark concession from the vice resort opponents imagined whenever they heard the word "saloon."

The distinction did not solve the political problem. The symbolism of mixing baseball and booze, beside the cemetery, with Ed Kripp's name on the paperwork, proved more potent than any assurance of decorum. On January 16, 1910, Kripp withdrew the application. The following day, the *Bee* reported that he had decided not to "fight the strong opposition which has arisen" against the establishment of a bar in his proposed ballpark. The decision had been made the previous night after a short telephone conference with Manager Graham. It was "considered poor policy to further antagonize the people who have opposed the placing of a bar in the stands and mixing baseball and booze," and the club had decided to abandon the feature rather than risk the whole project.

The park would still be built—but on revised terms. Kripp would receive $100 per month in rent from the Sacramento club in lieu of bar revenue, replacing the income he had expected from the saloon with a guaranteed payment from the team itself.[355]

Yet it marked an important shift. For most of Kripp's career, public opposition had been only one form of pressure among many—manageable, negotiable, rarely decisive on its own. This time, a petition bearing sixty signatures had forced him to change course. Not a court order, not a police raid, not a competing bid. Public sentiment, expressed through organized protest, had altered the calculations of one of Sacramento's most experienced businessmen. Kripp adapted, as he always had. But organized public opposition had accomplished what raids, lawsuits, and competitors never had: it forced him to change the economics of Buffalo Park.

On January 17, 1910, the *Sacramento Bee* announced: "Start Work on Ball Park. Baseball Club Gives Ed Kripp Cue to Commence." The Sacramento Club's board of directors approved the $100 monthly rental "in lieu of his privilege," and Kripp wasted no time. A crew arrived that morning to tear down fences and clear the property. The contractor expected to begin excavating for the concrete grandstand foundations the following Wednesday. The schedule was ambitious. Only unusually severe weather, the *Bee* reported, would prevent preliminary games before March.[356]

What emerged from the ground promised to be unlike anything Sacramento had attempted before. The grandstand would seat 2,400 spectators in covered individual opera chairs—"not benches," the *Bee* emphasized—while covered bleachers would accommodate another 4,400, giving the park a capacity approaching 7,000.[3] Every seat would command an unobstructed view of the field. Players would have modern dressing rooms. Reporters would work from press facilities equipped with telegraph connections. Private boxes and spacious concessions reflected a design intended not merely to host baseball games but to welcome thousands of paying spectators. The *Bee* declared the new grounds would be "up-to-date and modern in every detail," a park built to compare favorably with the finest on the Pacific Coast.[357]

Buffalo Park was larger, costlier, and far more permanent than any previous home of Sacramento baseball. Leased fields, borrowed grandstands, and temporary fences had sustained earlier clubs. Timber, grading, concrete, and enclosed grounds promised something different. Once completed, the park could not simply be dismantled or moved elsewhere. It represented the largest permanent commitment anyone had yet made to professional baseball in Sacramento.

Less than a month earlier, this same ground had been little more than a swamp littered with Sacramento's refuse. Kripp, Charley Graham, and a contractor picked their way across it in the December cold, marking out mains, streetcar access, and concrete foundations. Now the fences were gone. Excavation had begun. The newspaper headline had become a construction site.

Sacramento noticed. By February, the conversation had moved past the question of whether the park would exist to what it would host.[358]

By late February, confirmation arrived. The Chicago White Sox would travel west by special train, and Ban Johnson—president of the American League, one of the most powerful figures in professional baseball—would make the journey as the personal guest of White Sox owner, Charles Comiskey. Sacramento would open its new park not merely before a Coast League crowd, but before the man whose word, more than any other, determined what belonged in the game and what did not.[359]

Somewhere west of the Sierras, that train was already moving.
Ed Kripp had built a ballpark on a garbage dump. What happened next would depend on whether the institution of baseball was willing to meet him there.

Baseball at Buffalo Park.
Courtesy of Alan O'Connor. Private collection.

Baseball game at Buffalo Park.
Courtesy of the author.

CHAPTER 15

Eleventh and Y

1910

A FEW DAYS before the opening of Buffalo Park, the *Sacramento Bee* reported that "the first familiar sound of the approaching baseball season was heard at the Kripp grounds." Work crews rolled the diamond smooth and worked the outfield into shape, preparing the new field for its first game. Sacramento's Pacific Coast League club would soon take the field there, turning months of planning and construction into the city's new baseball home. The paper added—almost pointedly—that the new outfield would be "much superior to that at Oak Park."[360]

The comparison was deliberate. Oak Park had served Sacramento for years, but it was a borrowed ground owned by the street railway company. Buffalo Park was something different. It stood on land Ed Kripp owned outright.

On the morning of March 9, Sacramento began closing its doors early.

Shops along K Street pulled their shades at noon. Clerks were dismissed. Wholesale houses locked up so employees could join the crowds heading south toward Eleventh and Y Streets. For a few hours that afternoon, the business district thinned until it felt almost quiet. The city was rearranging itself around a baseball game.[361]

Before the first pitch there was a parade.

A procession of tally-hos carried the players, local officials, and visiting dignitaries through the streets. Sacramento's team rode together in new uniforms, waving to the spectators gathered along the route. The carriages eventually turned toward the streetcar lines that carried crowds out of downtown and toward the southeastern edge of the city.[362]

Then Sacramento began to move.

Streetcars clattered down Tenth Street, each car fuller than the last. Men in dark coats clung to the rear platforms. Boys ran alongside the tracks until conductors shouted them back. Women stepped carefully onto the dusty road and joined the steady stream of spectators walking toward the new park.

Not long before, the site had been a dumping ground where the city discarded its refuse. Now fresh lumber gleamed in the sunlight. The grandstand rose above the fence line, newly painted, the smell of cut wood and damp earth still hanging in the air.

Sacramento had been waiting for something like this.

For decades the city had struggled to hold onto professional baseball. Teams came and went. Ballparks appeared on borrowed land and disappeared just as quickly. Crowds arrived faithfully every season, but the infrastructure behind the sport remained temporary.

Kripp intended Buffalo Park to end that cycle.

The opening was arranged as something more than a routine exhibition. The Chicago White Sox arrived in Sacramento as part of their western spring tour, bringing one of the most recognizable clubs in major-league baseball. The team had crossed the continent by rail on a special train before continuing through Pacific Coast cities. Now that national circuit of travel had carried them to Sacramento.[363]

Their owner, Charles Comiskey, traveled with the club, along with American League president Ban Johnson. Their presence alone gave the opening a significance that no local exhibition could have achieved.

Sacramento's new ballpark would open under the eyes of the sport's national authorities.

The crowd arrived early.

An estimated 2,500 people—roughly double the attendance of the previous season's opening—settled into the stands. The covered grandstand filled with Sacramento's better-dressed spectators; the cheaper sections packed with clerks, laborers, and boys. The arrangement revealed the park's first real argument: not only that Sacramento could host professional baseball, but that it could sell it broadly—to fifty-cent fans under the roof and dime-a-seat boys crowding the bleachers.[364]

On the field, the Senators took their positions in blue.

Danzig anchored first base. Shinn, Haley, and Boardman spread across the infield. In the outfield stood Doyle, Zamlock, and Riggs—posted "in the gardens."[365]

Then the visiting White Sox appeared—also in blue—so that for a moment the two squads blurred together.

Governor James Gillett had been scheduled to throw the first ball but was called away from the city at the last moment. The absence mattered little. Ban Johnson occupied a place of honor, and Hugh Duffy—the former Boston star and one of the most respected figures in the game—stood on the field among the players.

Their presence mattered more than any ceremonial pitch.

It meant that the national leadership of baseball had agreed, at least for an afternoon, to treat Sacramento as legitimate.

Chicago's roster read like a map of professional baseball itself. Messenger in left field, Beall in right, Blackburn at shortstop, Waite in center, Block catching, Scott pitching, Zeider covering third.

The names did more than fill a column.

They announced Buffalo Park's status. A ground capable of receiving Ban Johnson and Charles Comiskey could also host a full American League lineup—and not look like a provincial stop on a goodwill tour.

When the game began, the crowd followed every play with nervous attention.

Midway through the contest Sacramento found its moment.

Hunt drove a sharp single into the field, and Doyle came racing home. For a second the new grandstand erupted. Hats lifted, boys shouted, and the sound rolled across the grounds in a wave of relief.

Sacramento could answer after all.

But experience eventually told. Chicago's hitters began wearing down Sacramento's pitching, pushing runs across one at a time. The White Sox finally edged ahead and held the advantage.

The final score was 6–5.

Yet the mood leaving the park was not disappointment.

It was vindication.

Sacramento had taken one of the American League's flagship clubs to the wire in a ballpark that had been a city dumping ground only weeks earlier. The *Sacramento Bee* captured the feeling the next day: "Everyone had a good word to say for the team and the new ball plant."[366]

In the weeks that followed, Buffalo Park settled into routine. Game stories appeared regularly in the sporting pages. Scores were posted. Standings were tracked.

The park—new and improbable—began to feel normal.

When the Senators traveled, other events began to appear on the calendar. Athletic meets, exhibitions, and eventually boxing tournaments drew their own crowds through the gates. Kripp had built the park with that flexibility in mind. A team might leave town. A schedule might falter. But the gates could still open.[367]

Buffalo Park, however, was only one part of Ed Kripp's world.

Another stood a few blocks away at the Columbia Café.

There his gambling establishment continued as a fixture of Sacramento's nightlife. In 1910 he converted several rooms above the café into apartments next to the operations.

During the renovations, the *Sacramento Bee* reported, Kripp chained his "favorite and rather gentle pet" on the back porch to a ring screwed into the floor.

The animal was a tiger.

Not the kind the newspapers used to describe his gambling rooms, but a living one.

Spectators gathered nearby to witness the pacing cat. The sight quickly became a neighborhood curiosity, drawing crowds who lingered outside the building. Kripp assured reporters that the animal was properly secured and "would not hurt anyone."[368]

The image bordered on allegory.

A civic ballpark had risen from a garbage dump at Eleventh and Y Streets, presenting Sacramento as a modern baseball city. Yet only blocks away, a gambling house lit by chandeliers and lined with green-felt tables, a chained tiger kept watch outside the building.

Inside the Columbia, everything spoke of order. Dealers ran the games with quiet efficiency. Whiskey flowed across polished bars. Debts were settled without dispute.

Outside, the tiger paced.

For the moment, Ed Kripp controlled both worlds.

It would not last.

GUSTAV POSTLER MEETS DEATH IN PISTOL DUEL WITH EDWARD L. KRIPP, A PROFESSIONAL GAMBLER

POLICE SERGEANT LENDS HIS PISTOL TO GAME KEEPER

LURE OF GAMING DRIVES MAN TO ROBBERY

Ruined Gambler Holds Up Men Who Won His Money and His Death Follows.

POLICE REVOLVER USED

Sergeant Donovan Now Faces Charges for Aiding Professional Gambler in Fight.

Coverage of the Postler shooting.
San Francisco Chronicle, January 28, 1911.

CHAPTER 16

Shooting at the Saratoga Club

1911

IN JANUARY 1911, Ed Kripp was living between two cities. Sacramento was where he had built Buffalo Park and established himself. In San Francisco, where his children were growing up, he was proprietor of the Saratoga Gambling Club.[369]

This was not a sudden expansion. Three years prior, as enforcement tightened in Sacramento and gamblers probed new ground in places like Oak Park, the *Bee* reported that Kripp himself was in Oakland, "making a book on the races," operating within a wider circuit that extended beyond any single city"[370]

Inside the so-called "incorporated club" of the Saratoga, protected by a carefully maintained legal fiction, police lookouts warned of raids, entry required membership, and warrants required advance notice. The courts demanded standards of proof that effectively guaranteed delay or dismissal. The result was a system designed to resist raids, prosecutions, and closure—and it usually succeeded.

For years, gambling along the Pacific Coast had functioned less as a series of isolated crimes than as a system. Poolrooms and gaming clubs operated openly. Police were posted nearby to watch them, but rarely to interfere. Newspapers protested, reformers demanded enforcement, and the games continued. Everyone understood the arrangement even when no one described it plainly: money moved, the machinery ran, and the law looked away so long as the balance held.

Up to this point, the story had unfolded at that level—institutions, accommodations, quiet understandings between operators and officials. But systems built on tolerance are stable only while nothing goes wrong. The shooting at the Saratoga Club would expose the cost of that invisible system.

The legal fictions surrounding the gambling houses worked so long as losses could be absorbed and grievances remained private. But gambling never distributes risk evenly. When fortunes collapse, they collapse somewhere—and on someone.

For Gustav Postler, the reckoning arrived at home.

The house had been gone for months.

Not physically. The structure still stood. But the ownership—the deed, the security, the right to call it theirs—had been mortgaged away to pay gamblers at a place the police had decided did not technically exist, that the courts had wrapped in legal fictions, and that the system had quietly agreed to leave untouched.

Portrait of Paul Postler.
San Francisco Call, January 28, 1911.

On the morning of January 27, 1911, Gustav Postler told his fifteen-year-old son Paul to accompany him downtown.

They drove in a buggy along Market Street. At Brittain's hardware store at Market and Mason, Postler purchased a .38-caliber revolver and a box of cartridges. The cost was $7.50. He had already lost far more than that at the Saratoga's tables.

"I am going to get my money back from the gamblers," he told his son.

Paul objected instinctively. "Oh, you can't get your money back."

His father said nothing.

At 149 Mason Street Paul sat holding the reins. The horse shifted its weight, stamped once against the pavement. Fog hung thick in the street, softening the edges of everything. The building rose in front of him, ordinary from the outside, its interior invisible.

Inside, the Saratoga Club was operating as it always did—tables full, money moving, lookouts watching the stairs.

And now Gustav Postler was inside, with a revolver in his pocket.

Paul waited.

"About ten minutes afterward," he testified, "I heard a noise inside the building which sounded like a shot."

The sound was muffled, distorted by walls and fog, but unmistakable. Paul tightened his grip on the reins.

"I then saw three men come to the windows at the top of the building and try to get on the fire escape."

Three men. Perhaps more. Moving fast. Fleeing.

Then another figure appeared.

"They went back, and soon after I saw a man—whom I afterward found out was Mr. Kripp—climb out a window on the top floor and run down the fire escape to the second floor. He then went inside and soon came out to the street."

Paul did not understand what it meant. He only knew his father was still upstairs.

Alarmed, he climbed down from the buggy. Sergeant James T. Donovan was standing near a cigar store on Mason Street.

"I told the sergeant that I thought there must be trouble upstairs, because I saw three men come to the window and another man come down."

As Donovan turned toward the entrance, Ed Kripp stepped into the street.

"There's a man holding up the game upstairs," Kripp said. "Give me your gun."

Donovan handed over his revolver.

Paul watched.

The boy quickly explained that his father was likely upstairs and that he had brought a gun. Kripp asked for a description, listened, and then said, "You better come up with me." After a pause, he added, "Maybe this boy can stop him."

They entered the building together. Paul later recalled riding up in the elevator and stepping off onto the top floor beside Kripp.

Inside, he saw his father standing just within the doorway of a large room. One hand remained in his pocket; in the other he held a pistol. He appeared agitated. Beyond him, several men paced or stood uncertainly among the tables.

Paul called out: "Pa, you better give them their money back and you better give me your gun, because this man has a gun too."

"My father then ordered me to come into the room," Paul said.

"I went inside and sat down at a table and began to cry."

Then Kripp entered.

"My father then said to Kripp, 'You come in here.' Then Kripp fired at my father, but did not hit him. Then my father began to fire at Kripp."

"I am sure that Kripp fired first at my father," Paul later stated, "but did not hit him."

The courts would never resolve the sequence that followed.

"I ran to the window and said to the men, 'Please let me out the window. I'm afraid I will get shot.'"

"I am afraid my father will shoot through the door."

"They told me to stay where I was, but I managed to open the window and I climbed down the fire escape and later went upstairs again with the police. Then I saw my father lying dead on the floor in the big room."

That was what Paul had seen. What he knew was narrower.

Paul Postler was fifteen years old when he witnessed the final moments of his father's life. He had seen Gustav Postler standing in a gaming room with a revolver. He had heard multiple shots. He had watched men flee through windows and down fire escapes. Later, he saw his father lying dead on the floor.

Contemporary newspapers reported that three bullets were recovered from Postler's body, even as suicide was advanced as a possible conclusion—an inconsistency no official account ever resolved. Some papers framed the death as self-inflicted; others described a pistol duel or an outright killing. None reconciled the number of wounds with a single, uncontested sequence of events.[371]

The coroner's jury split—seven voting suicide, six voting justifiable self-defense—mirroring the press's inability to settle the facts. The courts ultimately rendered judgment not on the shooting itself, but on its legal consequences. Criminal responsibility was avoided. Ed Kripp was charged not with homicide, but with operating an illegal gambling establishment. He pleaded guilty to a misdemeanor and was fined $1,000.

What happened in that room remained officially undecided.[372]

The shooting did not remain contained within courtrooms or editorials. Its consequences traveled outward—crossing cities, families, and the boundaries people believed might keep them untouched.

For Ed Kripp's ex-wife, Emma, distance had seemed like protection. By moving to San Francisco, she believed she had placed herself—and Ed's children—far enough from Sacramento's poolrooms and headlines for the noise to fade. The city was larger, the scandals more diffuse, the past easier to outrun. But the Saratoga shooting collapsed that illusion. Within hours, the name was in the papers. All boundaries dissolved the moment Ed Kripp stepped out of a San Francisco gambling room and into the public record again.

Anna Postler faced a different kind of battle.

In the days following the shooting, Mrs.Postler refused the explanation that others found convenient. In a statement published by the *San Francisco Examiner*, she traced her husband's destruction not to drink or temperament, but to gambling protected by the very authorities charged with stopping it. She described pleading with police days before the shooting, only to be told that nothing could be done—that gambling houses continued to operate because their proprietors enjoyed police protection secured through bribery. The law, she suggested, had not merely failed her husband; it had stood aside while he was dismantled piece by piece.[373]

The Postler Family.
San Francisco Call, January 28, 1911.

Her husband had carried life insurance and a fraternal benefit certificate intended to protect his family. The companies refused to pay. Their position was simple: Gustav Postler had committed suicide, and suicide voided the policies. The question that courts could not resolve inside a gambling room now followed the widow into courtrooms and offices, where it was reduced to clauses, paperwork, and precedent.

Anna Postler did not accept the verdict that others found convenient. She ordered an autopsy. She gathered testimony. She filed suit.

When claims went unanswered, she filed again. In January 1913, newspapers reported that she had sued the Travelers Insurance Company after furnishing proof of her husband's death nearly two years earlier and receiving no response. Later that year, she pursued payment from the Woodmen of the World, which had issued a benefit certificate shortly before her husband's death and then declined to honor it.[374]

The litigation dragged on. As late as August 1913, Anna Postler was still in court, seeking $1,100 from the Woodmen of the World—$1,000 in insurance and $100 designated for a headstone at her husband's grave. She had already presented her claim. She still could not collect.[375]

For more than two years, she pressed the same argument the coroner's jury had failed to settle: whatever had happened inside the Saratoga Club was not an act of self-destruction. The fight moved slowly, through motions and appeals, while her husband's death remained officially unresolved. When the United States Supreme Court ultimately declined to disturb a lower-court judgment in her favor, allowing it to stand, payment was finally compelled.

The victory was narrow and procedural. The cost was measured in years. What should have been protection became a test of endurance.[376]

The city, meanwhile, had made a show of reckoning.

Police Chief John F. Seymour vowed to cleanse the department and close the city's largest gambling resorts. Equipment was seized. Doors were shut. The machinery appeared, briefly, to have stopped.

Not for long.

The roulette wheels, faro layouts, chips, and tables seized from the

Saratoga Club remained in police custody only temporarily. Within months, the courts ordered the equipment returned. By April 1912, the same paraphernalia—identified in court as that restored after the Saratoga shooting—was found in use again, as Mack Wilson attempted to open a new gambling house at 215 O'Farrell Street. The system had paused. The cycle had continued.

In February 1911, the *San Francisco Examiner* reported on the collapse of gambling prosecutions tied to the same establishment, noting that cases brought in the wake of the shooting were dismissed for lack of evidence. Reform was promised. Raids were announced. But as with so many earlier efforts, the law stalled once it reached the courts..[377] The machinery had moved. It had not changed.

For Ed Kripp, what had once been managed through force now attracted scrutiny, and scrutiny was a kind of enforcement he could not outrun.

In the days after the shooting, Kripp did not hide. He appeared at the Columbia Café. He was seen on J Street. He attended to business as if the Saratoga Club had belonged to someone else.

But something had shifted in how he moved through the city.

The Saratoga Club had been carefully constructed. Lookouts were positioned. Signals were established. Connections to the police department had been cultivated over years. Everything that could be controlled had been controlled. And yet Gustav Postler had entered the room with a revolver, and the arrangement had not stopped him.

The coroner's jury split seven to six—an admission that even formal verdicts could not settle what had happened. The grand jury returned a misdemeanor rather than homicide.

By every measure, Kripp had survived intact. Yet the ambiguity unsettled him. Not because it was legally dangerous, but because it revealed a limit. For years he had believed that every contingency could be anticipated, every debt collected, every rule enforced. Gustav Postler had exposed the flaw in that belief. Kripp understood then that his power had never been absolute.

By morning, Kripp had made a decision. The Saratoga Club would be left to its fate. His San Francisco operations would contract. He would be present less, expose himself less directly.

But this was not retreat. It was adjustment.

A grandstand could burn. A lease could expire. But a ballpark stood in daylight. Its crowds were counted. Its receipts were printed. Its authority did not depend on whether anyone pretended not to see it.

The system in San Francisco had survived. But it had shown him its limits.

The packed grandstand at Buffalo Park.
Courtesy of the author.

CHAPTER 17

A City in the Stands

1911–1914

BUFFALO PARK was no longer an experiment by 1911. The boards had weathered into place. On summer afternoons, people moved toward Y Street as if they had always done so. What had once stood outside Sacramento's formal limits now functioned as one of its centers. That spring, Buffalo Park hosted something that felt larger than baseball. A touring team from Waseda University arrived from Tokyo as part of an early exchange between Japanese and American players.

Japanese passenger steamship Shinyo Maru, ca. 1911.
United States Navy, NavSource Naval History.

Their journey to Sacramento was not incidental—it was a statement of baseball's growing reach, and of California's place within it. They had endured a transpacific voyage—nearly two weeks of ocean travel—to stand on that field.

Word spread quickly beyond the usual sporting circles. On the afternoon they took the field, the grandstands filled not only with Sacramento's regular faithful—clerks, merchants, workingmen in shirtsleeves—but also with Japanese residents and visitors who came to see their countrymen play the American game on California soil.

Sacramento's college team entered as heavy favorites. Yet from the first innings, the tone unsettled expectation. The Japanese players moved with restraint. Their fundamentals were precise. When mistakes came, they did not protest or gesture. They returned quietly to position, composed enough that one paper described their bearing as "in the fashion of the Stoics."

The score widened to nine runs, but the margin obscured the point. What cost the visitors the game was fielding—the unfamiliar angles of a new diamond, misjudged hops, hurried throws. Observers conceded that without those errors, they might well have prevailed despite being outhit. The crowd did not remember defeat. It remembered discipline.

There were no arguments with umpires. No flared tempers. Both teams conducted themselves as gentlemen. Applause rose not only for clean hits but for clean conduct.[378]

Buffalo Park had hosted rivalries and resentments. That afternoon, it staged something else: an image of Sacramento as courteous, modern, capable of welcoming the world to its own ground. The park had become more than a venue, one of the few places capable of gathering the entire city.

It was a role he had not advertised, but one he increasingly understood. For Kripp, the moment confirmed something he had already begun to understand. The value of Buffalo Park did not lie solely in baseball itself, but in its ability to gather the city—to stage events that extended beyond the game and returned value in attention, reputation, and receipts. The exhibition was not his in origin, but it was his in effect. It passed through his gates, filled his stands, and reinforced the role he had carved out just beyond the city's edge.

And once the ground had proved it could hold the city's attention, it began to host everything the city wished to see reflected there.

The pattern had begun months earlier. Eighteen newspapermen from the *Bee*, the *Union*, and the *Independent-Leader* agreed to abandon their typewriters "in favor of the willow and the horse-hide."[379] The papers promoted the contest with cheerful self-mockery. It was billed less as sport than as a guarantee of comic incompetence. The city arrived already laughing.

Jack Stafford took the mound—a "veteran in politics, fraternities and baseball," whose friends were said to have equipped themselves with "a life insurance policy and a club for protection" against both his temper and his pitches. The box score would fade. The images would not. Buffalo Park had generated photographs, headlines, and stories, and the men who wrote Sacramento's daily narrative had spent an afternoon playing on Kripp's field.[380]

The park could hold spectacle. It could hold civic self-amusement. The games themselves were only part of what Buffalo Park was becoming. With every crowd and exhibition, the ground accumulated something harder to measure than gate receipts.

Kripp measured it anyway. Not precisely, but instinctively—tracking not only what the gate produced, but what repeated attention might sustain.

By 1912, Buffalo Park carried leverage.

Years earlier, the league's directors had chosen what they considered the safer course. Charley Graham and Bill Curtin were respectable operators, acceptable to the public and predictable to the league. Ed Kripp, whose reputation had been built in gambling rooms and aggressive promotion, was left outside the formal ownership structure.

Three seasons later, the situation looked different.

Buffalo Park had become the city's only modern baseball ground. Any club that wished to play professional baseball in Sacramento had to use it. The league might control the franchise on paper, but the physical home of the game—the grandstand, the gates, the diamond—belonged to Kripp.

That fact quietly altered the balance of power in Sacramento baseball.

But the park was not the only thing that had shifted the balance.

The Sacramento club had finished last in 1912, and dissatisfaction followed quickly. Rumors circulated that Graham, who effectively controlled the team's stock, would sell if the price could be met. The reports immediately produced speculation that Kripp might step forward.

After several disappointing seasons, Sacramento found itself looking once again toward the man whose clubs had won four consecutive California League pennants. No one since had restored the sustained success that had once made Sacramento the dominant club in California baseball.

For Kripp, the decision carried consequences beyond the dugout. Buffalo Park depended upon a club worth watching. In a city the size of Sacramento, victories did more than satisfy local pride—they filled grandstands. Every empty seat diminished the value of the investment he had built just beyond the city limits.

He did not deny his interest. "I would like to have the team," he told reporters. The asking price, however, was substantial—estimated at $15,000. In 1912, that was not speculative money. It was capital that could be tied up quickly and lost just as quickly. A club's value rose and fell with performance, attendance, and league maneuvering. Franchises shifted cities. Directors rebalanced schedules. A poor season could thin the gate. Even a strong one did not guarantee permanence.

Kripp declined. "It would take about $15,000... and I can't see that much," he said plainly.[381]

He already controlled Buffalo Park. Whoever played there paid him rent. If the club prospered, he benefited. If it faltered, he still held the ground. Ownership of the roster would have exposed him to league politics. Ownership of the park left him insulated from them.

Whether by calculation or simple reluctance to overpay, he chose to remain landlord rather than proprietor.

The park itself continued to draw the city. By April 1913, more than 4,500 spectators crowded Buffalo Park on a single afternoon, filling the grandstand and bleachers with a cross-section of Sacramento that few other events could assemble.[382]

Reports described a "new pull-together spirit" between players and fans—an alignment that suggested something more stable than the standings alone.

But the size of the crowd masked a quieter vulnerability.

In January 1913, Kripp went public with what he believed to be the park's single point of failure: transportation. If the location proved inconvenient, he warned, "baseball is going back in the Capital City"—back within Sacramento's municipal limits, to the smaller, less modern grounds that had preceded Buffalo Park.[383]

He treated the problem not as abstraction but as something measurable—minutes lost between the city and his gates, delays that could thin a grandstand as surely as a losing club. Rather than rely soley on complaints, Kripp tested the route himself. One afternoon he walked from Sixth and J Street to Buffalo Park—nearly twenty blocks—without a single streetcar passing him. [384] The experiment confirmed what he already suspected: on some days, a determined pedestrian could reach the ballpark as quickly as the transit system intended to serve it.

Buffalo Park sat deliberately outside municipal limits, beyond certain restrictions but also beyond easy access. Its success depended not only on the game, but on the city's ability to reach it.

"A 5-cent car service from every nook in Sacramento must be established," Kripp argued. Without it, receipts would collapse. Since the park's construction, he reminded critics, "receipts have grown five times larger" than in the days of Oak Park.

Transportation was not incidental. It was survival.

The league understood as much. In February 1913, after discussions with team owners and directors, Kripp secured a five-year extension of the lease with the Sacramento club. The "valuable piece of land" would remain a ballpark through at least 1919.[385]

For the moment, the ground was protected.

By October 1913, the park had something worth defending.

Harry Wolverton, a former major-league third baseman who had managed the New York Highlanders, had taken control of the Sacramento club.[386] His return to the Coast followed a disastrous one-year stint in New York, a reversal that brought him back into the Pacific Coast League just as Sacramento sought stability.[387]

Under his direction, the Senators climbed from the cellar into contention.

The shift was not abstract. It showed itself in results that the city could measure and in performances that filled Buffalo Park with a different kind of expectation. By early summer, Sacramento was no longer absorbing losses but delivering them. The Senators "bathed themselves in glory" in a decisive showing at Buffalo Park, a performance built on steady pitching and timely hitting that left little doubt about the team's improvement.[388]

For Kripp, such games translated directly into receipts. Victory did not belong to him, but the crowd it drew passed through his gates.

Days later, they followed with another emphatic victory, walloping Oakland and exposing one of the league's established clubs as vulnerable.[389] These were not isolated successes. They formed a pattern—wins that suggested structure rather than chance.

Even defeats carried a different tone. Losses were attributed not to collapse but to specific faults—ragged infield play, uneven support, moments that could be corrected rather than conditions that could not.[390] The language of the coverage shifted accordingly. The Senators were no longer described as overwhelmed. They were described as competitive.

By the closing months of the season, that transformation had taken statistical form. Sacramento ranked near the top of the league in batting, extra-base hits, and stolen bases, a combination that marked the club as both aggressive and efficient.[391] They were not simply improved—they were dangerous.

Buffalo Park absorbed that change. And Kripp absorbed what followed. He had declined the cost of ownership, but not the benefits of success.

Where earlier crowds had gathered out of habit or curiosity, they now arrived with expectation. The games mattered differently. A close contest carried consequence. A rally drew a response that was no longer ironic or detached. The park, which had already proven it could assemble the city, now held something more difficult: sustained attention.

Wolverton's team did not resolve the deeper instabilities of Sacramento baseball. But for a season, it altered the experience of the game itself. The Senators were no longer an obligation to follow. They were a team worth watching.

On October 22, in a tense contest against Portland, an argument over a call at third base escalated beyond the diamond. Wolverton and Big Bill James of the Beavers left the field and met behind the bleachers. What followed was described as a one-round fight—brief, violent, and visible enough that the crowd understood what had happened even without seeing it directly.

When the men reemerged, both were bloodied. Wolverton carried a cut over his eye. James bore a split lip and loosened teeth.[392]

The crowd erupted. It was spectacle in its rawest form. Loyalty made visible.

Harry Wolverton.
Morning Oregonian, June 18, 1916.

The game held, but the structure beneath it did not. Improvement on the field did not resolve the deeper instability. Wolverton's disputes with league officials—over contracts, finances, and control—continued to surface in the press, a reminder that success on the diamond did not guarantee stability beyond it.[393]

But spring training offered a different kind of continuity.

"Baseball On Boards at Buffalo Park To-Day," the *Bee* announced. "All the Boys Now Here."[394]

Instead of eruptions, repetition. Instead of arguments, drills.

Trainer Billie Burke, a former Pacific Coast boxer, approached conditioning with a fighter's discipline. From Marysville, he telephoned instructions back to Sacramento: players would be walked until they believed they were "out for cross-country honors."[395] Long hikes and enforced rest would harden them before the season began.

Camp kept Buffalo Park in the newspapers. It generated rental revenue. It extended anticipation beyond opening day. The park was no longer dependent on game day alone.

But beyond the fences, the pressure to convert land into something else was growing.

Developers saw not outfield grass but residential lots—a grid of houses where second base stood. The ground could be liquidated, turned from a recurring stream of small receipts into a single large return.

Kripp resisted that logic.

In February 1914, he proposed expanding Buffalo Park into something broader—a recreation complex that would extend beyond baseball entirely. Plans called for open-air moving pictures, vaudeville performances, and a large auditorium for dancing and boxing. It would be, he claimed, "the largest in this section of the State," surrounded by attractions that could draw crowds even when the team could not.[396]

If baseball faltered, something else would fill the boards.

The proposal was not speculative. It was conditional. Construction, Kripp noted, depended on improvements to infrastructure—double-tracking on Tenth Street, paving, and the removal of levee obstructions that limited access. The same problem remained.

Without reliable transit, a ballpark—or an amusement ground—was only a destination beyond reach. The plan stalled there, not for lack of vision, but for lack of access.

That reality surfaced publicly in March 1914, when frustration over streetcar service erupted at a hearing with Pacific Gas and Electric officials. Fans described delays that caused them to miss the opening innings, waits that stretched into twenty minutes after games, and a system that failed at the exact moments when demand was highest.

"The first inning is half the battle," Wolverton argued. If fans could not arrive on time, the experience itself was diminished.[397]

Kripp pressed for solutions. He understood what the city was only beginning to articulate: the crowd inside Buffalo Park depended on steel rails beyond it. If access could not be improved, the attraction itself had to be strong enough to overcome the inconvenience.

By late 1914, the limits of that equation had become clear.

The Senators threatened to move "bag and baggage" to Salt Lake City. The Pacific Coast League, always pragmatic, considered alternatives. If baseball failed, the grounds could be turned over to Kripp for amusement purposes.[398]

Buffalo Park had proven it could hold a city—Japanese exhibitions, newspapermen's follies, pennant races, streetcar protests, fights behind the bleachers. It no longer depended upon a single roster or even a single league.

The tenant was replaceable. The land was not. Baseball had built Buffalo Park. Now Buffalo Park would determine the future of Sacramento baseball.

It depended on access, schedule, and control. The ground, however carefully secured, could not compel a league to stay.

The Rivers-Wolgast fight in Vernon.
Los Angeles Times, July 5, 1912.

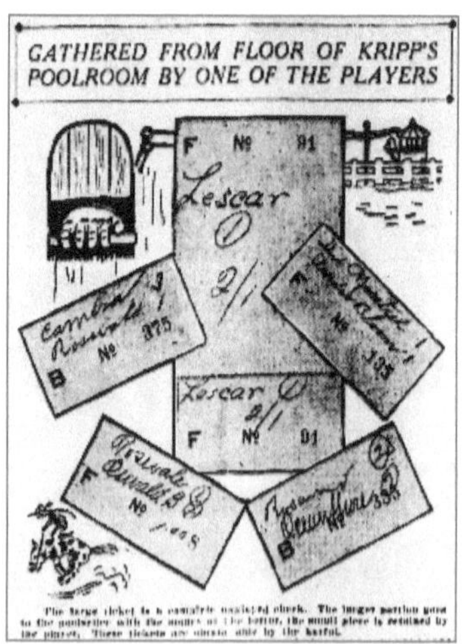

Betting slips from Kripp's poolroom.
Sacramento Bee, January 20, 1911.

CHAPTER 18

The Reckoning

1911–1917

THE RECKONING did not arrive in a single blow. For Ed Kripp, it came first through the gates at Eleventh and Y. Sacramento had not merely built a ballpark there. It had built an argument: that the city belonged in the Pacific Coast League.

For a time, the argument had held. On the right afternoon, when the heat settled over the grass and the crowd gathered close to the diamond, Buffalo Park made Sacramento look like a baseball city of consequence. The stands filled, the noise rose, and for nine innings the city could imagine itself part of the larger circuit moving up and down the Coast by rail, carrying players, scores, and ambitions from one town to another.

By the summer of 1914, that place had begun to come apart. League officials blamed attendance. Sacramento, they said, had failed to support its club. The charge landed hard because it was more than a business excuse. It was a civic judgment. If the league was right, then Sacramento had been weighed and found too small for the Coast League it had fought to join.

The local papers rejected that verdict sharply. The fault, they insisted, was not with Sacramento's baseball public. Buffalo Park had drawn a crowd. The city had supported the game. What fans would not support indefinitely was a club that lost its footing in July and never recovered.[399]

Behind the argument lay the harder problem. The club was in debt, and the debts could no longer be hidden behind hopeful talk of next season. Harry Wolverton and Lloyd Jacobs, the men then holding the Sacramento franchise, were ordered to raise the money necessary to keep the club alive. Reports varied on the amount required, but all of them made the same point: this was not a passing shortage. The franchise needed capital, and quickly.[400]

A campaign began to save the club. Sacramento businessmen were asked to come forward. Money would decide the fate of baseball in the city. If the backing could be found, Sacramento might hold its place. If it could not, the franchise would pass beyond local control.[401]

Kripp was not the owner whose debts had brought the club to this point, but the crisis unfolded on ground shaped by his own ambition. Buffalo Park had been built to root the game in Sacramento. A team could lose, owners could change, but the park itself had suggested permanence. The grandstand at Eleventh and Y was supposed to say that baseball had a place here.

Now the league was preparing to say otherwise.

In September, the break came. Sacramento's club collapsed in mid-season. The league assumed control of the franchise and shifted the team and Wolverton to San Francisco, where it finished the schedule as the Mission Wolves, a second club in a city already occupied by the Seals.[402] Sacramento's players were not entirely erased. They were refitted into another city's baseball map, while Buffalo Park stood empty of the league it had been built to hold.

The move did not settle the matter. Through the fall, the fate of the Missions moved through baseball offices and newspaper columns. Sacramento's future rested not with the fans who had filled its stands, but with league magnates weighing markets, debts, and schedules.[403] By late October, the verdict had hardened. Sacramento had been wiped off the Coast League map..[404] The following spring completed the removal. The franchise was sold and relocated again, this time to Salt Lake City.[405]

Buffalo Park remained. The grandstand did not vanish. The gates did not fall. The base paths could still be chalked, the grass cut, the seats filled when something worth watching came to Eleventh and Y. On a warm afternoon, the place could still sound like baseball. But the sound now carried a different meaning. The park could gather a crowd; it could no longer prove that Sacramento belonged.

That was the wound from which the rest of the reckoning followed. Kripp understood crowds. He understood the value of a place where people gathered, paid admission, and returned the next day. But the Coast League's decision showed how much the sporting world had changed around him. A crowd was not enough. A ballpark was not enough. Local pride was not enough. Baseball was becoming a business of franchises, capital, league politics, and cities with leverage beyond the gate.

Three years before the Coast League loss, the older world around Kripp had already begun to show itself in daylight. On January 20, 1911, the Sacramento Bee published a full-page attack under a headline that left no room for ambiguity: "No Honest Effort to Stop." The occasion was a series of raids on gambling rooms around the Western Hotel and along Sixth Street, including the world that gathered near Kripp's poolroom and the Columbia Café. Trustee Catlett had gone out the previous afternoon to see whether the city's anti-gambling campaign was being enforced. What he found was not a crackdown. It was a performance. The games were running. Men stood at the tables. Betting slips moved through the rooms. Officers who had been assigned to keep watch appeared to be doing just that—watching.

The *Bee* treated the scene less as revelation than confirmation. The slips gathered in the raids had not been seized in the manner of lawmen breaking open a hidden vice den. They had been collected afterward from the floor of Kripp's poolroom, scattered paper swept up by officers whom the paper suggested looked more like janitors than policemen. The rooms kept operating. The law entered, looked around, and stepped carefully over what it already knew was there.[406]

Five days later, the exposure became almost comic. Officer Thomas F. Patterson, a sworn member of the Sacramento Police Department, was found in full uniform outside the Columbia Café, the building he had been assigned to supervise. It was two o'clock in the afternoon, and Patterson was too drunk to walk properly. He leaned against the cigar stand on Sixth Street in plain view of everyone passing by. When he attempted to cross J Street, he could not manage it and turned back. Officers eventually found him in the back room of a nearby saloon.[407]

The image said enough: a uniformed officer, stationed outside a gambling establishment to represent the authority of the city, unable to keep his own feet beneath him. The poolrooms remained open. The gambling continued. But the public could now see how the system worked. The city was not shutting the rooms down so much as managing them, assigning officers to stand nearby while the games went on.

Kripp had built much of his success in the spaces Sacramento allowed but did not always admit existed: poolrooms, race betting, fight cards, and crowds drawn to the edge of respectability. He knew where people gathered and where money moved. He knew what the city would tolerate. But once those arrangements were printed in the newspaper, they became harder to protect. Reform did not have to end gambling to hurt men like Kripp. It only had to make the old tolerance visible.

That same winter brought the pressure into his private life. Clara Jessie Kripp, née Clara Glenn, had married Ed in San Francisco in 1902 after having already appeared during the wreckage of his first marriage. By 1906 she had left him and gone east, eventually pursuing theatrical ambitions. Kripp continued to support her, agreeing to pay $100 a month under a contract drawn up in Yolo County in December 1910. By early 1911, the arrangement had narrowed into settlement.

On February 1, the terms were placed in the public record. Clara was to receive $3,800, secured by a lien on Kripp's property at I and J Streets between Sixth and Seventh. In exchange, she waived any claim to alimony, any rights in his estate, and any grounds for divorce she might have asserted against him. He had already paid $1,000. The rest would come in installments, with the final payment due in 1913..[408] The divorce followed quickly. Kripp charged desertion, Clara answered the complaint the same day it was filed, and the decree was granted in San Francisco by Judge Cabaniss.[409]

The trouble reached beyond his own household. In February, newspapers reported that Mrs. Newton Kripp, wife of Ed's younger brother, had attempted suicide by drinking lysol at her father's home on Fifth Street. She survived, but another Kripp family crisis had entered the public prints during the same season that Ed's poolroom, marriage, and reputation were already under pressure.[410]

Taken separately, these episodes could be mistaken for unrelated misfortunes: a drunken officer, a divorce settlement, a family emergency. Together they marked a change in atmosphere. The police corridor was in the newspapers. The marriage was in the recorder's office. Family distress was on the city page.

Kripp did not stop moving. He rarely did. But after 1911, the ground beneath his ventures was less certain.

By 1912, boxing offered Kripp the clearest opportunity. If Sacramento's place in professional baseball had grown less secure, Buffalo Park could still be used for other things. The grounds had seats, gates, and room for spectacle. Through the Sacramento Athletic Club, Kripp was backing fight cards directly, including a twenty-round Mantell-Thompson contest at Buffalo Park on the evening of July 3. He put up the $2,500 purse himself and was already planning a permanent fight pavilion at the northeast corner of the park, where monthly cards could be staged.[411]

Local cards were not enough. That summer, Kripp wired Tom Jones, manager of lightweight champion Ad Wolgast, and offered $25,000 to stage a title fight between Wolgast and Joe Rivers in Sacramento on September 9. The terms were precise: $5,000 upon signing, $10,000 ten days before the fight, and the balance twenty-four hours before the bell. The fighters could take the guarantee or split the gate, with concessions included. It was not just an offer for a fight. It was an attempt to buy Sacramento onto the national sporting stage.[412]

Wolgast and Rivers had already made themselves worth chasing on the Fourth of July in Vernon, outside Los Angeles. More than fifteen thousand spectators packed Tom McCarey's arena to see the lightweight champion and his challenger. For thirteen brutal rounds the fight gave them action, argument, and the rising sense that the title might change hands. Then, in the final minute of the thirteenth, the arena seemed to lose track of what it was seeing. Rivers stepped in and landed a heavy right. Almost at the same instant, Wolgast struck low. Rivers went down. Wolgast fell forward over him.

The referee pulled Wolgast to his feet and started him toward his corner, but the champion collapsed again, apparently unable to continue. Rivers, meanwhile, had already risen. He stood in the ring waiting, while the count went on against him. When it ended, the decision belonged to Wolgast. The challenger was upright. The champion had been helped away. Still, Wolgast kept the title.[413]

The crowd erupted. Thousands protested what they believed they had seen: the challenger standing, the champion carried away, and the title still remaining with Wolgast. The controversy traveled beyond the arena. Within weeks, motion pictures of the fight were being advertised across the country, promising audiences the chance to judge the disputed ending for themselves.[414]

That was the kind of spectacle Kripp wanted for Sacramento: a crowd large enough to make the event national, a controversy valuable enough to travel, and a gate large enough to justify the risk. Jones's reply showed the distance between Sacramento's ambition and the market it was trying to enter. He would not consider any proposition outside Los Angeles unless Wolgast received more than he could get there: not less than $25,000, win, lose, or draw, plus half of the motion-picture rights, or $30,000 flat. Kripp answered that his $25,000 offer stood and that he would go no higher. Jones did not accept. The fight never came.

The failure revealed the hierarchy Kripp was trying to climb. Sacramento could offer money, Buffalo Park, and a public hungry for sport. But Los Angeles had the arena, the promoters, the scale, and the moving-picture market.

The year ended with a quieter loss. On December 31, 1912, it was reported that Beau Ormonde had dropped dead, apparently from a burst blood vessel. The paper called him the "pride" of Kripp's stable and noted that Kripp was mourning him.

Beau Ormonde was not just another horse. He had won six straight races in Chicago, broken records at Hawthorne and Harlem, held the six-and-a-half-furlong record at Tanforan, and once brought a $10,000 offer Kripp refused. Kripp had planned to take him to Kentucky for sale to a stock farm. Instead, the horse was gone before that plan could be carried out.[415]

The next blow came in July 1913, when racing officials of the British Columbia Thoroughbred Association, meeting in Vancouver, ruled Ed L. Kripp off the turf entirely. The decision followed testimony that

Jockey Grover Warren, riding for Kripp's stable, had attempted to bribe another jockey to pull a horse named Old Gotch, and that Kripp himself had suggested the bribe. The ruling barred Kripp and every horse in his stable.[416]

Among them was Orlin Kripp, named for his son. Only weeks earlier, Orlin had been winning. At Alan, Idaho, he came from behind in a six-furlong handicap and reached the wire first by a length. On June 17, the Spokane Press called him the champion three-year-old. Less than a month later, Vancouver took the stable off the track.[417]

Baseball had become uncertain. Prizefighting's largest prizes belonged to bigger markets. Now racing, too, had shown how quickly a ruling from officials could wipe out months of work. Kripp still knew how to gather a crowd. What he could no longer count on was control once leagues, promoters, commissions, and financiers began making decisions beyond him. Boxing offered another chance to make a venue matter.

By 1916, Buffalo Park had already outlived one of its central promises. The Pacific Coast League was gone from Sacramento, and the grounds at Eleventh and Y no longer guaranteed the city a place in the highest minor league in the West. But the park still had value. It had seats. It had gates. It had room for crowds. It could still be made useful whenever Sacramento wanted something large enough to justify gathering in public.

Ancil Hoffman understood that world. He had been active in Sacramento boxing circles for years, identified as Boxing Commissioner of the Sacramento Athletic Club as early as 1910, and he recognized the direction the sport was moving. Prizefighting could no longer depend only on backroom understandings, improvised cards, and local enthusiasm. It needed promoters, commissions, recognizable clubs, and venues that could survive scrutiny.[418]

Kripp brought what Hoffman needed: capital, the grounds, and experience filling a venue. Hoffman brought what Kripp increasingly needed: cleaner standing with boxing authorities and contacts among fighters who could draw. In September 1916, the Hoffman Club prepared a card at Buffalo Park with Willie Meehan against Henry Hendricks in the main event. The *Bee* described the program as one of the best four-round bills yet arranged in Sacramento. Ed Kripp was listed as president of the Hoffman Club. The card would be the last held at the ball grounds that season.[419]

Buffalo Park could still host a fight, but outdoor cards belonged to weather, daylight, and the seasonal limits of an open field. If boxing was to become more than a temporary use for a baseball park, it needed a home of its own.

Rumors first placed the proposed venue in the old pavilion at Sixth and M Streets, a building long condemned. Kripp corrected the report himself when the *Bee* asked. "It is not the old pavilion on the corner that we want," he said. "That building has been condemned and we know it. The building we seek is next to it and is known as the old armory. The walls are strong and the entire construction is such that there is no danger to any one." He added that no final decision had been made. They had another place in view and were choosing between the two.[420]

They chose a warehouse on L Street, between Second and Third, secured a lease and converted into Sacramento's first permanent boxing arena. It held four thousand seats. The building was not glamorous, but it had the essential quality Kripp had spent years trying to create in different forms: it could contain a paying crowd.

On November 18, 1916, the L Street Auditorium opened. In the days before the first card, Kripp spoke with the confidence of a man who understood what a successful opening required. The program, he said, was unquestionably the most attractive ever arranged in Sacramento in the four-round game. Matchmaker Fred Pearl reported unusual demand for seats all week, with orders arriving from cities up and down the valley.

That Saturday night, they came.

Three thousand people filled the converted warehouse on L Street, standing where there were no seats left, pressing toward the ring from every side, and turning the room into something Sacramento had not seen before indoors. The *Bee* called it the largest crowd ever to attend a four-round boxing show in the city. The air grew close with cigar smoke, heat, and noise. Willie Meehan, the San Francisco heavyweight, defeated Charley Miller in the main event, and when the crowd moved back into the November night, the auditorium stood behind them proven.[421]

The arena worked.

The crowd came.

Fourteen days later, it was over for Ed.

The failure did not come because the room was empty. The record does not say exactly why Kripp sold out so quickly, but the timing suggests that the pressure beneath his ventures may have been catching up with him. Running under the boxing enterprise was a financial obligation tied to land, notes, and capital he had counted on to keep moving. Kripp and his mother, Margaret, had sold a significant parcel of land to the West Sacramento Company, a reclamation enterprise, and accepted promissory notes totaling $18,000 as payment. Needing cash, Kripp had assigned those notes to a financier named A. Block. When payment stalled, Block sued to collect. The paper Kripp had treated as capital became a pressure against him.[422]

On December 4, 1916, the Sacramento Star published a brief notice under the headline "Kripp Quits Boxing Game." Ed Kripp had sold his entire interest in the Hoffman Athletic Club to Ancil and Charles Hoffman, who would guide the organization going forward. Another card was already being arranged for December 15 at the L Street arena. It would go on without him.[423]

The announcement was only a few sentences long. Kripp gave no public explanation.

Through all of it—the poolroom headlines, the divorce settlement, Beau Ormonde dead in his stall, Vancouver, the loss of the Coast League, the L Street arena sold almost as soon as it opened—the horses kept running.

He had named two of them after his children. Florence Kripp, a mare on the California and Utah circuits, won at Salt Lake in November 1912 before a large crowd, leading from start to finish under jockey Pauley. Orlin Kripp had been called the champion three-year-old in the West before Vancouver took him off the track.[424]

In an era when sporting records so often preserved the names of men and overlooked daughters, Kripp placed both children into the ledger, fixed in print. Whatever else disappeared, those names remained.

One thing had not moved through any of it. Buffalo Park was still standing at Eleventh and Y—the grandstand, the grass, the gates. The park could still admit a crowd when there was a game, a fight, a benefit, or any event strong enough to draw the city southward. Men and women could still sit in the bleachers on a warm afternoon, and when something close happened on the field, the sound could still rise the way it always had, sudden and collective, as if the park itself had come alive again.

But now the ground meant something different. It was no longer proof that Sacramento had secured its future in organized baseball. It was no longer proof that a crowd could make a venture safe. The Coast League had withdrawn its promise, but the park itself had not gone quiet. It had become something less certain, but not less alive: a ballpark, a boxing ground, a public stage, a place for crowds, benefits, and spectacles.

Still, the ground at Eleventh and Y endured—useful, adaptable, and stubbornly present, much like the man who had built it.

Portrait of Ed Kripp.
Sacramento Bee, January 31, 1913.

Game at Buffalo Park, ca. 1910s.
Courtesy of Alan O'Connor. Private collection.

CHAPTER 19

The New Terms

1915–1922

DURING the mid-1910s, Ed Kripp was no longer fighting to be noticed. He was fighting to remain legible. But the conditions that had once protected him were dissolving. What had long been handled through tolerance and private arrangement was now written down and carried forward. The moral wave he had named years earlier had not receded. It had learned to keep records.

He adapted where he could.

In June 1915, the *Sacramento Star* reported that Pacific Coast League clubs would begin playing regular Monday games at Buffalo Park, folding the city into the league's travel rhythm even without restoring Sacramento to the circuit. Teams arrived Sunday night by electric rail, played Monday, and continued on. Kripp no longer sold continuity; he sold access.[425]

Buffalo Park had become the center of Sacramento's sporting life—without a franchise attached. Soccer leagues centralized their schedules there. College teams followed. Stanford's all-stars appeared on Thanksgiving. On Sundays the Acorns, the Rovers, and the Dolphins played on the grass he had planted. The park endured not through prestige, but through constant use.[426]

The terms of access were changing as well. Automobiles had begun to alter how people moved through the city. Kripp himself appeared among Sacramento's registered auto owners, and by the mid-1910s the streets around the park carried more than streetcars and foot traffic.[427] The ground he had built at the edge of town was no longer remote. It was reachable.

Beyond the city, the terms were changing as well.

In June 1917, Kripp's son Orlin registered for the draft as the nation mobilized for war. In October 1918, he embarked for France with a U.S. Army motor transport unit, part of the massive late-war deployment to the Western Front. He arrived as the fighting reached its end and remained overseas during the unsettled months that followed, returning home marked by what he had seen.[428]

The war did not remain distant. It reordered movement, authority, and expectation—abroad and at home.

While his son served overseas, scrutiny tightened in Sacramento.

By 1918, the informal accommodations that had once governed enforcement—personal discretion, negotiated tolerance, and selective visibility—were collapsing. In their place came coordinated oversight and formal procedure.

That spring, the Sacramento County Grand Jury reopened its examination of gambling conditions in the city. The focus was unmistakable: Kripp's operation at Sixth and J. He was summoned to testify about games allegedly played in his rooms—and whether they violated state law. Will C. Davis of the *Bee* was called to recount what he had observed when he entered Kripp's rooms and "wrote a story on the games played there."[429]

This was not new terrain for him. For years he had operated in defiance of reformers, weathering the moral wave. As early as 1900, he blamed shifting public sentiment for losses in his gambling business, and by 1911 that wave had become routine opposition. Yet earlier enforcement had remained elastic. His poolrooms above the Columbia Café operated openly enough that uniformed officers on the beat sometimes served less as enforcers than as guides, "accommodatingly pointing with the thumb" toward the stairs.[430]

Even so, the city's usefulness to organized baseball had not disappeared. Sacramento's absence from the Pacific Coast League proved temporary—but not sentimental. After the 1917 season, when Portland dropped out, league officials restored Sacramento for 1918 not as a favor, but as a calculation: location, travel rhythm, and the stubborn usefulness of Buffalo Park as ready-made ground. For Kripp, the return confirmed what the withdrawal had already taught him: institutions could leave, but ground—if held and maintained—could wait.[431]

But ownership of ground no longer conferred immunity.

Coverage of the Grand Jury proceedings was brief. The implication was not. Ownership of Buffalo Park did not insulate him. Prominence did not erase suspicion. He owned the city's principal baseball ground and remained central to its sporting life—yet he continued to operate in rooms where the law was no longer inclined to look away.

Yet Sacramento had long operated under a different understanding of enforcement. Across the river in Washington, the older world still continued.

For nearly two decades, the Yolo Monte Carlo had operated as a "wide-open" establishment, surviving investigations, temporary closures, and shifting legal standards. From its earliest descriptions in the summer of 1903, newspapers acknowledged both its scale and the difficulty of suppressing it so long as local sentiment remained tolerant.[432] That tolerance mattered. Contemporary reporting noted that the steady flow of patrons filled houses in town and brought business to surrounding establishments. Enforcement, officials admitted, depended as much on public complaint as on statute.

By the early 1920s, however, tolerance was narrowing on both sides of the river.

In April 1921, the Monte Carlo again drew the attention of law enforcement when a raid led by the district attorney's office resulted in the arrest of several men involved in its gambling operations.[433] Such actions were no longer unusual. What was remarkable was that the enterprise persisted at all.

Sacramento, however, was no longer willing to look away. The breaking point came in August 1921.

On the night of August 6, Patrolmen F. McAllister, P.C. Gamble, E. Roberts, and W. Hanney moved through Sacramento's streets with deliberate purpose.[434] Their mission was to raid alleged gambling houses operating despite formal prohibition under state law.

They moved on two addresses at once: Kripp's place at 925 Sixth Street—just across from the Columbia Café—and the Greek-American Club at 1030 K Street. At Kripp's location, officers found no game in progress. But they found evidence. They reported discovering "gambling equipment of every description": race charts, poker chips, decks of cards, and a faro bank case—the apparatus of a working gambling room.

Fourteen guests were present. Kripp claimed they were "friends who had just dropped in for the evening." He was arrested on the charge of maintaining a gambling establishment.

On August 12, he appeared before Police Judge O.W. Anderson and pleaded guilty.[435] The judge fined him $250 or thirty days in the County Jail. Kripp paid the fine.

The coverage was routine. The message was not. Ed Kripp—owner of Buffalo Park—remained legally vulnerable, still subject to arrest and public judgment.

At fifty-three, Kripp could no longer continue as before.

On December 1, he sold Buffalo Park to Lew and Charlie Moreing, businessmen and relatives of former Sacramento player Cy Moreing, ending more than a decade of direct control.

Edward L. Kripp, known as E. L., unm to Nelson W. Chisholm. 0.694 acs at Y & 13th sts.

Nelson W. Chisholm known as N. W. unm to Lewis Moreing. 1.18 acs at Riverside Blvd.

Edward L. Kripp known as E. L. to Charles & Lewis Moreing. 5.567 acs at same.

Sale of park, as published in the newspaper.
Sacramento Union, December 2, 1921.

As part of the arrangement, he secured a lifetime pass to all baseball games.[436]

On January 1, 1922, workmen began dismantling Kripp's wooden structures. Newspapers described a modern concrete stadium—an investment of roughly $75,000—designed for scale and durability.[437] The new Moreing Field would seat 12,000 spectators, nearly doubling the park's capacity.[438] Expanded grandstands, a twenty-foot fence, automobile access, "comfort seats" with backs and arms, improved concessions, and architectural openings designed to admit Delta breezes beneath a high shaded wall.

The sale meant transformation—not only of the park, but of Kripp's position within the city. He no longer owned the ground. He passed through it.

In February 1922, Ed made a different kind of gesture. He offered a portion of the land at Tenth and Y Street to the city of Sacramento for municipal swimming baths.[439] The parcel—land he had previously planted in alfalfa—lay near Buffalo Park. He proposed donating half a block, noting that "Swimming baths can be built here very easily with little cost," and that earth from the Y Street levee could be used to create suitable surroundings. However, these baths were never built.

The ground he had shaped was already moving beyond him. On April 4, 1922, Moreing Field opened before a crowd of more than 10,000.

Baseball had once given Kripp legitimacy when gambling could not. Ownership of Buffalo Park tied his name to civic ritual and respectable crowds.

Aerial view of Moreing Field, ca. 1920s.
Courtesy of Alan O'Connor. Private collection.

By the early 1920s, credibility itself had changed. Baseball was governed, recorded, supervised. Visibility no longer absorbed scrutiny; it invited it. The same crowds that once protected him now made him easier to watch. Selling Buffalo Park was not an abandonment of respectability. It was a recognition of its new terms. The lifetime pass ensured he would remain present—without remaining accountable.

What endured was the instinct he had always followed: find where people want to gather, control the ground beneath them, and let the crowd do the rest. He had done it with Buffalo Park. He had done it, in a quieter way, with every room he had ever managed. The question now was whether he could do it again—and whether, this time, in a way the city did not merely tolerate but welcomed.

Ed Kripp had spent three decades in Sacramento operating in the margins between what the law permitted and what it looked away from. He had been raided, convicted, and accommodated in turns. He had built a ballpark that became a civic institution and sold it before it became a liability. He understood better than most how quickly the ground could shift beneath a man who stayed too long in one place.

The next move would have to be different in kind, not just in degree. Not another ballpark. Not another poolroom reconstituted under a new name. Something the city could not look at sideways. Something where respectable people entered as guests—not as evidence of tolerance.

In February 1923, he found it—on the corner of Sixth and I Streets, where the oldest church in California still stood.

PART THREE

THE ENDGAME

1923–1942

DREAMLAND

SACRAMENTO'S NEW $200,000
DANCING AUDITORIUM
SIXTH STREET—I AND J

Social Dances Tuesdays and Thursdays
LADIES FREE—GENTS 75c

Dreamland Dance Hall.
Sacramento Bee, March 22, 1924.

Another Job Well Done

We are proud of our part in the construction of this fine Musical and Dancing Auditorium for it is one of the finest in the entire west and one of which any city might well boast.

DREAMLAND

is but "Another Job Well Done" for us.

Many other examples of our ability as a builder are to be found throughout Sacramento in the form of some of her finest flats and apartment houses, on which we specialize.

G. E. Harvie

2212 "T" Street M. 586

GENERAL CONTRACTOR

(*Estimates Cheerfully Furnished*)

We Congratulate Mr. Kripp

on his excellent addition to our city in the way of a Musical Emporium and fine business structure, and we congratulate the young men and women of Sacramento in having this additional place of clean amusement and recreation for their pleasure.

GENTLEMEN:

Nothing will add so much to your enjoyment of the evening's dance as a fine

VIRGIN WOOL OVERCOAT

in the snappy new patterns that we are now showing.

Hirsh-Wickwire and other fine and fashionable garments are awaiting your choice.

Special Values, $25 to $[illegible]

Pickett-Atterbury COMPANY

624-26 J Str

Opposite Nat'l Bank of D.O.Mills

It was a pleasure to be identified with the building of Dreamland, insofar as it had to do with

Tile Work

H. O. Adams

915 26th St.

Main 2376W.

Endorsements for Dreamland.

Sacramento Union, November 20, 1923.

DREAMLAND-DANCING

CABLE ADDRESS HALE BROS. TELEPHONE MAIN 5100

HALE BROS., Inc.

NINTH AND K STREETS

Sacramento, California.

December 6, 1923.

Mr. Edward Kripp, Manager,
Dreamland Pavilion,
Sacramento, California.
Dear Sir:

In view of the splendid manner in which your new dancing pavilion is being conducted, we are pleased to confirm the arrangement whereby our employes are to enjoy the pleasure of a party at Dreamland on next Wednesday night, December 12th.

They are all looking forward to a good time on this occasion.

We desire to congratulate you, not only on the attractive pavilion that you have built, but on the splendid manner in which it is being conducted.

Yours very truly,
HALE BROS., INC.

RDC HAS

To Mr. R. D. Carpenter,
Hale Bros., Inc.,
Sacramento.

Your kind letter, emanating from one of the largest firms in Sacramento, is kindly appreciated, and shows the kindly interest of a firm whose payroll is probably the largest of its kind in this city, and appreciates a place where their employes may go and enjoy themselves in a wholesome atmosphere.

Dreamland, as you see, is now being conducted, will always, while under my ownership and control, be conducted in a first class manner; does not cater to any of the underworld or tough element, who are not admitted.

For this occasion, when probably one of the largest crowds of the season will attend, Dreamland will have special music and vocal selections by Leo Cashin, formerly with Feist Publishers, N. Y.; also the latest 1924 dance creations will be danced by Professor Walton of Saltair Pavilion, Salt Lake, and partner, Miss Lucille Shirley of Dreamland. Also a Free Grand March, breaking up into an old-time waltz quadrille at 9:15.

Sincerely yours,
E. L. KRIPP,
Owner Dreamland.

Sacramento, Dec. 11, 23.

Endorsement of Dreamland and Response.

Sacramento Union, December 12, 1923.

CHAPTER 20

Dreamland

1923–1938

THE NEWS landed on the front page of the *Sacramento Bee* on February 20, 1923, and it landed hard. "OLDEST CHURCH IN CITY TO GO," the headline read. Below it: "Kripp Buys Historic Congregational Property."[440] For readers who had grown up in Sacramento, the two facts together were almost impossible to absorb. The First Congregational Church at Sixth and I Streets had stood on that corner since 1854. It was not merely old. It was the oldest Protestant church in the state of California—the first institution of its kind to be permanently organized on the Pacific Coast.[441]

It had survived nearly every trial Sacramento had endured—fires that erased whole blocks, floods that drowned the streets, the upheaval of the Gold Rush years when the city itself seemed temporary. Through all of it the grey stone building remained, holding Sunday services for nearly seven decades.[442] Now a sport promoter had paid $35,000 for it and announced plans to build a boxing auditorium.

The idea was not entirely new. Nearly a decade earlier, Kripp had proposed something similar at Buffalo Park—a broader recreation ground of moving pictures, dancing, and exhibition, designed to draw crowds beyond baseball itself. There, the plan had stalled, not for lack of vision, but for lack of access. The park lay beyond the city's easy reach, dependent on streetcar lines that never quite kept pace with demand.

At Sixth and I, those constraints no longer applied. But the proposal carried a different weight there. It was no longer a speculative expansion at the edge of the city, but a transformation at its center.

First Congregational Church.
Center for Sacramento History.

The reaction across the city was immediate and not entirely unkind toward Kripp, though it was marked by a quiet sense of loss. The *Sacramento Union* ran an editorial two days later under the heading "Another Landmark Passes." The building, the paper acknowledged, had endeared itself far beyond the ranks of the denomination it housed—prima-donnas had sung there, budding artists had given their first public performances there, high school classes had graduated into the experiences of life within its walls.

The spirit of progress was upon Sacramento, the editorial conceded, and these changes had to come.[443] But there was something in the phrasing—"the old first church has about it traditions which are too rich to be subjected to this treatment"—that carried genuine grief.

The *Sacramento Star* was blunter in its headline: "Boxing Auditorium to Stand on Site of Historic Church."[444] The contrast was the story, and the papers knew it. What had housed hymns and prayer meetings and the moral aspirations of Sacramento's pioneer generation would now house fighters and nickel dances. Some who had grown up attending services on that corner found this difficult to accept. Others, reading the same news, simply noted that attendance had thinned for years and the congregation had already been searching for a new site.

Kripp, for his part, did not wait for the city to form its verdict. On April 25, he published an open letter addressed "To the People of the City of Sacramento." It was an unusual move for a man who had spent most of his career operating at the edges of civic respectability, and the tone was careful and direct. He laid out his plans in full. He intended to build an auditorium costing approximately $96,000—a story and a half of brick, fireproof, designed to serve the whole city. The dancing would be "the highest type of dancing amusement," and the moral arrangements would be entrusted to a lady who managed one of the largest dry goods departments in the city. Moving pictures would be offered at popular prices, no more than fifteen cents, and if possible ten, so that families of moderate means could come more often than they otherwise would. Children under eight years of age would be admitted free.

Then he disclosed something the city did not know. Mayor Albert Elkus, who had taken a public stand for the preservation of the church site, had been given a formal option to purchase the property—an exclusive right that ran until May 1st and formed part of the city's effort to save or relocate the building. Kripp had extended it himself. "I am not anxious to sell it," he wrote, "as I would much more prefer to keep it for the business purposes that I have outlined." He said that he considered the property worth $75,000—that he had in fact been offered a $10,000 profit on his purchase and had turned it down—because, as he put it, he was "putting a small margin of profit on the property because it was to be used for civic purposes and I do not care to block any move of a civic nature."[445]

The farewell services were held on April 15. They lasted all day. Pioneers and former members came from considerable distances—some traveling to Sacramento specifically for the occasion, drawn back by a building they had attended since childhood.[446] The *Sacramento Star* wrote that for sixty-nine years, every Sunday without exception, services had been held in that grey stone building.[447] The final sermon was preached that evening and the church's long continuity ended with a deliberate and unhurried goodbye. The *Union's* full-page farewell coverage ran photographs of the earliest pastors alongside images of the building itself, as if the paper were preserving in print what demolition would soon remove.[448]

Demolition began in April. The steeple that had anchored that stretch of skyline for nearly seven decades came down under sledgehammers. Pews were carried into the street and stacked for salvage. Brick dust settled along Sixth and I as the sanctuary became rubble. Then, beneath the cornerstone dated 1854, workers uncovered something older still: a Native American corn-pounding stone resting in the earth below the church's foundation. It lay there like a quiet reminder that every civic certainty rests upon something prior and largely forgotten. Kripp ordered it preserved.[449] He also announced that the church's bricks would be reused in the structure rising in their place.[450] Sacred wall would become secular shell.

What rose on that corner was not quite what the initial announcements had suggested. The plan had grown considerably in scope, and by the time Dreamland Dancing Auditorium opened its doors on the evening of November 20, 1923, it represented an investment of $200,000. The building was three stories of brick, with stores facing Sixth Street at street level, the basement given over to automobile storage, and the main floor—sixty by one hundred ten feet of spring-suspended maple—devoted entirely to dancing. Above it, a balcony fitted for auditorium purposes could seat a thousand people. The walls had been finished in a mottled effect of varied colors, the lighting fixtures made of silk, incandescent lamps adding warmth from every angle. Twelve ventilators and eight-foot exhaust fans changed the air in the entire building continuously. The stage was built into the side wall and constructed on the principle of a phonograph sounding box, with a spruce backing to act as a resonator, designed to project the orchestra's sound evenly to every corner of the hall.

The opening march was led by Mayor Elkus and Margaret, Kripp's own mother, who had made the journey overland by ox train in 1849. For the occasion she wore a wedding dress that had been purchased in 1861 at the original store of what was then the Nonpareil, considered one of the finest pieces of feminine apparel of its day. The program began at 7:30 p.m.[451] Sacramento was not merely opening a dance hall. The mayor and the owner's pioneer mother, in a dress from the Gold Rush era, were leading the city across a floor built on the foundations of its oldest church. The evening contained the whole of Sacramento's arc in a single gesture.

Within weeks the endorsements began arriving. The carpenters who had built Dreamland wrote Kripp a letter of thanks, published in the *Sacramento Bee* in December. Union rules allowed work already under contract to continue at the old wage scale. On September 1st the scale had increased by sixty-five cents per day. Kripp had made it effective immediately, absorbing the increase himself rather than holding his workers to the old contract. The members of Carpenter's Local No. 586 recommended "that Union labor in general extend their patronage" to Dreamland.[452]

Then came a letter from Hale Bros., the city's most prominent department store, dated December 6. The firm was bringing its employees to Dreamland for an evening party and wrote to say so in terms that carried the full weight of institutional approval. "We desire to congratulate you," the letter read, "not only on the attractive pavilion that you have built, but on the splendid manner in which it is being conducted.[453]

Kripp's reply was published alongside the letter in the *Sacramento Union*. "Dreamland," he wrote, "will always, while under my ownership and control, be conducted in a first class manner; does not cater to any of the underworld or tough element, who are not admitted."[454]

It was a sentence he would not have needed to write ten years earlier, because no one would have asked. A man with his history—the poolrooms, the negotiated tolerances, the years spent operating just outside what the city officially sanctioned—did not typically receive endorsements from department stores or have his fair treatment of laborers published in the newspaper. He was not merely being congratulated on a building. He was being recognized as someone the city's institutions could vouch for. That was new. And he was aware it was new, which is why he answered the letter the way he did: carefully, publicly, and on the record.

The *Union* captured the evening in a single telling detail: Kripp kept nothing. When society flocked to Dreamland on February 22, 1924, for the Community Chest benefit, he donated not just the hall but the orchestra too—every dollar raised that night went directly to the charity. The patronesses who attended were women whose names carried weight in Sacramento's civic life, and they came in evening frocks and afternoon gowns, filling the same floor that on any other Friday bore clerks and machinists and shop girls out for a night's pleasure. By dancing there, they folded Dreamland into their own social geography.

A splendid sum was raised for the Community Chest. The papers called the evening a great success. But Kripp had also done something worth noting: a man who had spent years in the business of baseball and ballparks had opened his new dance hall for free that evening, kept nothing, and handed everything over to the Community Chest. It was a different kind of ledger than the one he'd been keeping.[455]

This was not an isolated gesture. Dreamland was repeatedly turned over for charitable use—such as the Covered Wagon Club's charitable dance, for which Kripp donated both the hall and its musicians.[456] What Kripp lost in receipts he gained in something less tangible: the steady absorption of his hall into the city's institutional life.

The following year brought a different kind of evening altogether. In May 1925, the *Sacramento Bee* reported that Kripp had extended a personal invitation to the city's Civil War veterans—members of the Grand Army of the Republic, the fraternal organization of Union soldiers that had been a fixture of American civic life since the war's end—and the women's groups affiliated with them, to come to Dreamland and dance. Thursday night would be theirs. Jazz was pulled from the program entirely. In its place Kripp arranged old-time musical numbers, the kind the veterans would have known from their youth, along with vocal performances. A fife and drum corps that had been playing about the city was invited to offer a few numbers and set the mood. Five hundred balloons would be released from the ceiling. For veterans whose feet, as the paper put it, still responded to the rhythm of dance, it was an evening designed entirely around them. Kripp even thought ahead to those who might want something livelier: the more agile veterans, he said, were welcome to come back the following night for the regular social dance.

It was a small thing, in one sense. A Thursday night, some old songs, a balloon drop. But Kripp had looked out at the city and found a group of aging men who might not otherwise have a place on a modern dance floor, and he had cleared the room and handed it to them.[457]

The building proved elastic. It could be carnival or charity, contest or commemoration. By 1926 prize waltz contests offered cash awards,[458] and by 1927 novelty dances featured costumed orchestras performing comic fox trots beneath colored lights.[459] Dreamland adjusted to the city's appetite and in doing so became part of its seasonal rhythm.

When the market fell and the Depression tightened its grip, Kripp refused to dim the lights. In October 1930 he announced the installation of an indoor miniature golf course along the mezzanine level, a $10,000 investment featuring "unusual scenic effects" and designed not to interfere with dancing below.[460] The *Sacramento Union* praised the Trilby Indoor Golf Course as among the most scenic in the state,[461] and a columnist in the *Bee* commended Kripp's enterprise and described Dreamland as a "highly respectable institution."[462] Carnival balls continued. Balloon showers descended at midnight. Miss Margaret Ekdahl, Miss America of 1930, appeared on the Dreamland stage that New Year's Eve,[463] proof that Sacramento still imagined itself within the larger American spectacle.

On September 2, 1933, the *Bee* announced that the China Tea Garden would open that evening at 907 Sixth Street, occupying the entire second floor of the Dreamland Dance Pavilion. The establishment, "decorated to represent a Chinese garden," would serve Chinese and American dishes, provide private banquet halls for clubs and weddings, and offer continuous orchestra music until three o'clock in the morning.

The restaurant seated 240 patrons with twenty-seven private booths, offered six-course dinners for fifty cents and eight-course dinners for sixty-five, and remained open until four in the morning on Saturdays.[464] These were not the hours of a cautious experiment. They were the hours of confidence.

Nearly two hundred guests attended a pre-opening banquet. It was not a side venture. It was Dreamland extended upward.

Ownership was explicit: "Ed Kripp, owner of the building, will operate the restaurant," the article noted.[465] But authority was shared.

Advertisements during the 1934 State Fair made that visible. "E. L. Kripp (American), Sole Owner," appeared alongside "Benny Fong (Chinese), Manager." The layout did not obscure Fong's name. It featured it.

Fong himself was not an outsider. Athletic columns list him competing in amateur boxing bouts while simultaneously managing the restaurant floor.[466] He inhabited both spheres: the sporting culture that had long animated Kripp's world, and the Chinese culinary environment that now anchored it.

Advertisement for China Tea Garden.
Sacramento Bee, September 8, 1934.

The contrast with the 1890s was striking. In those years Kripp had operated gambling halls described in the papers as "Chinese lotteries," invoking Chinese gaming traditions as part of the commercial language of Sacramento's underworld. The label carried a mixture of familiarity and exoticism in a city where Chinese businesses and communities were already woven into everyday life. Yet his early career had also intersected with moments of coercion and enforcement directed at Chinese residents—episodes that reflected the unequal civic order of the time.

By the 1930s, the relationship had changed. Chinese identity was no longer merely an aesthetic or a marketing device. It had become integral to the success of the enterprise itself.

The shift from attacking Ah Lee to publicly elevating Benny Fong marked more than personal mellowing. It reflected a broader adjustment. In the 1890s, authority in Sacramento's sporting world had often been expressed through dominance. By the 1930s, it increasingly operated through partnership and visibility. The city's Chinese community had become more institutionally present in civic life, and Dreamland's upper floor functioned within that reality rather than against it.

Within Dreamland itself, another arrangement had taken shape. The China Tea Garden completed a design he had refined for four decades. Entertainment flowed downward and upward within the same building—music below, dining above, private booths opening into banquet halls, crowds dispersing gradually rather than abruptly. Money circulated instead of arriving in bursts. Spectacle lingered.

"Kripp's corner" required no advertisement. It endured as shared civic knowledge.

Yet something had begun to shift, less visible than the colored bulbs overhead but more permanent. By 1933 Dreamland was still drawing crowds on Saturday nights, the orchestra still counting off the first number and the maple floor still flexing beneath motion. But the city's posture toward such places had tightened in ways that a man with Kripp's history would have recognized immediately, even if they looked nothing like what he had navigated before.

On the evening of October 6, City Manager James S. Dean conducted a personal tour of Sacramento's public dance halls. He went alone, hat pulled low over his eyes to conceal his identity, moving from room to room without announcement. He did not stay long before being recognized.[467]

There were no arrests. No raid. No officers with warrants. Only a city official in a tilted hat moving quietly through lamplight. For decades, enforcement in Sacramento had announced itself loudly and then departed, leaving arrangements largely intact. This was something different. The authority was not negotiated. It simply observed, recorded, and remained.

In the months that followed, a new dance hall ordinance came before the city council, introduced as an emergency measure on behalf of the city manager. It called for a dedicated police officer to be stationed at the hall to enforce compliance—and the cost, at $200 per quarter in licensing fees. Kripp appeared before the council at an informal meeting and objected. The fee, he argued, was unreasonable.[468] Councilman Tom Scollan disagreed: the city should not bear the cost of regulating a private business, and the license fee existed precisely to cover the officer's wages.

It was a civic argument, conducted through civic channels, by a man who a decade earlier would have handled such matters through entirely different means. That was the change, and it ran in both directions. The city now moved through paperwork rather than through tolerance and discretion. And Kripp, in turn, had become the kind of man who appeared before city councils to contest licensing fees—not the kind who paid someone to make the problem disappear.

By December 1938, it was over. A brief notice in the *Union* on Christmas Day recorded that the city council would act on an application to transfer the Dreamland dance hall license, held by Ed Kripp, to two new operators.[469] That was all. No farewell was organized. The building that had replaced the oldest church in California passed out of his hands through paperwork.

He had run it for fifteen years. He had outlasted the reform campaigns and the city manager's undercover tours and the licensing disputes and the ordinances, and in the end, it was not any of those things that ended it. He was simply sixty-eight years old.

What came next was the quietest passage of his life. He had spent fifty years in Sacramento moving from one enterprise to the next, always with something under construction or under negotiation. Now there was nothing to negotiate. The question that had driven him since the 1890s—where will people gather, and how do I own the ground beneath it—had finally run out of new answers.

CHAPTER 21

After the Turnstile

1935–1942

YEARS OF CHANGE had reshaped Ed Kripp's place in Sacramento by the mid-1930s, though he had not disappeared. His influence did not vanish; it contracted. The ventures grew smaller, more provisional, pressed into a civic climate less tolerant of improvisation than the one that had allowed him to thrive. The instinct for opportunity remained. The latitude did not.

In the spring of 1936, police ordered the closure of two newly opened horse-race betting rooms—one operated by Joe Gedeon, the other by Kripp at 608 J Street, directly across from the block where his Columbia Café and earlier gambling quarters had once been concentrated.[470] The *Bee* reported the matter during City Council questioning over enforcement, noting that complaints had been issued and the establishments shuttered.[471] Police Chief William Hallanan made clear that the city had grown weary of proliferation. Kripp's room closed with the others. He denied that pressure had forced his hand, insisting the business had simply failed to attract sufficient trade.

The episode revealed how far the terrain had shifted. Newspapers invoked his name during council hearings, but no longer as accusation against an active manipulator of events. "Kripp" had become shorthand for an earlier order of negotiated tolerance. The question was no longer who he was. It was why the arrangement once associated with him had proven so persistent.

Across the river, that arrangement had never entirely disappeared. In September 1935, the *Woodland Daily Democrat* reported that the "Chinese Monte Carlo" near the Yolo County end of the M Street bridge continued to operate as a thriving gambling house. The article alleged that California State Treasurer Charles G. Johnson had lost heavily at its tables—an accusation supported by affidavits cited in the report, though publicly denied by Johnson.[472] The tone treated the establishment not as revival, but as continuity. The culture that had taken root across the river during Kripp's ascendancy endured beyond his direct involvement.

He had receded. The ecosystem had not.

In the years after Lewis Moreing's death, the park Kripp once built and dominated passed fully into a new order. Moreing Field was renamed; affiliation replaced independence; and by the mid-1930s Sacramento's club had been formally folded into the St. Louis Cardinals' developing farm system. What had once operated under local leverage now functioned within a national hierarchy.

In later years, family members remembered that one opportunity had lingered with him. His granddaughter, Carol, would later say that declining the Pacific Coast League franchise had been his greatest regret.[473]

In January 1938, he reappeared publicly—not as operator, but as claimant. When the sale of the field to the St. Louis Cardinals was confirmed, Kripp announced his intention to sue, asserting that his earlier agreement with Lewis Moreing entitled him to lifetime passes and a six-seat box.[474] The dispute did not restore control, but it revealed something essential: even as baseball formalized into corporate affiliation and national structure, he continued to assert rights rooted in personal contract—an older grammar of ownership in which privilege had been negotiated face to face.

By 1941, he appeared in print primarily as recollection. A retrospective in the *Sacramento Union* identified him as the Gilt Edge business manager and credited his gambler's instinct in bringing national notice to Sacramento baseball.[475] The tone was reflective rather than adversarial. He had entered civic memory.

The Sacramento metropolitan district had grown by more than twenty-five percent in a single decade, rising from roughly 127,000 residents in 1930 to nearly 159,000 by 1940.[476] Growth was no longer concentrated within the old city limits; more than a third of the population now lived outside the city proper.[477]

Scale altered governance. Practices once regulated by familiarity—by reputation, proximity, and negotiated tolerance—could not function unchanged in a city that sprawled beyond its historic core. What had once been contained by knowing looks and quiet agreements required departments, ordinances, and public enforcement.

He had lived long enough to watch the city refashion itself. The river that once dictated survival had been caged by levees. Gaslight had yielded to electric glare. Horses gave way to streetcars, and streetcars to automobiles that loosened the city from its rails. Gambling that once operated by wink and nod was indexed and licensed. Baseball arranged by handshake had hardened into bylaws, capital deposits, and distant offices. For decades he had survived by reading the terms of a city that kept changing them. What began as improvisation became infrastructure. What began as tolerance became oversight. And the ground he had fought to hold no longer belonged to his world alone. It had outlived him, taking on new names, new owners, and new crowds, while preserving in concrete and record the older city that had made it possible.

On February 20, 1942, Ed Kripp died at seventy-two.[478]

He was buried in the Sacramento City Cemetery among the men who had dredged levees, raised streets, and imposed civic order.

Across from the cemetery stood the ballpark; the wooden grandstand he built in 1910 had long since been replaced by concrete. It would outlive whatever came next.

The newspapers ran obituaries. They remembered him as the creator of Dreamland, a pioneer of Sacramento baseball, a man who understood what the city wanted before the city understood it itself. They remembered what he had built; everything else was allowed to fade.

Monument marking the grave of Ed Kripp, Sacramento City Cemetery.
Courtesy of the author.

The turnstile had done its work. It had counted who entered and who did not. Behind it lay the negotiations, the risks, and the moral accommodations. Those compromises were absorbed into structures and rules—into boards, capital deposits, and league authority. What remained was the game, ordered and regulated, no longer dependent on the man who had once held it together.

PART FOUR

FATES & MYSTERIES

CHAPTER 22

Where the Current Carried Them

TIME DID what leagues, courts, and public ceremony could not. It stripped away titles and reputations, leaving only outcomes—some documented, others unresolved. The men and women who once orbited Ed Kripp's world of ballparks, gambling rooms, and civic ambition did not leave the stage together. Some fell spectacularly. Some faded. Some reinvented themselves. What follows is a reckoning with what became of them once the system that had sustained them began to harden.

The Fall of "Doc" Henesey

Henesey had once embodied the professional respectability that Sacramento's baseball promoters hoped to project. For readers who recall the 1897 incorporation of the California League at the Baldwin Hotel, Henesey was the "respectable" face of the Gilt Edges—the player turned League Director who sat beside Kripp to draft the corporate bylaws of California baseball. He was the man presented with a diamond-studded charm for his civic service, a figure of athletic grace and professional promise. By 1910, he was a physician, but his reputation was permanently shattered by a brutal assault on actress Lucy Lyle Jones.

The attack was a calculated act of revenge fueled by rejection. Jones had recently ended a relationship with Henesey and refused to see him. On the night of September 18, 1910, Henesey purchased a four-ounce bottle of carbolic acid and traveled by automobile to the Miles Hotel with the express purpose of destroying the actress's beauty and ending her stage career.[479]

Henesey did not go alone. He was accompanied by Netta Bluhm, the manager of the Hotel Cecil, who acted as a lure to bring Jones into the hotel parlor where Henesey was waiting.[480] Because Jones had been avoiding Henesey, Bluhm entered the hotel and sent word for the actress to come down, effectively delivering the victim to her attacker. After Jones refused a final plea to accompany him to the Cliff House, Henesey confronted her and threw the caustic chemical onto her face and neck. Witnesses described the aftermath as a scene of horror, with Jones left "groping and stumbling" like she was half-blind.[481]

The ensuing legal drama revealed a man physically powerful but mentally unraveled. Henesey's defense relied on a "temporary insanity" plea, claiming that his return to heavy drinking after three years of abstinence had left him "not himself." Eight "friendly witnesses" testified to his erratic behavior, and the jury was reportedly swayed by the fact that Jones's scars had significantly faded by the time of the trial.

While Netta Bluhm was exonerated citing no evidence she knew of Henesey's violent intent, Henesey's own escape from justice was more cynical. On May 9, 1911, a jury rendered a verdict of not guilty by reason of insanity. Walter "Doc" Henesey walked out of the courtroom "scott-free," a dark conclusion to a life that had once been defined by the "good old days" of baseball glory and corporate respectability.[482]

Jay Hughes: The Long Descent

Jay Hughes represented the rare player whose talent briefly escaped the instability of Western baseball. Following the 1902 season—the exceptional pitcher developed by the Gilt Edge signed with Seattle in the newly formed Pacific Coast League. The move marked the end of his National League career, not from decline, but from choice: the PCL offered competitive salaries, geographic stability, and a level of control increasingly unavailable to Western players in Eastern leagues. In his first season with Seattle, Hughes posted a 34–15 record with a 2.35 ERA across 444 ⅔ innings, vindicating his decision to remain on the West Coast.

Yet his later years were marked by personal decline. A salary dispute cost him an entire season in 1905. Arm injuries ended his pitching career. His marriage deteriorated. Mary Hughes filed for divorce in 1915.

On June 2, 1924, Hughes's body was discovered at the bottom of a railroad trestle in Sacramento, the victim of a fall that fractured his skull. He was 50.[483]

His major league record—83-40 with a .675 winning percentage—suggested that only his preference for California stood between Hughes and eventual greatness. Whether the fall was accident or intent, the record does not say.

Dreamland's Fate

Dreamland did not disappear abruptly after Ed Kripp's era, but it survived only by adapting to a regulatory climate that increasingly constrained nightlife. By the early 1950s, the dance hall at 917 Sixth Street was operated by new owners, including Michael Campanella and Charles Morgan, who ran Dreamland as a licensed beer-serving dance hall. In June 1953, city authorities fined the operators for employing so-called "B girls" and imposed a thirty-day suspension, with municipal officials noting that revocation of the establishment's license and closure were under consideration.[484] "B girls" were commission-based drink solicitors employed by dance halls, a practice increasingly prohibited under mid-century municipal ordinances.

By the mid-1960s, Dreamland's survival was threatened less by vice enforcement than by urban redevelopment. In April 1966, Joseph

Giacomo requested a permit to remodel property at 821 J Street in order to relocate Dreamland from Sixth Street, stating that the dance hall was being displaced by redevelopment. City officials responded that a license transfer would be required before any move could be approved, leaving both the relocation and the building permit in limbo.[485] Two years later, the Sacramento City Council scheduled a public hearing on Giacomo's proposal to move Dreamland to J Street, confirming that the displacement was ongoing and unresolved.[486]

By the early 1970s, Dreamland appeared only in retrospective commentary rather than current listings. A 1973 the *Sacramento Union* column referring to Ed Kripp's world treated Dreamland as part of a vanished nightlife ecosystem rather than an operating venue, signaling that the dance hall had passed fully into memory.[487]

The Resilience of Laura Vice

Laura Vice has been described as one of the earliest female owners associated with a professional baseball club. The failure of the 1891 Sacramento venture, however, did not define her career. If the loosely organized structure of early baseball exposed her to risk, Vice responded not by retreating but by redirecting her influence into Sacramento's fraternal and charitable institutions—spaces that offered more durable forms of authority.[488]

By the late 1890s she had become a prominent figure within the city's network of fraternal orders. As an officer in Wenonah Council, No. 2, she helped organize large public events, including the twenty-ninth annual ball at Turner Hall. These gatherings drew wide attendance from Sacramento's civic and social circles.[489]

In June 1898, members of her circle organized a surprise party in her honor, attended by prominent figures from what newspapers called the city's "Gilt Edge" set. The event was described as lively and well attended—a sign that whatever disappointment accompanied the 1891 baseball episode, Vice's standing in Sacramento had not diminished.[490]

If early baseball had been unstable, the fraternal world proved steadier ground. Laura Vice moved from a speculative sporting enterprise into institutions that were structured, visible, and enduring.

Angus Ross, The Last of the Knightly Gamblers

Ross remained where Kripp had begun. Co-owner of the Yolo Monte Carlo, Angus Ross, never escaped the world that Ed Kripp eventually left behind. A professional gambler by trade, Ross appeared repeatedly in early twentieth-century newspapers as an operator of faro games in Sacramento and Washington, often named alongside Kripp during the height of the poolroom wars. Unlike Kripp, whose ambitions extended into sports, entertainment, and later civic gestures, Ross remained rooted in gambling as a vocation, continuing to operate under his own name even as enforcement tightened.

By the final years of his life, the reputation that had once sustained him offered little protection. In November 1914, Ross died at the age of fifty-two, his passing noted quietly in the press as that of one of "the last of the romantic line of knightly gamblers." He was ill, impoverished, and largely forgotten by a city that had once known his name.[491] Ross's fate stood in quiet contrast to Kripp's survival: two men who had helped build the same system, only one of whom found a way out.

The Price of the Ring

Boxing, like early baseball, consumed its heroes quickly. Ad Wolgast and Joe Rivers—the champion and challenger whose 1912 contest and contested aftermath unfolded beyond Ed Kripp's reach—left the ring with reputations intact, but futures already narrowing.

Ad Wolgast had been built for an era that did not know how to stop.

Smaller gloves. Longer rounds. Fewer rules. He fought the way the sport demanded—forward, unguarded, absorbing punishment and returning it with interest.

That style carried him to the top. In February 1910, after fighting Battling Nelson at Point Richmond, one of the costs was already visible in the record.[492] It was not merely a fight but an ordeal: forty rounds fought under a California sun, with no meaningful defensive pauses and no medical intervention until Nelson was effectively blind and the referee stopped the contest.[493] Contemporary newspapers marveled at Wolgast's endurance and brutality.

Adolph Wolgast, ca. 1910.
Bain News Service, Library of Congress.

By 1912, he was wealthy, famous, and celebrated—one of boxing's defining figures.[494]

But the accumulation of punishment was unmistakable even then. As Wolgast's fame peaked, observers began to notice changes. He became impulsive and withdrawn before suffering a breakdown that led to his commitment to a state hospital in 1917.

Long before the condition had a name, Wolgast became one of the earliest documented victims of what would later be called chronic traumatic encephalopathy (CTE), the neurological price paid by fighters whose careers were built on absorbing punishment rather than avoiding it. When he died in 1955 in Camarillo, California, he had outlived both his fame and the brutal era that had demanded everything from his body and left little behind to protect his mind.[495]

Joe Rivers' fate was quieter, but no less revealing.

Joe "The Mexican" Rivers, ca. 1910.
Bain News Service, Library of Congress.

Born José Ybarra in Los Angeles, Rivers rose quickly after turning professional in 1910, known for speed and relentless pressure.

After his July 4, 1912 fight against Wolgast, he continued fighting. He earned a living, but the title never returned. The sport moved on.

By the 1950s, Rivers was living alone in a windowless Los Angeles apartment with a naked lightbulb hanging from the ceiling, largely forgotten. He had little to his name other than his most valued possession—a violin that had belonged to his father—an object from a life before the ring. He died in 1957, remembered faintly by a world that had once believed he was its future.[496]

Together, their lives revealed what boxing in Kripp's era could not yet admit. Glory was immediate. Damage was cumulative. The ring made men famous—but it offered no protection from what it took in return.

Charles Doyle: Custodian of the Game

Charlie Doyle represented the transformation of baseball from personality-driven enterprise to organized institution. For Doyle, the years after his playing career unfolded with a steadiness that set him apart from many of his contemporaries. While the era that produced the Gilt Edges and Buffalo Park had begun to change, Doyle remained visibly and productively connected to baseball in Sacramento. On January 10, 1920, he was announced as secretary of the Senators.[497] The title *secretary* carried far more authority than its name suggests. In practice, Doyle functioned as the club's chief baseball executive, overseeing finances, contracts, and league relations in a role equivalent to what would later be called a general manager, a capacity in which he continued to be identified throughout the 1920s and into the mid-1930s.[498]

Throughout this time, he continued to appear in local coverage as a respected voice within Sacramento's baseball community. Sports columns treated him as a figure of continuity—someone who bridged the city's early professional ambitions with its more modern, organized forms.[499] Unlike former players whose post-baseball lives faded into obscurity, Doyle remained present, useful, and consulted, his reputation grounded less in past heroics than in ongoing contribution.

That respect endured into later decades. By the late 1940s, as Sacramento prepared to open a new park and take stock of its baseball lineage, Doyle was selected for public honor. Plans were announced for a Charlie Doyle Night, intended to recognize his long association with the city's teams and his role during the Buffalo Park years.[500] The event was postponed following a fire at Edmonds Field, which left the city without a suitable venue for such a celebration. The postponement did not diminish the intent.

Newspapers noted that Doyle was "entitled to have a great night in the new park," a phrase that framed his recognition as a certainty rather than a consolation.

In an era when so many figures from Sacramento's early baseball world were remembered chiefly for scandal, ambition, or decline, Doyle's fate was quieter—and rarer. He did not vanish. Instead, he remained: a working presence, a keeper of memory, and a man whose relationship to the game matured into stewardship rather than legend.

The Brothers and the Mother: Power and Survival

Although also marred by controversy, Ed's brother Newton made the news less often than his brothers. He died in 1943 after working for the Southern Pacific Railroad for 25 years before retiring.[501]

Where Ed adapted, his older brother performed the old system long after it stopped working. Fred Conrad Kripp continued to drift along the margins of the law long after Ed had turned his instincts toward lasting structures. In February 1917, Fred—by then a former city detective—was accused of extortion while operating off duty in Chinese and Japanese restaurants, threatening arrest without proper authority. Though formally cleared, city officials issued a sharp public rebuke, condemning his conduct as an abuse of public trust.[502] Three years later, he was fined for impersonating a federal marshal after attempting to collect money while presenting himself as a deputy of the United States.[503] Fred Conrad Kripp died in 1934 following an extended illness, his passing marked quietly in the local paper as that of an ex-police officer, a native son who never fully escaped the gravity of his past.[504] Where Ed ultimately converted informal power into fixed institutions, Fred remained bound to its performance—relying on titles, badges, and residual status long after their protections had thinned.

If Fred Kripp's life reflected the volatility of his era, their mother,

Margaret Ann Kripp Landsburg, embodied endurance of a different order. Born in 1842, she arrived in Sacramento in 1849 as a child, crossing the plains by wagon with her parents and witnessing the city's earliest years at ground level.

In May 1922, Margaret appeared publicly among the city's surviving pioneers at a reunion of forty-nine early settlers, an event that gathered men and women who had come west by wagon train and lived to see Sacramento raised, rebuilt, and regulated.[505]

She had remarried after the death of her husband Frederick. By December 1932, the *Sacramento Bee* marked her ninetieth birthday by noting that she had lived in the city for more than eight decades—long enough to have seen Sacramento rise from flood-prone settlement to modern capital.[506] When she died five years later, at age ninety-four, the paper identified her as the oldest living resident of the capital, a woman whose memory stretched back to ox teams, raised streets, and the city's first hotels.[507] She outlived her husband, her son Fred, and nearly all of the world that had shaped her children. In a family marked by risk and ambition, Margaret Kripp's legacy was not power or notoriety, but continuity—the rare authority of having seen it all and endured.

Emma Hables' Reinvention

Emma's life after the divorce revealed a different kind of survival. By 1905, she had moved to San Francisco. That year, Emma Kripp appeared in the Sacramento press as a professional hairdresser, though she was then residing and working in San Francisco. Her advertisement did not introduce her services; it addressed former clients, inquiring whether they remained in Sacramento and inviting continued patronage. The notice assumes an established clientele, suggesting that her reputation had been built locally before her relocation. She was sustaining a professional identity across cities.[508]

In August of 1907 Emma had married Samuel Hables, an Austrian immigrant and entrepreneur who could offer her the stability and fidelity that Kripp had never provided. Orlin and Florence lived with their mother and stepfather in the city.[509]

Emma (holding child) with family, ca. late 1920s.
Author's collection.

Emma's move to San Francisco signaled her transformation into a sharp commercial strategist. No longer a passive observer, she actively managed the family's assets, securing clear ownership of prime Mission District real estate at 24th and Treat Avenue.[510] Before Sam became an automotive pioneer, he was rooted in the city's elite merchant culture, managing high-end grocery and retail operations linked to legendary institutions like the White House department store.[511]

Sam transitioned from auctioning livestock at his Folsom Street stables to securing a prestigious five-year contract for the Tennessee-built Marathon car. By 1913, the couple had moved their expanding automobile agency into a modern showroom located on Golden Gate Avenue.[512]

Florence and Orlin Kripp: The Next Generation

Beneath all the monuments and the business acumen, Ed Kripp was also a father. After his divorce from Emma, Florence and Orlin grew up in the household of Emma and her husband, Samuel, but with frequent visits from Ed.

Orlin Kripp with his family.
Author's collection.

Florence Kripp.
Sacramento Bee, March 28, 1914.

His son, Orlin Arthur, served in the military and was among the generation that went to war during World War I.

He returned from the war, and in February 1920 married Bertha, known as Betty. Together they raised two children, Robert Moore, born 1921 and Carol Ann, born 1926, whom they raised in San Francisco.

Ed's daughter, Florence, became an accomplished singer, eventually balancing her artistic talents with a professional career.

As an adult she was living in San Francisco and working as a school teacher, yet she remained a sought-after performer in her hometown. A notable highlight of her singing career occurred on March 28, 1914, when she returned to Sacramento as a featured guest for the Sacramento Society of Pioneers.

She was married to Dr. William Morris Cohn, though they later divorced. She lived the rest of her life in a quaint home in San Francisco. Multiple generations of her family hold fond childhood memories of their gentle and kind "Aunt Florence."

Yolo King: The Legend Persists

In May 1964, demolition crews arrived to tear down Edmonds Field to make way for a Gemco discount store...[513] The excavators dug into the earth near the location of the old diamond, they discovered something that seemed to validate fifty years of local legend.

Back in the height of his gambling days, when Ed Kripp was still young, he owned his beloved champion racehorse named Yolo King. The horse was named after the county that had been so generous to him with land and fortune during the reclamation years.

When the horse died—whether from age or illness, the records don't say—Kripp made a decision that defied convention.

He had the horse's body transported to Buffalo Park and buried on the grounds.

The exact burial location became the subject of local legend. Some accounts placed it under first base. Others claimed it was near home plate. Still others insisted it was in center field. For decades, people visiting the park imagined the champion horse lying beneath the field where Sacramento's great moments would unfold, a tangible connection between the gambling kingpin and the monument he had created.

When the construction crews excavated the site in 1964, local lore says they found the skeletal remains of a horse. The skull still contained the gold tooth that Kripp had reportedly given the animal.[514] A final, glittering connection between Ed Kripp's personal ambition and the public legacy he had left behind. The truth was never confirmed. Perhaps it was real. Perhaps it was the city's way of making sense of a man who had lived his entire life in that same ambiguous space—between legitimacy and the underworld, between gambling and baseball, between destruction and creation.

The legend persisted not because the gold tooth could be proven, but precisely because it could not be. It was the kind of detail that revealed the character of a man: someone so consumed with making monuments of everything he touched that he would gild a horse's tooth and bury the animal beneath his most sacred creation. Whether it was true or merely whispered into being by the city's collective imagination, the story endured. It said less about what could be proven than about the kind of man people took him to be.

The Enduring Mystery

The ambiguity that surrounded so many moments in Kripp's life found its most enduring embodiment in the Postler case. The coroner's jury split seven to six—unable to agree even on whether the death was suicide or justifiable homicide. Contemporary accounts reported that three bullets were recovered from Postler's body, a fact that sat uneasily beside every official explanation offered. What remained was not a conclusion, but a question.

The episode lingered in the city's memory as one of those stories that refused resolution. Decades later, in 1947, a San Francisco columnist returned to the Saratoga shooting, listing it among the city's enduring "Unfashionable Mysteries."

The continued public interest, long after Kripp had achieved respectability through Dreamland, confirmed that the incident had never been fully absorbed into the past. It was too strange, too contradictory, and too resistant to tidy narrative to disappear.

The bullets, like the verdict, never lined up.

The Buffalo Brewing Tray

Among the objects that survived Ed Kripp is a tray.

Buffalo Brewing Company tray owned by Ed Kripp.
Author's collection.

It is a turquoise blue Buffalo Brewing Company serving tray, circular and lithographed, showing a flower-crowned woman lifting a narrow glass beneath the words *"For Health and Cheer."* Around its edge runs *Buffalo Brewing Co., Sacramento, California.*

The image at its center is noticeably worn, softened by repeated use, while the outer border remains comparatively intact.

It was not a display piece. It was used.

The tray belongs to the author. In the family, its purpose was never uncertain. Kripp's granddaughter—who knew him personally—said it had been used to serve beer at the ballpark.

The historical record neither confirms nor fully denies that claim. During Kripp's ownership of Buffalo Park, his application for a county liquor license was denied. Contemporary reporting makes clear that alcohol at sporting grounds was a contested issue, shaped by the "moral wave" Kripp so often spoke about—one that would soon culminate in Prohibition. What the record does *not* show is an article announcing that beer was sold at games, or that a liquor license was ever approved during the period in which Kripp owned Buffalo Park, a park that bore the name of Buffalo Brewing Company itself.

Silence, in this period, is not evidence of absence.

The tray does not prove where beer was served, or under what authority. It only suggests repetition: something passed from hand to hand often enough to wear away its center.

In a life spent negotiating what could be seen and what could not, some truths left no documentary trace at all—only an object, and a memory that endured.

The tray is a reminder that much of Kripp's world survives not in headlines or approvals, but in what was quietly done, carefully remembered, and never written down.

Perhaps this was Kripp's truest legacy: not the certainty of his accomplishments, but the mystery that surrounded him. A man who had lived his entire life in ambiguity—between law and lawlessness, between shadow and light—left behind a city full of questions. The Postler shooting. The exact location of the buried horse. Money that appeared when needed and vanished just as cleanly. Protection that arrived before warrants did. Deals struck without paper. All of it remained suspended in Sacramento's imagination, waiting for someone to prove what had actually happened.

That day has never come.

CHAPTER 23

When the Systems Hardened

THE MEN who built Sacramento baseball did it by personality—by leverage, by instinct, by favors traded in private and threats delivered in daylight. For a time, that was enough. The game could be held together by operators who knew where to stand, when to press, and who to call.

Then the game outgrew them.

What replaced the early order was not a new generation of local strongmen, but a structure. Baseball began to behave like an institution: governed by contracts instead of handshakes, stabilized by affiliations instead of loyalties, protected by rules that made the sport harder to bend. The power that once lived in Sacramento's personalities migrated upward—into league offices, parent clubs, and systems designed to endure without the men who first proved California could sustain the game.

This is the story of that hardening: how Buffalo Park became Moreing Field, then Cardinal Field, then Edmonds Field—how lights were installed, names were removed, and Sacramento's baseball identity was folded, piece by piece, into a machine larger than the city that had once invented its own terms.

The League That Outlived Its Builders

The incorporated California League formed at the Baldwin Hotel in 1897 became the direct ancestor of the Pacific Coast League, established in 1903.[515] Over the next half-century, the PCL grew so stable and professional that West Coast fans often regarded it as their own major league—a self-contained system rivaling the prestige of the eastern circuits until Major League Baseball finally expanded west in 1958.[516]

That durability was not accidental. The league's founders understood that baseball would survive only if it outgrew the men who first bent it to their will. Contracts replaced handshakes. Franchises replaced personalities. Authority migrated upward. The framework formalized because it was designed to do so.

Yet its foundations were laid by men who thrived before such an arrangement existed.

Ed Kripp's "Gilt Edge" method—controlling space, shaping schedules, managing crowds, turning spectacle into routine—created the proving ground on which organized West Coast baseball learned to function at scale. Long before league stability, he demonstrated that California could sustain professional teams, reliable attendance, and profitable operations year after year.

The irony was that the very success of that model made it unnecessary—and eventually undesirable—for the league to retain its original builders.

Sacramento's later franchises cycled through capable stewards, but none wielded the combination of standing, leverage, and local control that had once made the city dominant under Kripp's management. The Pacific Coast League chose permanence over personality. In doing so, it traded volatility for consolidation.

But the PCL became a pipeline for greatness. Before they were icons in New York or Boston, Joe DiMaggio played for the San Francisco Seals, and Ted Williams emerged as a teenage phenom with the San Diego Padres—players shaped within a regional system that had grown from California's early territorial experiments.[517]

Even many of Kripp's own players would pass east through this pipeline, absorbed into the national game.

The league endured.

The builders faded.

That, too, was part of the design.

When the Lights Came On

Concrete improved the park. But concrete was not enough. In 1930, Lew Moreing made a decision that altered not just Sacramento baseball, but the rhythm of the game itself. He understood what traditionalists resisted: working people could not attend weekday afternoon games. By the time they left their jobs, the innings were nearly finished.

Moreing had observed experiments with artificial lighting in eastern leagues. Sacramento would become his laboratory. Only a handful of parks had attempted night baseball, and none had yet proven it could sustain a professional schedule.

On June 5, 1930, as dusk settled, automobiles lined the surrounding streets. Nearly a thousand people gathered with their faces tilted upward. Something unprecedented was about to happen.

At 8:31 p.m., Moreing threw the switch.

Banks of lights mounted on wooden poles flooded the field with 180,000 watts of brilliance. Darkness dissolved. The park blazed beneath artificial suns so bright that one writer remarked that "Old Sol was never more neatly eclipsed by the moon than he is by the new lights at Moreing Field."[518]

A ball rose into the glow. The first pitch traveled cleanly from the pitcher's hand to the center fielder's glove. The crowd erupted.

Five days later, the Senators hosted the Oakland Oaks in the Coast League's first official night game. Bryan delivered a shutout before 12,000 fans.[519] Attendance surged that season, placing Sacramento first in Pacific Coast League attendance.[520] Baseball had been restructured around labor schedules and electric current. The game now belonged to workers who could finally see it.

After the Name Came Down

Lew Moreing and Margaret Castle at the lighting switch, June 4, 1930.
Courtesy of Alan O'Connor. Private collection.

Lew Moreing, who had invested nearly $200,000 of his own money into the park, watched as the block letters spelling "MOREING FIELD" were removed from its entrance.

Sports columnist Steve George called the act "an outrage against gratitude and common decency to deprive Lew Moreing of all he has left in baseball—his name."[521]

Moreing died the following year, his name already gone.[522] In 1936, the park was rechristened Cardinal Field.[523]

The new name signaled more than cosmetic change. Sacramento entered formal affiliation with the St. Louis Cardinals, folding the city's baseball identity into a national development pipeline. Talent, contracts, and authority now flowed through a parent club. The park remained a civic gathering place, but its function had been standardized. It was no longer improvised by local strongmen. It functioned as an outpost of an organized machine.

That same year, the club formally adopted the Solons name, transforming a newspaper shorthand into a legal identity drawn from Solon, the ancient Greek lawgiver. Under Pacific Coast League rules, regular-season finishes and postseason championships often diverged.[524] Sacramento finished first in 1937 but fell in the playoffs. In the Pacific Coast League, the regular-season pennant and the postseason championship were separate prizes.

The seasons were long—often stretching to 180 or even 200 games—and the playoffs were added to keep fan interest alive late in the year, create a dramatic championship series, and generate additional gate revenue..[525] Sacramento captured the postseason title in 1938 and 1939 without winning the pennant, and only in 1942 did the club unite both—securing the franchise's sole true Coast League pennant.[526]

Edmonds Field

Stability remained fragile.

By 1943, rumors circulated that the franchise would be sold and moved to Tacoma. Sacramento faced the loss not merely of a team, but of its place within organized West Coast baseball.

Richard J. Edmonds, the thirty-year-old sports editor of the *Sacramento Union*, refused to concede it. Declaring he "would not care to live in Sacramento" without its Pacific Coast League franchise, he rallied investors and raised $52,000 in forty-eight hours during wartime. Racing through a snowstorm to reach the league meetings, they persuaded the directors to keep the franchise in Sacramento. The price of the club was reduced to $40,000, and a local group soon arranged to purchase the ballpark for $50,000, securing the team's future in the city.[527]

For a brief period, the park was renamed Doubleday Park, invoking baseball's mythical founder. The Solons opened their 1944 season there against Seattle under that name.[528]

Edmonds' victory was short-lived. He contracted pneumonia and died in July 1945.

Within weeks, a public campaign began to rename the park in his honor. On September 9, 1945, between games of a doubleheader, the stadium was officially christened Edmonds Field.[529]

The Fire at Edmonds Field

On July 11, 1948, the wooden era ended.

A discarded cigarette near the press box ignited a blaze that consumed the structure Moreing had built. Firefighters arrived quickly but could do little more than contain the perimeter. Newspapers described an "ocean of flame" lighting the sky above Riverside Boulevard as embers drifted across nearby streets.[530]

Fire at Edmonds Field.
Center for Sacramento History.

Thirty-eight years of accumulated memory—bleachers, press box, light poles—collapsed into ash.[531]

The park was rebuilt in concrete for the 1949 season. It was functional, modern, and stark. Without a roof, fans endured the harsh Sacramento sun. By the late 1950s, minor league economics were faltering. Television siphoned attention. Attendance declined. In 1960, the franchise was sold and moved to Hawaii.[532]

Professional baseball faded from the site.

By 1964, a Gemco department store opened on the property. Later it became a Target. The land that had once drawn thousands under electric light was absorbed into commercial routine.[533]

Today, shoppers pass a commemorative plaque marking the ground where Buffalo Park once stood.

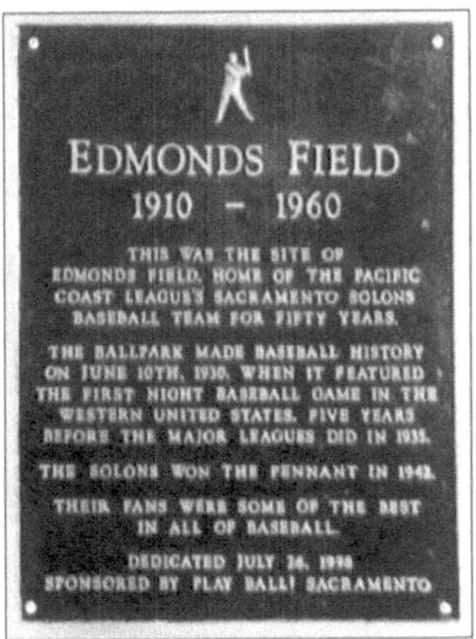

Commemorative plaque at Target store on Riverside.
Courtesy of the author.

Across the street, in the quiet of the cemetery, Ed Kripp and Dick Edmonds rest—men separated by decades, united by their conviction that Sacramento required spectacle, continuity, and a place to gather.

Hughes Stadium

Between 1964 and the mid-1970s, Sacramento possessed no true professional baseball park. When the Solons briefly returned in the

1970s, they played at Hughes Stadium, a football facility leased from the Los Rios Community College District..[534]

Hughes was not a successor to Buffalo Park or Edmonds Field. It was a refuge—an improvised setting that kept the game alive while Sacramento searched for a permanent home.

Major Leagues come West

In 1958, Major League Baseball permanently altered the national landscape when the Brooklyn Dodgers relocated to Los Angeles and the New York Giants to San Francisco. For decades the sport's western boundary had stopped in St. Louis. Now it crossed the continent.[535]

The move was driven not only by aging eastern ballparks but by the explosive growth of television and California's expanding markets. Broadcast revenue, suburban population growth, and new stadium construction made the West newly attractive to the major leagues.[536]

For the Pacific Coast League, the consequences were immediate. Long operating as a quasi–major league with "open" classification, the PCL saw its premier territories absorbed into Major League Baseball's centralized structure.[537]

The West gained the highest level of play.

It lost its autonomy.

Regional dominance gave way to national consolidation.

The System Consolidated

By the time that consolidation was complete, Ed Kripp was no longer required. Affiliations, contracts, standardized schedules, and farm structures reduced dependence on personality and informal command. The game no longer needed a man who could control space and shape a crowd. It needed continuity.

Yet even the most permanent structures rest on proof. Long before affiliations and parent clubs, someone had to demonstrate that California could sustain professional baseball—that crowds would return week after week, that land beyond the city grid could be made central, that spectacle could become routine.

That proof existed before the structure did.

Sutter Health Park in West Sacramento.
Photograph by Quintin Soloviev.

Gilt Edge open air club inside Sutter Health Park.
Courtesy of Sutter Health Park.

EPILOGUE

The River Cats and the Legacy

ALMOST A CENTURY after Ed Kripp opened Buffalo Park on the edge of town, professional baseball found another edge of Sacramento. In 2000, the River Cats, as part of the Pacific Coast League, began play in West Sacramento, just across the river from the old city. The location felt familiar—just outside the traditional city limits, yet inseparable from it. Different ground. Same instinct. The crowds did not need to be convinced. They arrived in numbers that startled the rest of minor league baseball.[538]

In 2025, the Athletics made Sutter Health Park their temporary home while awaiting completion of a stadium in Las Vegas.[539] For the first time in the city's history, Major League Baseball was played in Sacramento. The moment had been building for generations.

Sacramento never permanently secured a major league franchise. What it sustained instead was something quieter and more durable: the habit of gathering. Through relocations, renamings, financial collapses, wars, reform movements, and ownership changes, the city kept showing up.

The most tangible bridge between Kripp's era and the present stands inside Sutter Health Park itself. At the edge of the outfield sits the Gilt Edge Club. Nearby stretches the Solon Club, elevated beneath shade, looking toward the skyline.

The names are not decorative. They are acknowledgments.

The Gilt Edge Club recalls the championship empire Kripp built in the 1890s, when wooden grandstands shook beneath shouting crowds. The Solon Club honors the generations who followed—the Sacramento

Solons who carried Pacific Coast League summers for decades. Memory is embedded in signage, in the architecture of gathering.

A few miles away, on Riverside Boulevard, a plaque in the parking lot of a Target marks the site of Edmonds Field, once Buffalo Park. From 1910 to 1960, thousands passed through its gates. Championships were celebrated. Names were raised and lowered from the marquee. The grandstands are gone now. Asphalt covers the diamond.

The marker remains.

Kripp understood something fundamental about Sacramento: if you built a serious park and treated the game as an event worth attending, the city would respond. He built outside the municipal core, invested heavily, and trusted that spectacle and seriousness could coexist. He was right.

Nearly a century later, River Cats owner Art Savage made a similar wager. He financed a modern ballpark largely through private capital and trusted that Sacramento would sustain it. It became one of the most successful franchises in Triple-A baseball. Different era. Same wager.[540]

Sacramento remains a baseball town—though not one defined only by league status. The wooden fences are gone. The lights have grown brighter. The names on the jerseys have changed.

But the game endures.

It lives in summer nights at the park. In families who return year after year. In stories passed down—of the night the lights came on, of Buffalo Park glowing beneath electric suns, of impossible pennants and narrow escapes.

Ed Kripp's legacy persists there. Not as a statue. Not as a clean moral tale. But as a current running beneath the surface of the city.

The conviction that a place can remake itself; that vision, capital, and will can shape institution.

The field changed names. The leagues shifted. The lights evolved.

The crowd remained.

AFTERWORD

By R.E. Graswich

Journalist, media expert, and author of *Vagrant Kings*

I FELL FOR ED KRIPP when I learned he buried his favorite racehorse at Buffalo Park, the stadium Kripp built over a garbage dump for the baseball team he owned in Sacramento.

The horse was entombed at Broadway and Riverside, 6 feet under home plate. Or first base. Or centerfield. Years passed. Memories dimmed.

Kripp was not a normal sportsman. He was a high-roller businessman who operated gambling parlors in cigar shops and a dance hall called Dreamland.

He settled arguments with his fists and bet on anything that moved. He never seemed to sleep. Two big weaknesses were baseball and the stallion he buried at Buffalo Park, a champion router named Yolo King.

Yolo King had another name—the Big Horse with the Gold Tooth. When Yolo King developed an infected incisor, Kripp hired the best dentist in town to extract the animal's tooth and replace it with a golden bridge. Or so legend says.

I fell for Kripp because it's impossible to imagine anyone like him today.

He was honestly dishonest and wildly successful. He never hid his addiction to vice. He was loyal to friends. Enemies were scorned. Or punched in the face.

Among his friends were sober judges and crooked cops, Irish priests and tattooed prostitutes, bald-headed bartenders and French jockeys, boxers with smashed noses and baseball players with mutton-chop sideburns.

Kripp was a capitalist whose financial skill made professional baseball viable on the West Coast. Without his ability to conjure sandlot baseball into a marketable, professional attraction as the early 1900s unfolded, the San Francisco Giants and Los Angeles Dodgers might not have left New York and Brooklyn a half-century later. Never mind the Padres, Angels and Athletics.

Today nobody remembers Ed Kripp.

His name looks like a typo. No streets, schools or libraries honor his legend. But there was a time when anything anyone did for fun in Sacramento, illicit or legitimate, in darkness or on bright Sunday afternoons, likely involved an enterprise shaded by Kripp.

Now Ed Kripp lives again. With her book *The Gilt Edge of Ambition*, Lisa Jonsson, Kripp's great-great-granddaughter, examines an extraordinary man whose life straddled the gutters, baseball offices, courthouses, boxing rings and racetracks of adolescent California.

Her story is remarkable in foundation and prose. Jonsson transforms exhaustive research into a narrative that begs for Hollywood script treatments.

As she chronicles Ed Kripp's life, Jonsson tracks a brute, scoundrel, gambler, merchant, husband, father and sporting tycoon who encompassed California's golden, two-fisted ambitions from the 1890s into World War II.

Kripp hands Jonsson a lens to explore grimy, forgotten alleys in California history. A century ago, he was a household name around Northern California.

Local newspaper reporters loved him and tracked his triumphs and troubles. Sometimes journalists embellished. Jonsson dissects conflicting news reports with a surgeon's precision. A relentless historian and captivating writer, she acknowledges what she can't prove.

Historians fall into categories. Some are intense researchers and ponderous writers. Others are slick wordsmiths who glide over factual roadblocks. Before Jonsson began to dig and write, they all missed the goldmine left behind by Ed Kripp.

Jonsson is a descendant with an important story to tell. Familial love and loyalty stir no hesitation as she presents ugly examples of her great-great-grandfather's attitudes and behavior.

She confirms he could be an awful person. Her story's heart is baseball, but her scope illuminates a deeper California netherworld obscured by time and turned to dust.

Ed Kripp died in 1942, age 72. He's buried in Sacramento City Cemetery, across Riverside Boulevard from the former garbage dump that became Buffalo Park, where Kripp buried Yolo King.

Now the site holds a Target store, parking lot and a story that finally found its voice. There could be a horse's gold tooth planted there. Lisa Jonsson isn't sure, but she may discover it yet.

Author's Notes

This work of historical narrative nonfiction is grounded in extensive primary research, including newspaper accounts, archival records, legal documents, and family materials. All significant events, dates, and factual claims are drawn directly from the historical record. Some historical photographs have been digitally restored for clarity.

The research draws on more than five hundred primary-source citations. Where the historical record contains contradictions—split juries, conflicting testimony, or inconsistent reporting—the narrative preserves that ambiguity rather than imposing artificial certainty. Silence in the record is treated not as absence, but as evidence of how informal power often operated.

Ed Kripp's life spanned from the Gold Rush era through the years leading up to the Second World War. He witnessed Sacramento's transformation from a frontier town into a modern city. He was both a product of that transformation and a catalyst for it. His story is Sacramento's story—a tale of ambition, reinvention, and the shifting systems that shaped the modern American West.

Historical Photographs

Margaret Conrad, Ed's mother, (second from right, first row) with her mother Mary and her siblings, ca 1870s.
California History Section Picture Catalog, California State Library.

M Street Bridge, predecessor to the Tower Bridge, 1910.
Photograph by McCurry Foto Co., California State Library.

Brewery of the Buffalo Brewing Company, ca. 1890s.
Photograph by Varney. Sacramento Public Library.

Oakland Commuters leaving the Statehouse Hotel for their first Pacific Coast League game against Sacramento, 1903.
California Historical Society.

Ruhstaller's Gilt Edge beer label.
Courtesy of Alan O'Connor. Private collection.

K Street with electric streetcar, Sacramento, 1910.
California State Library.

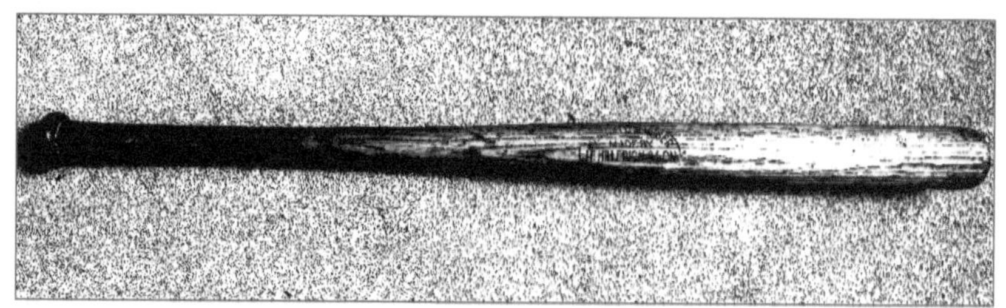

1897 Louisville Slugger bat.
Photograph courtesy of Alan O'Connor. Private collection.

Poster advertising a Gilt Edge game at Snowflake Park, 1898.
Photograph courtesy of Alan O'Connor. Private collection.

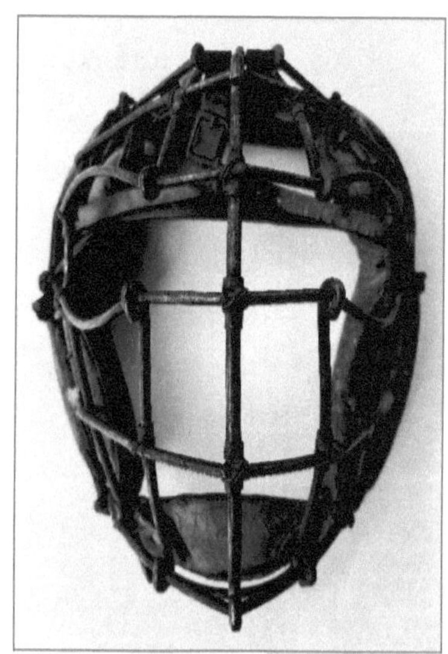

Sacramento Senators catcher's mask used at Buffalo Park.
Photograph courtesy of Alan O'Connor. Private collection.

Image Credits

Augustus Koch, Bird's Eye View of the City of Sacramento, State Capital of California (San Francisco: Britton & Rey, 1870). David Rumsey Map Collection.

Downtown Sacramento, 1890. Photograph by Frank Appleton. Sacramento Room Photograph Collection, Sacramento Public Library, MC7 Album 1-23.

China Slough, Sacramento, 1878. Central Pacific Railroad photograph. Old Central Pacific Depot and trestle bridge over China Slough. Digital image courtesy of NoeHill.com.

Sacramento flood of 1862, K Street at Fourth Street, looking west. Photograph by Eugene Hepting. Center for Sacramento History, catalog no. 1985/024/1605.

Washington Hotel, Washington Township, Yolo County, California, 1955. Photograph by Ralph H. Shaw. Center for Sacramento History, catalog no. 1998/726/0029.

Ed Kripp, detail from team photo, ca. late 1890s. Courtesy of Alan O'Connor. Private Collection.

Gilt Edge Baseball Club and manager Ed Kripp. Courtesy of Alan O'Connor. Private collection.

Frank Ruhstaller, ca. 1885. Center for California History.

Baldwin Hotel, San Francisco, 1879. San Francisco Public Library, San Francisco Historical Photograph Collection.

Portrait of Jay Hughes, 1899. Author's collection (family scrapbook).

Sacramento Gilt Edge Baseball Club portrait. Courtesy of Alan O'Connor. Private collection.

"Crowd Entered the Diamond," *Evening Bee* (Sacramento), April 25, 1898.

"Hughey Fears for His Life," *San Francisco Examiner*, October 24, 1898.

Oakland Greenhood & Moran baseball club, ca. 1880s.*Always on Sunday: The California Baseball League 1886–1915* by John E. Spalding (Ag Press, 1992).

Gilt Edge Baseball Club, 1898–1900. Sacramento Room Photograph Collection, Sacramento Public Library, PH-2019-47.

Gilt Edge Baseball Club, ca. 1899–1900. Courtesy of Alan O'Connor. Private collection.

Oak Park, Sacramento, showing trolley cars, ca. 1900. California Historical Society Collection, USC Libraries Digital Library.

Gilt Edge Baseball Team.*San Francisco Call*, December 3, 1899.

Oak Park with streetcars, Sacramento Library.
Mr. and Mrs. Jay Hughes. *Evening Bee* (Sacramento), April 14, 1900.
Portrait of Mike Fisher. *Evening Bee* (Sacramento), September 22, 1905.Charley Graham, ca. 1920s. Courtesy of Alan O'Connor. Private collection.
Columbia Café, Sixth and J Streets, Sacramento, ca. 1909. *Sacramento Bee*, December 11, 1909.
Ormonde, sire of Beau Ormonde. Thoroughbred Heritage.
Baseball at Buffalo Park. Courtesy of Alan O'Connor. Private collection.
Baseball game at Buffalo Park. Courtesy of the author.
Coverage of the Postler shooting. *San Francisco Chronicle*, January 28, 1911.
Portrait of Paul Postler. *San Francisco Call*, January 28, 1911.
The Postler family. *San Francisco Call*, January 28, 1911.
The packed grandstand at Buffalo Park. Courtesy of the author.
Japanese passenger steamship *Shinyo Maru*, ca. 1911. United States Navy, NavSource Naval History.
Harry Wolverton. *Morning Oregonian*, June 18, 1916.
The Rivers–Wolgast fight, Vernon, California. *Los Angeles Times*, July 5, 1912.
Betting slips from Kripp's poolroom. *Sacramento Bee*, January 20, 1911.
Deed for park. *Sacramento Union*, December 2, 1921.
Portrait of Ed Kripp. *Sacramento Bee*, January 31, 1913.
Game at Buffalo Park, ca. 1910s. Courtesy of Alan O'Connor. Private collection.
Aerial view of Moreing Field. Courtesy of Alan O'Connor. Private collection.
Dreamland Dance Hall. *Sacramento Bee*, March 22, 1924.
Endorsements for Dreamland. *Sacramento Union*, November 20, 1923.
Endorsement of Dreamland and response. *Sacramento Union*, December 12, 1923.
First Congregational Church, Sacramento. Frank Christy Collection, Center for Sacramento History.
Advertisement for China Tea Garden. *Sacramento Bee*, September 8, 1934.
Monument marking the grave of Ed Kripp, Sacramento City Cemetery. Author's collection.
Ad Wolgast. Bain News Service, Library of Congress, Prints and Photographs Division.
Joe "The Mexican" Rivers. Bain News Service, Library of Congress, Prints and Photographs Division.
Emma (holding child) with family, ca. late 1920s. Author's collection.

Orlin Kripp with family. Author's collection.

Florence Kripp. *Sacramento Bee*, March 28, 1914.

Buffalo Brewing Company tray owned by Ed Kripp. Author's collection.

Lew Moreing and Margaret Castle at the lighting switch, Moreing Field, June 4, 1930. Courtesy of Alan O'Connor. Private collection.

Commemorative plaque at Target. Courtesy of the author.

Fire at Edmonds Field. Center for Sacramento History.

Sutter Health Park, West Sacramento. Photograph by Quintin Soloviev, Wikimedia Commons, CC BY 4.0.

Gilt Edge open-air club inside Sutter Health Park. Courtesy of Sutter Health Park.

Margaret Conrad with her mother Mary and siblings, ca. 1870s. California State Library.

M Street Bridge (predecessor to the Tower Bridge), ca. 1910. Photograph by McCurry Foto Co., California State Library.

Brewery of the Buffalo Brewing Company, Sacramento, ca. 1890s. Photograph by Varney. Sacramento Public Library.

Opening Day 1903: Oakland commuters leaving the Statehouse Hotel for their first Pacific Coast League game against Sacramento. California Historical Society, Dick Dobbins Collection.

Ruhstaller's Gilt Edge beer label. Courtesy of Alan O'Connor. Private collection.

K Street with electric streetcar, Sacramento, ca. 1910. California State Library.

1897 Louisville Slugger bat. Photograph courtesy of Alan O'Connor. Private collection.

Broadside advertising a baseball game at Snowflake Park. Photograph courtesy of Alan O'Connor. Private collection.

Sacramento Senators catcher's mask used at Buffalo Park. Photograph courtesy of Alan O'Connor. Private collection

Endnotes

---

[1] "The Flood," *Evening Bee* (Sacramento), December 12, 1861, 4; "Local News," *Evening Bee* (Sacramento), November 21, 1861, 2; "Local News," *Daily Bee* (Sacramento), December 24, 1861, 3.

[2] "Give Us a High Grade," *Daily Bee* (Sacramento), December 10, 1861, 1; "All on the Level," *Daily Bee* (Sacramento), August 18, 1866, 3; G. J. Cross, contractor, advertisement, Daily Bee (Sacramento), March 29, 1870, 1.

[3] "Births," San Francisco Chronicle, April 18, 1869: 3.

[4] Margaret Ann Conrad, FamilySearch Family Tree profile, FamilySearch.org, person ID KDMV-L64, including listed children Frederick Conrad Kripp, John Kripp, Alice Louisa Kripp, Edward Lukens Kripp, George W. Kripp, and Newton Booth Kripp, accessed February 6, 2026; Clark, Booth & Yardley Funeral Home, Mortuary record for Edward Lukens Kripp, San Francisco, February 20, 1942; digitized in "Sacramento, Sacramento, California, United States records," FamilySearch (image 112 of 544), accessed February 7, 2026; "Local Matters," *Sacramento Weekly Bee,*, November 10, 1883, 5.

[5] U.S. Census, 1860, California, population schedule, Sacramento County, Frederick Kripp; *Daily Bee* (Sacramento), October 15, 1860, 4; *Daily Bee* (Sacramento), September 4, 1860, 3; October 15, 1860, 4; "Local Matters," *Daily Bee* (Sacramento), November 10, 1883, 5.

[6] "Marriages," *Daily Bee* (Sacramento), June 14, 1861, 3.

[7] "Sale of a Yolo Ranch," *Sacramento Daily Record-Union*, September 21, 1895, 4.

[8] "Bad for Gas," *Daily Bee* (Sacramento), November 9, 1889, 5; "Trustees Meeting: The Second Street Extension Matter Postponed," *Daily Bee* (Sacramento), October 29, 1895, 2. Classified advertisements, *Daily Bee* (Sacramento), July 20, 1899, 3.

[9] "The Japanese: They Are Gaining a Strong Foothold in This City," *Weekly Bee*, (Sacramento), July 9, 1892, 2; U.S. Census Bureau, *Statistics of the Population of the United States* (1880, 1890, 1900); and Sanborn-Perris Map Company, *Fire Insurance Maps of Sacramento, California* (1895);

10 U.S. Congress, Report of the Joint Special Committee to Investigate Chinese Immigration, 44th Cong., 2d sess. (Washington, DC: Government Printing Office, 1877); Gordon H. Chang and Shelley Fisher Fishkin, "The Chinese and the Iron Road: Building the Transcontinental Railroad" (Stanford, CA: Stanford University Press, 2019).

11 Judy Yung, "Unbound Feet: A Social History of Chinese Women in San Francisco's Chinatown" (Berkeley: University of California Press, 1995); Benson Tong, "Unsubmissive Women: Chinese Prostitutes in Nineteenth-Century San Francisco" (Norman: University of Oklahoma Press, 1994); Melvyn S. Weiss, *Valley City: A Chinese Community in America (1974), 47–48;* John C. Jenkins, "Sutter Lake or China Slough," *Golden Notes,* December 1966; *Sacramento Union,* July 31, 1884, 2*; Pacific Bee,* August 25, 1887, 5.

12 Dorene Askin, "The Chinese in Sacramento Through the Acts of the City Council," 1849–1900 (1979), 5–6.

13 "Constables on Deck," *Record-Union* (Sacramento), September 2, 1890, 2.

14 John C. Jenkins, "Sutter Lake or China Slough," Golden Notes, December 1966, 1–3.

15 "The Bold Bent," *The Pacific Bee* (Sacramento, CA), July 27, 1892, 3; "Officer Kripp's Chinatown Cognomen," *Evening Bee* (Sacramento), January 17, 1894, 1.

16 "Collector Kripp," *Sacramento Daily Record-Union,* April 17, 1891, 3.

17 "Ah Lee" may not have been the man's full or actual name. In many Chinese dialects, "Ah" (阿) functions as a familiar or informal prefix attached to a given name rather than a surname or honorific. In late-nineteenth-century California newspapers and police records, Chinese defendants were frequently identified by abbreviated, generic, or phonetic names assigned by English-speaking officials, often without regard for individual identity. The records preserve the violence and the charge with precision, but not the man himself.

18 "A Palatial Roadside Inn," *Saturday Bee* (Sacramento), July 3, 1897, 1; "They Were Married," *Weekly Bee,* (Sacramento), August 12, 1891, 3.

19 "Kripp Hated to Leave," *Weekly Bee* (Sacramento), October 21, 1891, 5.

20 David L. Durham, California's Geographic Names: A Gazetteer of Historic and Modern Names of the State (Clovis, CA: Quill Driver Books, 1998), 455; Winters Express, October 11, 1901, 2.

[21] Woodland Daily Democrat, March 30, 1896, 4.

[22] California Department of Transportation, Historic Property Survey Report: Broadway Bridge Project (May 2021).

[23] "Wild and Drunken Orgies in Washington," *Daily Bee* (Sacramento), February 15, 1893, 6.

[24] Carol Ann Kripp Olson (grandmother of the author), in multiple conversations with the author, various dates.

[25] California, Sacramento County, Marriage Record for Edward L. Kripp and Emma A. Waldren, 10 December 1891; *FamilySearch*, California, Marriages, 1850–1945 (entry for Edward L. Kripp and Emma A. Waldren); California, Sacramento County, Supplemental Birth Report (Florence Adele Kripp); and World War I Draft Registration Card (Orlin Arthur Kripp), accessed December 28, 2025.

[26] "Ten Men Are Selected," *Evening Bee* (Sacramento), April 11, 1893, 2.

[27] "Officer Kripp's Chinatown Cognomen," *Evening Bee* (Sacramento), January 17, 1894, 1.

[28] "Kripp and Alter. The Grand Jury Ignores the Charges Against Them," *Evening Bee* (Sacramento), January 18, 1894, 2.

[29] "Officer Kripp's Close Call: A Highbinder Attempts to Shoot Him Last Night," *Sacramento Daily Record-Union*, January 17, 1894, 6.

[30] "Kripp Arrested: A Plea of Guilty for the Battery Upon Scott," *Evening Bee* (Sacramento), February 9, 1894, 2.; "Ex-Officer Kripp Is Fined for Hitting Scott," *Evening Bee* (Sacramento), February 15, 1894, 1.

[31] "An Unexpected Visit," *Weekly Bee* (Sacramento), September 7, 1893, 1; "An Invalid Clause," *Weekly Bee* (Sacramento), August 22, 1893, 4.

[32] "Gamblers are Happy," *Weekly Bee* (Sacramento), August 23, 1893, 5; "A Lively Scrimmage," *Evening Bee* (Sacramento), April 12, 1894, 1.

[33] "Kripp Wants $10,260 Damages," *Sacramento Daily Record-Union*, April 24, 1894, 4.

[34] "Edward Kripp's Trial," *Evening Bee* (Sacramento), April 17, 1894, 2.

[35] "Kripp is Acquitted," *Evening Bee* (Sacramento), April 18, 1894, 1; "Hustling for News," *Evening Bee* (Sacramento), April 18, 1894, 4.

[36] "Fined for Gaming," *Sacramento Daily Record-Union*, November 30, 1895, 3; "Arrested for Gaming," *Sacramento Daily Record-Union*, November 28, 1895, 6.

[37] "The Courts Criticized," *Evening Bee* (Sacramento), November 1, 1895.

[38] "A Bank Gets Judgement," *Evening Bee* (Sacramento), December 23, 1895, 5.

[39] "Gamblers Fined," *Evening Bee* (Sacramento), December 26, 1895, 2.

[40] "Personal Notes," *Evening Bee*, (Sacramento) June 10, 1895, 8.

[41] "Racing News," *San Francisco Examiner*, December 8, 1905, 13; "Racing at Oakland," *Evening Bee* (Sacramento), January 31, 1905, 2; "Care of Racing Stock," *Courier-Journal* (Louisville, KY), November 2, 1912, 10.

[42] Kripp & Co Advertisement, *Sacramento Daily Record-Union*, April 16, 1896, 3.

[43] "A Baseball Franchise," *Weekly Bee* (Sacramento), August 16, 1893, 7.

[44] "Not in It. Sacramento Must Struggle Along Without League Baseball," *Sacramento Daily Record-Union*, February 3, 1892, 5; "The New Baseball League," *Evening Bee* (Sacramento), April 1894; *Sacramento Daily Record-Union*, July 14, 1893, 3.

[45] "Sacramento Will Cross Bats with Oakland To-Day," *Sacramento Daily Record-Union*, August 17, 1893, 6.

[46] "Nicol and Knell Did It," *Oakland Times*, April 15, 1893, 5.

[47] "Uncle's Hoodoo Still With Him," *Evening Bee* (Sacramento), July 23, 1900, 4.

[48] "The Baseball League," *Fresno Weekly Expositor*, January 15, 1890, 9.

[49] "Ten Innings and a Riot," *San Francisco Examiner*, June 30, 1893, 5; "The Panic Spreads," *Sacramento Record-Union*, May 1893, 3.

[50] "Trying to Boom Baseball," *Evening Bee* (Sacramento), April 12, 1894, 6.

[51] Whitten, David O. "The Depression of 1893." *EH.Net Encyclopedia of Economic and Business History*, Economic History Association. Accessed February 9, 2026. https://eh.net/encyclopedia/the-depression-of-1893.

[52] "Local Brevities," *Woodland Daily Democrat*, September 21, 1895, 3.

[53] "Record of Deeds," *Winters Express*, May 16, 1896.

[54] George B. Kirsch, "Baseball in Blue and Gray: The National Pastime during the Civil War" (Princeton, NJ: Princeton University Press, 2003), 3.

[55] Albert G. Spalding. "America's National Game" (New York: American Sports Publishing Company, 1911), 64–66.

[56] "Brief Notes," *Sacramento Daily Record-Union*, January 3, 1895, 6.

57 "Base Ball Notes," *Sacramento Daily Record-Union*, May 24, 1897, 3; "Local Brevities," *Sacramento Daily Record-Union*, May 31, 1897, 4;

58 "Baseball Notes," *Evening Bee* (Sacramento), July 9, 1897, 4; "Base Ball," *Sacramento Daily Record-Union,* June 30, 1897, 6; "Base Ball," Sacramento Union, July 1, 1897, 4.

59 "Baseball," *Evening Bee* (Sacramento), June 26, 1897, 11; "Base Ball," *Sacramento Daily Record-Union,* June 26, 1897, 5; "Base Ball," *Sacramento Daily Record-Union,* June 28, 1897, 4.

60 "Guilt Edges Prove Too Much for the Visitors," *Evening Bee* (Sacramento), June 28, 1897, 2; "A Gilt Edge Victory," *Sacramento Daily Record-Union,* June 11, 1895, 6. "Brief Notes," *Sacramento Daily Record-Union,* January 3, 1895, 6.

61 "Baseball To-Morrow," *Sacramento Daily Record-Union,* October 15, 1892, 8.

62 "Evolution of 19th Century Baseball Rules," *19th Century Base Ball,* accessed October 19, 2025, http://www.19cbaseball.com/rules.html.

63 Baseball-Reference Bullpen, "1890s," accessed October 19, 2025, https://www.baseball-reference.com/bullpen/1890s.

64 "Baseball Notes," *Evening Bee* (Sacramento), June 24, 1898, 5.

65 "Silent Harvey and McLaughlin Will Play with Them," *Sacramento Daily Record-Union,* May 5, 1899, 3; Retrosheet, "Harvey Zaza Player Record," accessed October 27, 2026, https://www.retrosheet.org/boxesetc/H/Pharve101.htm.

66 "Jay Hughes," *Evening Bee* (Sacramento), December 2, 1897

67 "Gilt Edge All Through," *Sacramento Daily Record-Union,* November 15, 1897, 3; "Won the Game in the Ninth," *Evening Bee* (Sacramento), November 15, 1897, 7.

68 "Score Twelve to Three," *Sacramento Daily Record-Union,* August 16, 1897, 4; "The Score Was 15 to 6," *Evening Bee* (Sacramento), August 30, 1897, 3; "Personal Mention," *Sacramento Daily Record-Union,* November 16, 1898, 5.

69 "Snowflake Park Opening," *Sacramento Daily Record-Union,* August 14, 1897, 4; "Sacramento Baseball," *San Francisco Examiner,* August 21, 1897, 4.

70 "It Was Really Gilt Edge," *Sacramento Daily Record-Union,* July 12, 1897, 3.

71 "Fresnos Had a Walkover," *Sacramento Daily Record-Union*, August 1, 1897, 3.

72 "Was Nearly a Whitewash," *Sacramento Daily Record-Union*, November 22, 1897, 4.

73 Jack Sullivan, *"The Thomas Hall Story Almost Ended Before It Began,"* Those Pre-Pro Whiskey Men, May 1, 2015.

74 "Snowflake Park One of the Best in the State," *Evening Bee* (Sacramento), August 7, 1897, 12; "All Ready to Play Ball," *Sacramento Bee*, August 14, 1897, 1; "Baseball Park War Is Revived," *Sacramento Bee*, October 8, 1897, 8.

75 "Ball Tossers Enlist for Charity," *Evening Bee* (Sacramento), September 29, 1897, 8.

76 "Baseball Park War is Revived," *Evening Bee* (Sacramento) October 8, 1897, 8.

77 "Boy Boys Couldn't Stand Up Against the Home Nine," *Evening Bee* (Sacramento), August 23, 1897, 2.

78 "Sacramento Baseball," *The San Francisco Examiner*, August 21, 1897, 4.

79 "They Downed Los Angeles," *Sacramento Daily Record-Union*, September 14, 1897, 3.

80 "Reliance Affairs," *Oakland Tribune*, August 25, 1897, 8.

81 "At Snowflake Park To-Day: Gilt Edges and Union Iron-Workers to Meet," *Sacramento Daily Record-Union*, August 29, 1897, 3.

82 "Gilt Edge Won the Game," *Evening Bee* (Sacramento), December 20, 1897, 7.

83 "The Offer Was Spurned," *Evening Bee* (Sacramento), September 24, 1897, 1.

84 "Have Formed a New Ball League," *Evening Bee* (Sacramento), September 21, 1897, 1.

85 "Four O'Clock—First Contest in New League," *Evening Bee* (Sacramento), September 25, 1897, 12; "New Deal in Baseball Effected," *San Francisco Call*, September 25, 1897, 14.

86 Hubert Howe Bancroft, *Chronicles of the Builders of the Commonwealth: Historical Character Study* (San Francisco: The History Company, 1892), 2:371–373.

87 "New League Formed," *Oakland Times*, September 25, 1897, 1.

[88] "New Baseball League Formed," *San Francisco Call*, September 29, 1897, 12.

[89] "California League Formally Organized," *Evening Bee* (Sacramento), September 29, 1897, 2.

[90] "Adieu To Manager Henesey," *Sacramento Daily Record-Union*, August 31, 1897, 5.

[91] "Had a Banquet," *Evening Bee* (Sacramento), August 31, 1897, 6.

[92] "Plans for the New Baseball League," *San Francisco Chronicle*, January 22, 1900, 8.

[93] "The Olympics Outclassed," *Sacramento Daily Record-Union*, September 27, 1897, 3.

[94] "Trustee Tozar Was Spectacular," *Evening Bee* (Sacramento), November 22, 1897, 8.

[95] "We Lost One and Won One," *Evening Mail* (Stockton, CA), November 22, 1897, 5.

[96] National Baseball Hall of Fame and Museum, "Hughie Jennings," accessed January 15, 2026, https://baseballhall.org/hall-of-famers/jennings-hughie; National Baseball Hall of Fame and Museum, "John McGraw," accessed January 15, 2026, https://baseballhall.org/hall-of-famers/mcgraw-john.

[97] "Smith Was Knocked Out in the Game," *San Francisco Call*, November 22, 1897, 10.

[98] "Orioles Play at Napa" *San Francisco Call*, November 24, 1897, 2.

[99] "Borland's Freak Hit for Three Bases," *San Francisco Chronicle*, November 29, 1897, 8.

[100] "Corbett Hit Hard," *Buffalo Times* (Buffalo, NY), November 26, 1897, 7.

[101] "Gilt Edges Defeat the Baltimore Team at Sacramento Thanksgiving Day," *Evening Mail* (Stockton, CA), November 26, 1897, 2.

[102] "Oh, We Don't Know You're Not So Warm," *Evening Bee* (Sacramento), November 26, 1897, 2.

[103] "Orioles Defeated in Sacramento," *Baltimore Sun*, November 26, 1897, 2.

[104] "Corbett Hit Hard," *Buffalo Times*, November 26, 1897, 6.

[105] "Baltimore Now Claims Him," *Evening Bee* (Sacramento), December 2, 1897, 5.

106 The *Sacramento Daily Record-Union* later published under the masthead *Sacramento Union*. For clarity, the narrative refers to the paper as the *Sacramento Union* throughout, while endnotes preserve the original masthead used at the time of publication.

107 "Gilt Edges Winner of the Baseball Trophy," *Sacramento Daily Record-Union*, November 29, 1897, 3; "Balltossers Get an Enjoyable Banquet," *Evening Bee* (Sacramento), November 29, 1897, 1.

108 "The Pennant Comes Here," *Sacramento Daily Record-Union*, November 29, 1897, 3.

109 "Around the Festal Board," *Evening Bee*, (Sacramento) November 29, 1897, 1; "At the Banquet Board," *Sacramento Daily Record-Union*, November 29, 1897, 3.

110 "Gilt Edge Ball," *Sacramento Daily Record-Union*, January 1, 1898, 4.

111 "Crowd Entered the Diamond," *Evening Bee* (Sacramento), April 25, 1898, 2.

112 "Gossip About Baseball," *Evening Bee* (Sacramento), April 21, 1898, 8.

113 "Ballplayers on Strike," *Evening Bee* (Sacramento), April 20, 1898, 5.

114 The *Evening Bee* later published under the masthead *Sacramento Bee*. For clarity, the narrative refers to the paper as the *Sacramento Bee* throughout, while endnotes preserve the original masthead used at the time of publication.

115 "Kripp Puts Up Gold," *Evening Bee* (Sacramento), April 22, 1898, 5.

116 "The Pennant Race," *Evening Bee* (Sacramento), October 10, 1898, 2; *San Francisco Call*, December 3, 1899, 12.

117 "Baseball Managers on a Strike—They Want a Share of the Gate Receipts," *Evening Bee* (Sacramento), September 18, 1897, 12.

118 "State Baseball League Organized," *Evening Sentinel* (Santa Cruz, CA), February 18, 1898, 3.

119 "Is the Colonel Trying to Win 'Em?," *Evening Bee* (Sacramento), April 7, 1898, 5.

120 John E. Spalding, *Always on Sunday: The California Baseball League 1886–1915* (Ag Press, 1992); Dick Dobbins and Jon Twichell, *Nuggets on the Diamond: Professional Baseball in the Bay Area from the Gold Rush to the Present* (San Francisco: Woodford Press, 1994).

[121] "Colonel Robinson Sets Fire to the Pennant of 1889" *Morning San Francisco Call,* June 29, 1891, 8.

[122] "A Pitcher's Work," *Oakland Tribune,* July 3, 1898, 6.

[123] "Baseball Sayings—The Colonel Will Have to Negotiate for More Pitchers," *The Morning Times* (Oakland), September 4, 1891; "Now for the Pennant—Reorganization of the Team," *The Oakland Times,* August 31, 1892; "Police Court News," *Oakland Enquirer,* November 20, 1891; "Oakland Is a Winner," *The Morning Times* (Oakland, CA), May 30, 1891, 3.

[124] "News of the Baseballers," *Evening Bee* (Sacramento), March 22, 1898, 5.

[125] "Pacific States League Opening," *San Francisco Examiner,* March 28, 1898, 11; "Baseball Schedule," *Evening Bee* (Sacramento) March 21, 1898, 6.

[126] "News of the Baseballers," *Evening Bee* (Sacramento), March 22, 1898, 5.

[127] "Consolidation Now Proposed," *Evening Bee* (Sacramento), April 26, 1898, 5.

[128] "Baseball At Snowflake Park," *Evening Bee* (Sacramento), April 2, 1898, 8; "Consolidated Leagues Open Season," *San Francisco Chronicle,* May 2, 1898, 10.

[129] "California League Affairs," *Evening Bee* (Sacramento), June 24, 1898, 5.

[130] "Gilt Edges Were the Winners," *Evening Bee* (Sacramento)August 22, 1898, 7.

[131] "The Baseball Season: Eight Clubs to Compose the State League," *San Francisco Chronicle,* February 14, 1898, 8.

[132] "Baseball Campaign of '98," *Sacramento Daily Record-Union,* March 21, 1898, 3.

[133] "State League Games to Be Played During the Season," *Evening Bee* (Sacramento), March 21, 1898, 6.

[134] "Baseball Excursion," *Sacramento Daily Record-Union,* August 18, 1899, 3.

[135] "Gilt Edges Give the Oaklands Quite a Drubbing," *San Francisco Chronicle,* April 18, 1898, 8.

[136] "Sand Crabs Wouldn't Down," *Santa Cruz Surf,* August 1, 1898, 3; The Pace Was Too Fast, *Santa Cruz Surf,* August 15, 1898, 1;" Sand Crabs Wouldn't Down," *Santa Cruz Surf,* August 1, 1898, 3.

137 "A Hot Old Baseball Game—It Almost Ended in a Bloodshed," *Evening Bee* (Sacramento), May 23, 1898, 7.

138 "Snappy Ball Sunday Afternoon," *Evening Bee* (Sacramento), August 15, 1898, 4.

139 "Hughey Fears for His Life," *San Francisco Examiner*, October 24, 1898, 4.

140 "The Baseball Trouble," *Santa Cruz Daily Sentinel*, September 22, 1897, 1.

141 "Difference of Opinion," *Sacramento Daily Record-Union*, July 25, 1898, 4.

142 "A Lively Scrimmage," *Sacramento Daily Record-Union*, July 25, 1898, 4.

143 "Sacramento Style," *Evening Mail* (Stockton, CA), July 25, 1898, 8.

144 "Will Not Apologize," *Evening Bee* (Sacramento), August 6, 1898, 8.

145 "Equally Matched Teams," *Santa Cruz Daily Sentinel*, November 8, 1898, 3.

146 "Gilt Edges are Champions," *San Francisco Call*, December 17, 1898, 3.

147 Advertisement for Oak Park real estate, *Evening Bee* (Sacramento), November 20, 1894, 2; "Five Blocks! That New Subdivision at Oak Park," advertisement, *Sacramento Union* (Sacramento), December 31, 1895, 7.

148 "Local Brevities," *Evening Bee* (Sacramento), December 16, 1898, 8.

149 City of Sacramento, *Oak Park Historic District Plan* (Sacramento: City of Sacramento Community Development Department, 2019), 283; "Robin Datel," *Central Oak Park Walking Tour* (Sacramento: Department of Geography, California State University, Sacramento, 2010), 8.

150 "Ed. Kripp Says He Has Enough," *Evening Bee* (Sacramento), January 22, 1900, 7.

151 City of Sacramento, Oak Park Historic District Plan, 283; "Robin Datel," Central Oak Park Walking Tour, 8.

152 "Baseball on Sunday," *Evening Bee* (Sacramento), March 3, 1899, 8; "Gilt Edges and Seattles," *Evening Bee* (Sacramento), March 6, 1899, 2.

153 "On the Diamond: Gilt Edges Win the First Game Played," *Sacramento Daily Record-Union*, April 2, 1899, 1.

154 "Gilt Edges Beaten," *Sacramento Daily Record-Union*, April 17, 1899, 1.

155 "Didn't Have Them," *Sacramento Daily Record-Union*, April 14, 1899, 1.

156 "The Gilts Carry Off the Plums in Two Close Brushes," *Santa Cruz Surf*, April 10, 1899, 1.

157 "Gilt Edges Own the Banner," *Evening Bee* (Sacramento), May 1, 1899, 7.

158 "Hoodoo Has Been Lifted," *Sacramento Daily Record-Union*, May 8, 1899, 7.

159 "Luck With the Sand Crabs," *Santa Cruz Surf*, May 22, 1899, 1.

160 "Manager Kripp Is Criticised," *Evening Bee* (Sacramento), May 22, 1899, 4; "The Signing of Eagan," *Sacramento Daily Record-Union*, May 7, 1899, 3.

161 "Pitcher Andrews Won the Day for San Jose," *Santa Cruz Surf*, July 17, 1899, 4.

162 "Crestfallen 'Dudes'," *Santa Cruz Surf*, August 21, 1899, 4.

163 "A Chance to Gain Second Place," *Santa Cruz Surf*, September 19, 1899, 1.

164 "The League Race," *Santa Cruz Surf*, October 26, 1899, 4.

165 "The League Race," *Santa Cruz Surf*, November 2, 1899, 4.

166 "Uncle Is Hoodoo—Still With Him," *Evening Bee* (Sacramento), July 23, 1900, 4, using "Frisco" to refer to San Francisco.

167 "How Doyle Saved the Day," *Sacramento Daily Record-Union*, August 14, 1899, 3.

168 "Baseball Prediction," *Santa Cruz Daily Sentinel*, November 3, 1899, 3.

169 "Little Hope for the Locals," *San Francisco Chronicle*, November 4, 1899, 8.

170 "The Baseball Honors Go to Sacramento," *San Francisco Chronicle*, November 25, 1899, 8.

171 "The Pennant Remains with Sacramento," *Evening Bee* (Sacramento), November 27, 1899, 8; "No Change in the Clubs' Standing," *San Francisco Chronicle*, November 18, 1899, 8.

172 A. C. Herrick, "Gilt Edges and the Oaklands," *Evening Bee* (Sacramento), December 11, 1899, 7.

173 "Pennant Winners Lose to Eastern Visitors," *San Francisco Examiner*, December 1, 1899, 11.

174 "All-Californias Won Again," *San Francisco Call*, December 26, 1899, 9.

175 "Eastern Men May Have 'Claimed' Them," *Evening Bee* (Sacramento), January 9, 1900, 8.

176 "And Next We Lose Harvey!," *Sacramento Daily Record-Union*, October 10, 1899, 4.

177 "Pitcher Harvey's Last Game Here," *Santa Cruz Surf,* November 24, 1899, 4.

178 "Doyle Goes to Louisville," *Santa Cruz Surf,* October 28, 1899, 4.

179 "Some Fresh Baseball Talk," *Evening Bee* (Sacramento), February 1, 1900, 5.

180 "Eastern Men May Have 'Claimed' Them," *Evening Bee* (Sacramento), January 9, 1900, 8.

181 "Something About the Gilt Edge's Twirling Trio," *Sacramento Daily Record-Union,* November 21, 1899, 3.

182 "1899—Louisville Colonels," Society for American Baseball Research, SABR Game Project: September 7, accessed December 26, 2025.

183 "Local Brevities," *Evening Bee* (Sacramento), March 20, 1900, 8.

184 Columbia Café Advertisement for Opening Day, *Evening Bee* (Sacramento), September 10, 1898, 2.

185 "Sued for Divorce," *Evening Bee* (Sacramento), November 22, 1897, 14.

186 Newspaper clippings preserved in family scrapbook, author's collection.

187 "Expensive Illumination for the City Streets," *Los Angeles Evening Express,* August 6, 1900, 5.

188 "Settlement Made in Kripp Divorce Suit," *Evening Bee* (Sacramento), November 27, 1900, 5.

189 "Suit for Divorce and Restraining Order," *Evening Bee* (Sacramento), May 16, 1900, 9.

190 "A Noble Building: A Magnificent Monarch of Masonry," *Los Angeles Daily Herald,* February 24, 1889, 2.

191 "That Gun Play," *Los Angeles Times,* July 14, 1900, 7.

192 "Made a Break for a Pistol," *Evening Bee,* (Sacramento), July 6, 1900, 8.

193 "Kripp Battery Case Dismissed," *Evening Bee,* (Sacramento), July 17, 1900, 5.

194 "Settlement Made in Kripp Divorce Suit," *Evening Bee,* (Sacramento), November 27, 1900, 5.

195 "Ed. Kripp Says He Has Enough," *Evening Bee* (Sacramento), January 22, 1900, 7.

196 "Sacramento Phenomenon Going East," *Los Angeles Evening Express,* March 5, 1900, 6.

[197] "Farewell Banquet to Thomas Sheehan," *Evening Bee* (Sacramento), March 1, 1900, 2.

[198] "Some Fresh Baseball Talk—Management of the Gilt Edges Still Unsettled," *Evening Bee* (Sacramento), February 1, 1900, 5.

[199] "Organizing A New Nine," *Evening Bee* (Sacramento), March 5, 1900, 8.

[200] "Beebe Says There is No Difference," *Evening Bee* (Sacramento), April 18, 1900, 9.

[201] "Pitcher Hughes to His Parents Rescue," *The Brooklyn Daily Times*, December 12, 1899, 8; "Close of the Season's Play on the Field," *The San Francisco Call*, November 25, 1899, 8; "Silent Harvey, the Star Twirler, His Last Appearance," *Evening Bee* (Sacramento), November 25, 1899, 8.

[202] "Pitcher Hughes Signs with the Gilt Edges," *The San Francisco Call Bulletin*, April 14, 1900, 2; "Beebe Says There Was No Difference," *The Evening Bee* (Sacramento), April 18, 1900, 9.

[203] "Pitcher Hughes Signs with the Gilt Edges," *San Francisco Call*, April 14, 1900, 2.

[204] "Gilt Edge Club on Upgrade," *Evening Bee* (Sacramento), April 30, 1900, 4.

[205] "Shanahan Has Received an Offer to go East," *Evening Bee* (Sacramento), November 9, 1899, 5; "The Gilts Suffer Defeat," *Sacramento Daily Record-Union*, March 13, 1899, 4 (lineup listing Shanahan in center field).

[206] "Tim Shanahan Seriously Ill," *Evening Bee* (Sacramento), August 8, 1900, 3.

[207] "State League Baseball Games," *Evening Bee* (Sacramento), August 25, 1900, p.8.

[208] "Oakland Loses to Stockton in a Slow Contest," *San Francisco Call*, June 17, 1900, 2; *"Reliance Club Notes—Plans— West Oakland Club,"* Oakland Tribune, June 6, 1900, 8.

[209] "Baseball Player Returns," *Evening Bee* (Sacramento), September 20, 1900, 2.

[210] "Gilts Have Stopped Sliding," *The Evening Bee* (Sacramento, CA), October 15, 1900, 5.

[211] "Baseball Umpire Has Resigned," *The Sacramento Bee* (Sacramento, CA), October 31, 1900, 2.

[212] "Uncle Henry a Very Bad Loser," *San FranciscoCall,* October 29, 1900, 5.

213 "Gilt Edges Too Far Ahead to Be Caught—The Pennant Already Virtually Belongs to the Capital City Men," *San Francisco Chronicle*, November 11, 1900.

214 "Gilt Edges – The Four Time Winners," *Evening Bee* (Sacramento), December 3, 1900, 7.

215 "1899 National League Standings," *Baseball-Reference.com*, accessed March 18, 2026, https://www.baseball-reference.com/leagues/NL/1899.shtml (showing Brooklyn Superbas finished first).

216 "Amateur Won Battle for Gilt Edges," *Evening Bee* (Sacramento), April 29, 1901, 2.

217 "Michael Fisher," *Baseball Manager*, *Evening Bee* (Sacramento), January 23, 1902, 7.

218 "Sacramento Is No Longer Wide Open," *San Francisco Examiner*, February 13, 1900, 13.

219 "Sacramento's Population Now Reaches 40,000 Mark," *Evening Bee* (Sacramento), October 11, 1906.

220 City of Sacramento, *Oak Park Historic District Plan* (Sacramento: City of Sacramento Community Development Department, 2019), 283.

221 "Defendant Says the Moral Wave Cost Him Money," *Evening Bee* (Sacramento), June 8, 1900, 8.

222 "Mayor Clark and the Chief Know Nothing About Poolrooms," *Evening Bee* (Sacramento), November 14, 1900, 4.

223 "Why is Kripp for Clark?," *Evening Bee* (Sacramento), November 4, 1901,8.

224 "Where Is Edwin K. Alsip?" *Evening Bee* (Sacramento), January 11, 1898, 8.

225 "Notice of Sale by Commissioner," *Evening Bee* (Sacramento) March 29, 1898, 6.

226 "Mrs. E. K. Alsip Turns Over All," *Evening Bee* (Sacramento), February 3, 1898, 1.

227 "Capt. Bradley Spoke to Edwin K. Alsip," *Evening Bee* (Sacramento), January 15, 1898, 12; "Edwin K. Alsip Is Missing," *Daily Record-Union* (Sacramento), January 12, 1898, 3.

[228] "Alsip Took Little Money With Him," *Evening Bee* (Sacramento), January 14, 1898, 8.

[229] "Saw E. K. Alsip on Sunday Last," *Evening Bee* (Sacramento), January 13, 1898, 8.

[230] "Warrant Out for Alsip's Arrest," *Evening Bee* (Sacramento), January 20, 1898, 8.

[231] Real estate transfer notice, *Sacramento Star*, April 23, 1909, 7.

[232] "Edwin K. Alsip Is Buried Here," *Evening Bee* (Sacramento), June 16, 1915, 5.

[233] "Baseball Management—Kripp Said to Be Anxious to Reassume It," *Evening Bee* (Sacramento), December 1, 1900, 4; "Baseball Franchise Suit," *Evening Bee* (Sacramento), January 21, 1901, 5; "Local Brevities," *Evening Bee* (Sacramento), March 16, 1901, 5.

[234] "Kripp and Beebe Compromise: Former Keeps an Interest and Latter Runs the Team," *Evening Bee* (Sacramento), April 2, 1901, 2.

[235] "Beebe Says They Must Obey Rules," *Evening Bee* (Sacramento), June 19, 1901, 1.

[236] "New League Being Formed," *Evening Bee* (Sacramento), August 22, 1901, 8.

[237] "Beebe's Men May Go to Honolulu," *Evening Bee* (Sacramento), August 14, 1901, 8.

[238] "Beebe Wants a Guarantee" *Evening Bee* (Sacramento), Aug. 17, 1901, 5.

[239] "Baseball Gossip," *Evening Bee* (Sacramento), July 31, 1902, 7.

[240] "Beebe May Have to Fight for Franchise," *Evening Bee* (Sacramento), January 3, 1902, 5.

[241] "Michael Fisher, Baseball Manager—Secures Franchise for the Sacramento Team," *Evening Bee* (Sacramento), January 23, 1902.

[242] "Beebe Intends Filing a Suit," *Evening Bee* (Sacramento), April 2, 1902, 6.

[243] "Mike Rejoices in His New Team," *Evening Bee* (Sacramento), March 18, 1903, 1.

[244] "Baseball Gossip," *Evening Bee* (Sacramento), July 31, 1902, 7;

[245] "Baseball Standing," *Evening Bee* (Sacramento), September 25, 1902, 3; "Baseball Standing," *Evening Bee* (Sacramento), October 18, 1902, 6; "Baseball Gossip," *Evening Bee* (Sacramento), November 1, 1902, 2.

246 William J. Weiss, *The Pacific Coast League Record Book, 1903–1969* (Pacific Coast League, 1969).

247 "Pacific Coast League," *Berkeley Gazette*, September 10, 1902, 6.

248 "Coast League Is Legally Formed," *San Francisco Chronicle*, December 30, 1902, 4; "Pacific Coast League Is Formed," *Oakland Tribune*, December 30, 1902, 6.

249 "Pacific Coast Baseball League—It Has Been Fully Organized," *Evening Bee* (Sacramento), December 30, 1902, 7.

250 "Manager Fisher Is Signing Players," *Evening Bee* (Sacramento), December 20, 1902, 12.

251 "Baseball Gossip," *Pittsburgh Press*, April 27, 1901, 7; *Pittsburgh Post*, May 5, 1901, 14.

252 "Doyle's Pitching Defeats Portland," *Evening Bee* (Sacramento), August 31, 1903, 9.

253 "Henry Harris Sends Reassuring Telegram," *Evening Bee*, (Sacramento), March 20, 1903, 5.

254 "An Unlucky Day for the Big Ballplayers," *Evening Mail* (Stockton), March 21, 1903, 6; "Fisher Uses Law to Hold His Players," *Oakland Tribune*, March 20, 1903, 11; "Baseball War Causes Two Arrests," *San Francisco Examiner*, March 20, 1903, 1.

255 "Fisher's Plan Meets Approval," *Evening Bee* (Sacramento), November 12, 1903, 7.

256 "Shall the Nine Go or Stay?" *Evening Bee* (Sacramento), November 28, 1903, 2.

257 "Mike Fisher Pulls Up Home Stakes," *Evening Bee* (Sacramento), December 12, 1903, 8; "Mike Fisher Is Now a Tiger," *Evening Bee* (Sacramento), December 14, 1903, 2.

258 "Members of Old Tacoma Tigers Making Good," *Evening Bee* (Sacramento), August 10, 1908, 8.

259 "Portland Takes Opening Game," *Fresno Morning Republican* (Fresno), April 8, 1906, 7.

260 "Fisher's Team Here Next Year," *Spokesman-Review* (Spokane), September 30, 1905, 3.

261 "Sports," *Fresno Bee* (Fresno), November 2, 1906, 6.

262 "Mike Fisher Has Quit Fresno Ball Club," *Fresno Morning Republican* (Fresno), November 2, 1906, 12.

263 "Coast League Standing," *Fresno Evening Democrat*, November 2, 1906, 6.

264 "Diamond Talk," *Fresno Herald*, June 21, 1909, 6.

265 "Baseball Gossip," *Evening Bee* (Sacramento), April 18, 1903, 2

266 "Another Suit Against Kripp," *Evening Bee* (Sacramento), September 28, 1900, 8.

267 "Kripp's Billiard Table and Barware Sold," *Evening Bee* (Sacramento), October 31, 1900, 5.

268 "Caesar Young's Stable in Form," *San Francisco Call*, February 25, 1901, 6; "Cesar Young Gets Pool Privilege," *Evening Bee* (Sacramento), August 10, 1901, 5.

269 "Kripp Dropped a Thousand," *T Evening Bee* (Sacramento), August 16, 1901, 8; "Edward Kripp Is a Stayer," *Evening Bee* (Sacramento), August 17, 1901, 8.

270 "Poolrooms Are Running Apparently Without Fear of Police Interference," *Evening Bee*, March 15, 1902, 5.

271 "Gambler Kripp Roasts Police," *Sacramento Star*, February 27, 1912, 1.

272 Carol Ann Kripp Olson (grandmother of the author), in multiple conversations with the author, various dates.

273 "Sacramento Wide Open for the Gamblers," *Evening Bee* (Sacramento), November 2, 1904, 3.

274 "Poolrooms Have Started Up for the Winter Season," *Evening Bee* (Sacramento), November 16, 1905, 5.

275 "Really Raided a Gambling Place," *Sacramento Star*, September 21, 1906, 1.

276 "No Honest Effort to Stop," *Sacramento Bee*, January 20, 1911, 12.

277 "Washington Poolrooms to Reopen," *Evening Bee* (Sacramento), November 13, 1902, 8; "Poolrooms Are Running Apparently Without Fear of Police Interference," *Evening Bee* (Sacramento), March 15, 1902, 5.

278 "Washington gambling exposé," *Evening Bee* (Sacramento), August 5, 1901, 6.

279 "Yolo County Officials Calmly Indifferent to Outlawed Gambling Games," *Evening Bee* (Sacramento), January 8, 1904, 2.; "Service Denied," *Woodland Daily Democrat*, May 19, 1904, 4.

280 "Angus Ross' Joint Raided by Police," *Evening Bee* (Sacramento), January 10, 1907, 10.

281 "Paid $100 for Selling Pools in Yolo's Monte Carlo," *Evening Bee* (Sacramento), April 29, 1903, 3.

282 "Yolo's Monte Carlo," *Winters Express*, July 17, 1903, 1.

283 "Gambling Games," *Woodland Daily Democrat*, July 13, 1903, 2.

284 "What Do the People Say," *Winters Express*, July 24, 1903, 3.

285 "Poolroom Man Fights Editor," *San Francisco Call*, November 10, 1901, 25.

286 "Kripp Denies It," *Woodland Daily Democrat*, November 11, 1901, 2.

287 "Poolroom Man Fights Editor," *San Francisco Call*, November 10, 1901, 25.

288 "Newspaper War," *Woodland Daily Democrat*, November 18, 1901, 1.

289 "Gorton Still at It," *Davisville Enterprise* (Davis, CA), November 14, 1901, 1.

290 "After the Gamblers – Editor Gorton Swears Out Nine Complaints," *Davisville Enterprise* (Davis, CA), December 5, 1901, 1.

291 "Yolo Gamblers Under Arrest," *Evening Bee* (Sacramento), December 4, 1901, 5.

292 "Edward Kripp Paid Respects to Yolo Court," *Evening Bee* (Sacramento), December 10, 1901, 4.

293 "Yolo Message Changes Hands," *Evening Bee* (Sacramento), November 18, 1901, 4.

294 "Service Denied," *Woodland Daily Democrat*, May 19, 1904, 4.

295 "Yolo Monte Carlo," *Woodland Daily Democrat*, November 18, 1904, 1.

296 "Poolrooms to Resume: Washington Gamblers to Do Business Despite the Boycott," *Woodland Daily Democrat*, June 15, 1904, 4.

297"Keno!' 'Keno!' Rings in Yolo," *Evening Bee* (Sacramento), August 5, 1901, 6.

298 "Kripp Arrested for Battery," *Evening Mail* (Stockton, CA), November 22, 1904, 3.

299 "Edward Kripp Heavily Fined," *Evening Bee* (Sacramento), December 12, 1904, 6.

300 "Sports Have the Laugh on Chief Denny," *Evening Bee* (Sacramento), December 5, 1906, 5.

301 "Kripp Tells Why He Moved Down Riverside Road," *Evening Bee* (Sacramento), January 30, 1906, 5.

302 "Thinks Too Much of New Chief: Kripp Tells Why He Moved Down Riverside Road," *Sacramento Bee*, January 30, 1906, 5; "Throw Open the Faro Games—Why Not?" *Sacramento Bee*, August 2, 1906, 4; "Gamblers May Play for Hams, Bacon or Any Thing but Coin," *Sacramento Bee*, August 2, 1906, 1.

303 "Beau Ormonde (USA) ch. H," PedigreeQuery.com, accessed January 23, 2026, https://www.pedigreequery.com/beau+ormonde/.

304 "Ed Kripp Buys a Thoroughbred," *Evening Bee* (Sacramento), January 23, 1903, 5; "Kripp Loses a Valuable Horse," *Davis Enterprise*, January 4, 1913, 1.

305 "Enterprising Land Owners Make Important Purchase," *Evening Bee* (Sacramento), November 22, 1905, 3.

306 "Beau Ormonde Smashes Record," *Inter Ocean* (Chicago), May 21, 1903, 4.

307 "Ormonde," *Thoroughbred Heritage*, accessed January 23, 2026, https://www.tbheritage.com/Portraits/Ormonde.htm.

308 "Lycurgus Shows Poor Form in Saddle," *San Francisco Bulletin*, October 31, 1907, 8; "Local Items Briefly Told," *Woodland Daily Democrat*, October 4, 1907, 4.

309 "Horse Owner Gets Buncoed; Men Arrested," *San Francisco Chronicle*, August 8, 1904, 1.

310 "Sacramentan Is Buncoed," *Evening Bee* (Sacramento), August 4, 1904, 10.

311 "Czar's Gave Money on Worthless Pawn Ticket," *San Francisco Chronicle*, August 4, 1904, 1.

312 From a retrospective by Bill Conlin, *Sacramento Union*, May 22, 1964, 13.

313 "Enterprising Landowners Make Important Purchase," *Evening Bee* (Sacramento), November 22, 1905, 3.

314 "Railroad After Property on Yolo Side," *Evening Bee* (Sacramento), September 29, 1905, 2.

315 "Levee Break Drenches Yolo," *Sacramento Star*, February 8, 1907, 1; "Yolo Levee Breaks," *The Evening Bee*, (Sacramento), Feb. 8, 1907, 2; "Yolo Levee Broke," *Davis Enterprise* (Davis, CA), February 9, 1907, 1.

316 "Yolo Levee Breaks and 700 Acres Are Inundated," *Evening Bee* (Sacramento), February 8, 1907, 1; "Hundreds of Acres Were Flooded," *The Union* (Grass Valley, CA), February 9, 1907, 1.

317 "Bright Side of the Picture," *Sunday Evening Leader* (Sacramento), February 10, 1907, 1; "Yolo Levee Breaks," *The Evening Bee*, February 8, 1907, 2.

318 "Kripp Saves Stock," *Evening Bee* (Sacramento), February 8, 1907, 2.

319 "Yolo Levee Broke," *Davis Enterprise* (Davis, CA), February 9, 1907, 1.

320 "Needed River Improvement Pointed Out to Engineers," *Sacramento Star*, January 20, 1908, 7; "Road and Levee Improvements," *Evening Bee* (Sacramento), February 10, 1908, 1; "Will Wharf the River Front," *Evening Bee* (Sacramento), April 24, 1907, 1.

321 "Levee Breaks Drenches Yolo," *Evening Bee* (Sacramento), February 8, 1907, 1.

322 "Railroads Acquire 700 Acres in Yolo," *Evening Bee* (Sacramento), April 12, 1907, 1; "Kripp Ranch Reported Sold," *Evening Bee* (Sacramento), April 11, 1907, 12.

323 "Condemnation Suits Filed," *Evening Bee* (Sacramento), February 13, 1907, 6; "Twenty Condemnation Suits Filed," *Evening Bee* (Sacramento), February 13, 1907, 6; "Railroads Begin Condemnation Proceedings," *Evening Bee* (Sacramento,) March 28, 1907, 1.

324 "Repair That Levee Break," *Sacramento Star*, September 4, 1907, 2; "Kripp Break to Be Closed," *Sacramento Star*, September 16, 1907, 5; "Plan to Close Kripp Break," *Sacramento Star*, October 7, 1907, 7; "State Aid Is to Be Given," *Evening Bee* (Sacramento), November 30, 1907, 12; "Yolo Supervisors Will Not Aid Kripp Levee Break Repairing," *Sacramento Bee*, September 4, 1907, 6.

325 "The Offer Was Spurned," *Evening Bee* (Sacramento), September 24, 1897, 1, (identifying J. Cal Ewing as manager of the Oakland Reliance).

326 "Getting Ready for Coast League Baseball Here," *Sacramento Star*, July 14, 1908, 7.; "Lots of Ball," *Los Angeles Evening Post-Record*, July 16, 1908, 6; "Coast League to Give Franchises," *Fresno Herald*, July 14, 1908, 5; "Coast League Expands Circuit at Meeting," *Oakland Tribune*, July 16, 1908, 10; "Baseball League Enlarges to Six Clubs for Season of 1909," *San Francisco Chronicle*, July 16, 1908, 8; "Coast League Standing," *Los Angeles Evening Express*, July 13, 1908, 12; "Tomorrow the Oaks Play the Shamrocks," *Stockton Daily Evening Record*, July 17, 1908, 4.

327 Kripp Wants to Back Coast League Team," *Sacramento Star*, April 20, 1908, 2.

328 Dennis Snelling, *The Greatest Minor League: A History of the Pacific Coast League, 1903–1957* (Jefferson, NC: McFarland, 2011), 1.

329 Says Sacramento Has No Franchise," *Sacramento Bee*, August 29, 1908, 1; "Sacramento Not Sure of Franchise," *Independent-Leader* (Sacramento), August 30, 1908, 8.

330 "Opposition League Prepares to Fight," *Independent-Leader* (Sacramento), June 14, 1908, 5.

331 "Grant Ed Kripp Sacramento Franchise," *Sacramento Star*, July 16, 1908, 7.

332 "Baseball Budget: Late Diamond Gossip from All Around the Circuit," *Sunday Leader* (Sacramento), June 14, 1908, 5.

333 "Begin Work on New Diamond," *Sacramento Star*, May 25, 1908, 7; "Rival Leagues Prepare for War," *Independent-Leader* (Sacramento), July 5, 1908, 4.

334 "Sport Notes," *Sacramento Star*, September 11, 1908, 7.

335 "Kripp's Gone to Get His Franchise," *Sacramento Star*, September 16, 1908, 7.

336 "Magnate M'Credie Stands by Guns," *The Bulletin* (San Francisco), September 18, 1908, 9.

337 "Kripp Can't Get Franchise," *Sacramento Star*, November 5, 1908, 7.

338 "Ewing Says Kripp Can Not Have a Franchise Next Year," *Sacramento Bee*, October 10, 1908, 20.

339 "Putting Another Team Here," *Sacramento Bee*, January 6, 1909, 11.

340 "Opposition League Prepares to Fight," *Sunday Leader* (Sacramento), June 14, 1908, 5.

341 "Are Handing It to Graham and Curtin," *Sacramento Star*, January 6, 1909, 7.

342 "Sacramento Formally Given the Franchise," *Sacramento Star*, January 23, 1909, 2.

343 "Coast League Season Opens Next Tuesday," *Sacramento Star*, March 27, 1909, 7.

344 "Good Ship Baseball Launched on Journey," *Sacramento Bee*, March 30, 1909, 1.

345 "Declare Kripp Is After the Coast League Franchise," *Sacramento Star*, August 20, 1909, 7.

346 "Declares Randle is Mistaken," *Sacramento Bee*, February 8, 1910, 14; "Railroads Acquire 700 Acres in Yolo," *Evening Bee*, April 12, 1907, 1.

347 "Will Ask Yolo and Sacramento to Share the Cost," *Evening Bee*, July 16, 1910, 19.

348 "Controversy on Baseball Grounds," *Sacramento Bee*, January 6, 1910, 5.

349 U.S. Bureau of the Census, Twelfth Census of the United States: 1900 and Thirteenth Census of the United States: 1910, Sacramento population schedules.

350 "Land Values on the Rise," *Sacramento Union*, May 28, 1974, 9; *Sacramento Bee*, March 4, 1912, 3.

351 "Coast League Has Caused Outlaw Baseball," *Sacramento Bee*, December 14, 1907, 16.

352 "Go Over Site for Proposed Ball Park," Sacramento Bee, December 28, 1909, 11.

353 "Ed Kripp Ready to Construct $25,000 Baseball Park Here," *Sacramento Bee*, December 22, 1909, 3.

354 "Booze and Baseball," *Sacramento Star*, December 28, 1909, 1.

355 "Ball Park Next to Cemetery Opposed," *Sacramento Star*, January 4, 1910.

356 "Controversy on Baseball Grounds," *Sacramento Bee*, January 6, 1910, 5.

357 "Are Looking into Kripp's Proposal," *Independent-Leader* (Sacramento), January 9, 1910, 5.

358 "Kripp Decides to Withdraw Application for Bar License," *Sacramento Bee*, January 17, 1910, 8; "The New Ball Park," *Independent-Leader* (Sacramento), January 9, 1910, 5.

[359] "Start Work on Ball Park. Baseball Club Gives Ed Kripp Cue to Commence," *Sacramento Bee*, January 17, 1910, 8.

[360] "Ed Kripp Ready to Construct $25,000 Baseball Park Here," *Sacramento Bee*, December 22, 1909, 3.

[361] "White Sox Soon to Come West," *Sacramento Bee*, February 9, 1910, 2.

[362] "White Sox Reach State Tuesday," *Independent-Leader* (Sacramento), February 27, 1910, 5.

[363] "The First Sound of Baseball Season," *Sacramento Bee*, March 7, 1910, 11.

[364] "Sacramento Falls Before Chicago White Sox," *Sacramento Bee*, March 9, 1910, 11.

[365] "White Sox Won in the Seventh Frame," *Sacramento Star*, March 9, 1910, 7.

[366] "Comiskey to Open Sacramento Park," *San Francisco Call*, March 8, 1910, 10.

[367] "Big Crowd at Second Game," *Sacramento Star*, March 9, 1910, 9.

[368] "Senators Line Against Sox in New Park," *Sacramento Star*, March 8, 1910, 7.

[369] "Sacramento Falls Before Chicago White Sox," *Sacramento Bee*, March 9, 1910, 11.

[370] "S. A. C. Gets Lease on Baseball Grounds," *Sacramento Bee*, July 30, 1910, 22; "Boxers of the Olympic Club Capture the P.A.A. Tourney," *Sacramento Bee*, November 23, 1910, 10.

[371] "Kripp Ties His Tiger Outside," *Sacramento Bee*, October 26, 1910, 11.

[372] "Proprietor of Saratoga Club Gives His Version of Shooting," *San Francisco Chronicle*, January 28, 1911, 2; "Ed Kripp, Gambler, Kills a Hold Up Man in His 'Club,'" *Bakersfield Californian*, January 27, 1911, 1.

[373] "No Gambling for Astredo," *Sacramento Bee*, February 17, 1908, 5.

[374] "Ed Kripp Slays Man in a Gambling Club Row at San Francisco," *Sacramento Bee*, January 27, 1911, 11; "Crazed by Loss in Police-Protected Gambling Resort, Victim Dies in Duel," *San Francisco Examiner*, January 28, 1911, 1.

[375] "Sensational Gambling Club Holdup Uncovers Big Police Scandal," *San Francisco Call*, January 28, 1911, 2.

[376] "Widow Tells of Gambling Curse," *San Francisco Examiner*, January 28, 1911, 2.

377 "Slain Man's Widow Sues for Benefit," *Bulletin* (San Francisco), August 22, 1913, 9.

378 "Widow Wants Headstone," *San Francisco Chronicle*, August 22, 1913, 10.

379 "Suit for Life Insurance," *Bulletin* (San Francisco), January 26, 1913, 24.

380 "Gambling Trial Against Police is Dropped," *San Francisco Examiner*, February 11, 1911, 2.

381 "Waseda Nine Lose Hard Game," *Independent-Leader*, October 2, 1910, 5.

382 "Tragedy Billed at Buffalo Park," *Independent-Leader* (Sacramento), October 2, 1910, 5.

383 "Notes of the Game," *Sacramento Bee*, October 22, 1913, 10.

384 "Too Much Money Says Ed Kripp," *Sacramento Star*, July 18, 1912, 2.

385 "4,500 Enthusiastic Fans Cheer Senators to 5 to 2 Victory," *Sacramento Bee*, April 2, 1913, 11.

386 "Pow-wow on Ball Park Soon: Ed Kripp Sees Drawbacks," *Sacramento Bee*, January 31, 1913, 12.

387 "Bradley Kicks at Slow Street Cars," *Sacramento Bee*, February 5, 1914, 1; Shawn Turner (Sacramento Historical Society), conversation with the author, March 24, 2026.

388 "Buffalo Park: Five-Year Extension Agreed Upon," *Sacramento Bee*, March 14, 1913, 14.

389 Dennis Snelling, *The Greatest Minor League: A History of the Pacific Coast League, 1903–1957* (Jefferson, NC: McFarland, 2011), 46, 57.

390 "Wolverton Enroute 'Home,'" *Sacramento Bee*, February 3, 1913, 9.

391 "Major League Ball at Buffalo Park; Senators Bathe Selves in Glory," *Sacramento Bee*, June 18, 1913, 10.

392 "Senators Wallop Oaks; Shinn Disabled and May Be Out of Game a Month," *Sacramento Bee*, June 20, 1913, 12.

393 "Slow Game Is Lost by Our Senators; Too Much Football; Munsell Hurt," *Sacramento Bee*, May 15, 1913, 13.

394 "Sacramento's Baseball Team Has High Place in All Departments of National Game," *Sacramento Bee*, November 15, 1913, 23.

395 "Notes of the Game," *Sacramento Bee*, October 22, 1913, 10.

[396] "Wolverton Working Quietly," *San Francisco Call Bulletin*, December 30, 1913, 7.

[397] "Baseball on Boards at Buffalo Park To-Day," *Sacramento Bee*, February 3, 1913, 9.

[398] "Senatorial Camp Begins to Look Like Business," *Sacramento Bee*, February 18, 1914, 10.

[399] "Plans Amusement Grounds on Present Buffalo Park Site," *Sacramento Bee*, February 7, 1914, 8.

[400] "Britton Admits Car Service Is Bad," *Sacramento Star*, March 27, 1914, 1.

[401] "Fans Figuring on Diamond Sport During 1915," *Sacramento Bee*, December 25, 1914, 13.

[402] "League Tries to Shift Blame," *Sacramento Bee*, September 2, 1914, 1.

[403] "Sacramentans to Launch Campaign to Secure Financial Backing," *Sacramento Bee*, September 26, 1914, 12.

[404] "Money Campaign to Decide Fate of Baseball Here," *Independent-Leader*, September 27, 1914, 5.

[405] "Mission Wolves, Our Boys No. 2, Make Good in New Home," *San Francisco Chronicle*, September 7, 1914, 8.

[406] "What's To Be Done with Missions," *Sacramento Bee*, September 22, 1914, 11; "Fate of Sacramento Coast League in Hands of Baseball Magnates To-day," *Sacramento Bee*, October 26, 1914, 12.

[407] "Sacramento Is Wiped Off the Diamond Map by the Coast Moguls," *San Francisco Call Bulletin*, October 27, 1914, 6.

[408] Dennis Snelling, *The Greatest Minor League: A History of the Pacific Coast League, 1903–1957* (Jefferson, NC: McFarland, 2011), 57; "Leavitt Thinks Well of Harry Wolverton," *San Francisco Chronicle*, October 29, 1914, 10.

[409] "No Honest Effort to Stop," *Sacramento Bee*, January 20, 1911, 12.

[410] "Policeman Too Drunk to Walk Along Streets," *Sacramento Bee*, January 25, 1911, 1.

[411] "Mrs. Kripp Gets $3,800 as Share," *Sacramento Bee*, February 1, 1911, 2.

[412] "Ed Kripp Gets Divorce Decree in San Francisco," *Sacramento Bee*, March 3, 1911, 1; "Ed Kripp Is Given Divorce," *Sacramento Star*, March 3, 1911, 1.

413 "Seeks Surcease from Her Woes," *Sacramento Bee*, February 20, 1911, 16; "Mrs. Kripp Attempts Suicide," *Sacramento Star*, February 20, 1911, 4.

414 "Ed Kripp Is Backing Mantell-Thompson Scrap," *Sacramento Bee*, June 24, 1912, 12.

415 "Wolgast Wants Purse of $25,000, Win, Lose or Draw," *Sacramento Bee*, July 10, 1912, 10.

416 "Rivers-Wolgast Battle Ends in Near-Riot," *Los Angeles Times*, July 5, 1912, 23.

417 "Rivers-Wolgast Battle Ends in Near-Riot," *Los Angeles Times*, July 5, 1912, 23; Advertisement for motion picture of Wolgast-Rivers fight, *Lancaster Daily Intelligencer*, September 3, 1912, 5.

418 "Beau Ormonde Runner, Falls Dead," *Sacramento Bee*, December 31, 1912, 10.

419 "Ed Kripp Is Ruled Off Vancouver Track: Attempted Bribery," *Sacramento Star*, July 9, 1913, 9.

420 "Ed Kripp's Horse Wins Another Race," *Sacramento Bee*, June 18, 1913, 10; "Orlin Kripp Is Champion 3-Year-Old," *Spokane Press*, June 17, 1913, 9.

421 "Hoffman Goes to Get Talent for Dec. Card," *Sacramento Star*, December 6, 1910, 7.

422 "Willie Meehan to Fight Next Main Event Battle Here," *Sacramento Bee*, September 22, 1916, 14.

423 "Boxing Promoters Do Not Seek the Old Pavilion, Says Kripp," *Sacramento Bee*, November 1, 1916, 15.

424 "Willie Meehan to Fight Charley Miller Tonight," *Sacramento Bee*, November 18, 1916, 13.

425 "Suit for $18,000 Being Tried by Judge Anderson," *Yolo Independent*, November 23, 1917, 5.

426 "Kripp Quits Boxing Game," *Sacramento Star*, December 4, 1916, 6.

427 "Florence Kripp a Feature Winner," *San Francisco Call Bulletin*, November 8, 1912, 14; "Orlin Kripp Is Champion 3-Year-Old," *Spokane Press*, June 17, 1913, 9.

428 "Coast League Teams to Play at Buffalo Park on Mondays," *Sacramento Star*, June 19, 1915, 6.

[429] "Sacramento Fans Will Honor Returning Star," *Sacramento Bee*, September 13, 1916, 11.

[430] "Official List of Auto Owners," *Sacramento Star*, March 25, 1916, 14; "Automobiles Collide," *Sacramento Star*, July 11, 1916, 5.

[431] Orlin Arthur Kripp, World War I Draft Registration Card, June 5, 1917, Sacramento County, California; Passenger List, Motor Truck Company No. 381, sailing October 23, 1918; National Archives and Records Administration.

[432] "Grand Jury Continues Case of Ed Kripp," *Sacramento Star*, May 7, 1918, 8.

[433] "Ahern Still Protects the Law Breakers," *Sacramento Bee*, January 23, 1911, 5.

[434] "Sacramento Gets Place in Pacific Coast League," *Sacramento Bee*, December 17, 1917, 1; "Training Season of Senators Opens Here Next Monday," *Sacramento Bee*, March 2, 1918, 12; "Solons Make Debut Here Tomorrow in Battle with Tigers," *Sacramento Bee*, April 1, 1918, 10.

[435] "Yolo's Monte Carlo," *Winters Express* (Winters, CA), July 17, 1903, 1.

[436] "Monte Carlo is Run for Casino," *Woodland Daily Democrat*, April 11, 1921, 2.

[437] "No Game in Progress," *Sacramento Union*, August 7, 1921, 1.

[438] "Kripp Fined $250 For Having Gaming Equipment," *Sacramento Bee*, August 12, 1921, 11.

[439] "Steve's Sports Shelf," *Sacramento Union*, February 21, 1942, 4.

[440] "Sacramento's New $75,000 Ballpark Nearing Completion," *Sacramento Union*, February 4, 1922, 5.

[441] "Moreing Announces Plan for $75,000 Baseball Stadium," *Stockton Daily Evening Record*, November 12, 1921, 12.

[442] "Ed Kripp Offers Land to City to Be Used for Municipal Baths," *Sacramento Bee*, February 2, 1922, 14.

[443] "Oldest Church in City to Go," *Sacramento Bee*, February 20, 1923, 1.

[444] "Last Services Today in Oldest Protestant Church in State," *Sacramento Union*, April 15, 1923, 18.

[445] "Last Hymn to Be Sung in Oldest Church," *Sacramento Star*, April 13, 1923, 4.

[446] "Another Landmark Passes," *Sacramento Union*, February 23, 1923, 4.

[447] "Boxing Auditorium to Stand on Site of Historic Church," *Sacramento Star,* February 21, 1923, 8.

[448] E. L. Kripp, "An Open Letter Concerning Congregational Church Site," *Sacramento Bee,* April 25, 1923, 31.

[449] "Pioneers Coming to Farewell Service in Old Church," *Sacramento Bee,* April 13, 1923, 18.

[450] "Last Hymn to Be Sung in Oldest Church," *Sacramento Star,* April 13, 1923, 4.

[451] "Last Services Today in Oldest Protestant Church in State," *Sacramento Union,* April 15, 1923, 18.

[452] "Old Church Cornerstone Found," *Sacramento Bee,* June 16, 1923; "Relics Dug Out of Church Ruins by New Owner," *Sacramento Union,* June 17, 1923, 4.

[453] "Will Build with Old Brick," *Sacramento Bee,* May 5, 1923, 39.

[454] "$200,000 Dance Pavilion to Open To-Morrow Night," *Sacramento Bee,* November 19, 1923, 2.

[455] Members of Carpenter's Local No. 586 to E. L. Kripp, November 10, 1923, published in "Dreamland-Dancing," *Sacramento Bee,* December 11, 1923, 4.

[456] Hale Bros., Inc. to Edward Kripp, December 6, 1923, published in "Dreamland-Dancing," *Sacramento Union,* December 12, 1923, 4.

[457] E. L. Kripp to R. D. Carpenter, Hale Bros., Inc., December 11, 1923, published in "Dreamland-Dancing," *Sacramento Union,* December 12, 1923, 4.

[458] "Society Gives Response to Charity Call! Dreamland Thronged," *Sacramento Bee,* February 23, 1924, 1.

[459] "Covered Wagon Club Will Give Charity Dance at Dreamland," *Sacramento Bee,* February 4, 1925, 14.

[460] "Veterans Invited to Take Part in Dance," *Sacramento Bee,* May 19, 1925, 10.

[461] "Big $25 Prize Waltz Contest," *Sacramento Bee,* January 23, 1926, 29.

[462] "Dreamland To Feature Novelty Dances To-night," *Sacramento Bee,* June 25, 1927, 30.

[463] Kripp To Install Miniature Golf Course at Dance Auditorium," *Sacramento Bee,* October 21, 1930, 17.

[464] "Trilby Indoor Golf Course Opens at Dreamland," *Sacramento Union*, November 28, 1930, 9.

[465] "Commenting on Passing Events," *Sacramento Bee*, December 10, 1930, 10.

[466] "Dreamland Plans Big Celebration on New Year's Eve," *Sacramento Bee*, December 27, 1930, 2.

[467] "Nothing Like It Anywhere — State Fair Visitors Don't Fail to See This Famous Restaurant," *Sacramento Bee*, September 8, 1934, 4.

[468] "China Tea Garden to Open To-Night," *Sacramento Bee*, September 2, 1933, 4.

[469] "All Are Game," *Sacramento Bee*, February 19, 1936.

[470] "City Manager Goes Sleuthing in Dance Halls," *Sacramento Bee*, October 7, 1933, 1.

[471] "Regular Police to Watch Dances," *Sacramento Bee*, December 2, 1933, 6.

[472] "News of Sacramento Told in Brief," *Sacramento Union*, December 25, 1938, 9.

[473] "Hallanan Orders Two Bookmakers on Races to Close," *Sacramento Bee*, May 1, 1936, 5.

[474] "Bookie Ban Is Sidetracked in Council Meeting," *Sacramento Bee*, May 15, 1936, 5.

[475] "Treasurer Lost in Yolo Monte Carlo Games," *Woodland Daily Democrat*, September 27, 1935, 1.

[476] Carol Ann Kripp Olson (grandmother of the author), in multiple conversations with the author, various dates.

[477] Kripp, Former Owner, Says He'll Sue," *Sacramento Union*, January 12, 1938, 9.

[478] "Cardinals Buy Solons' Field," *San Francisco Examiner*, January 12, 1938, 21.

[479] "Census Shows Big Gain in Sacramento Area," *Sacramento Bee*, January 21, 1942, 10.

[480] "Area Growth Alters City Pattern," *Sacramento Union*, November 25, 1942, 12.

481 Clark, Booth & Yardley Funeral Home, Mortuary record for Edward Lukens Kripp, San Francisco, February 20, 1942; digitized in "Sacramento, Sacramento, California, United States records," FamilySearch (image 112 of 544), accessed February 7, 2026.

482 "Grand Jury Returns True Bill Against Dr. Walter J. Henesey," *San Francisco Chronicle*, October 8, 1910, 4.

483 "Henesey's Victim is Ready to Testify," *San Francisco Chronicle*, April 21, 1911, 20.

484 "Says Henesey Wants Meeting," *San Francisco Chronicle*, October 1, 1910, 4.

485 "Dr. Henesey 'Crazy' Is Jury's Verdict," *San Francisco Call*, May 10, 1911, 18.

486 "Jay Hughes, 50, Former Baseball Hero, Found Dead," *Sacramento Bee*, June 2, 1924, 1.

487 "Dreamland Dance Hall Operators, B Girls Are Fined," *Sacramento Bee*, June 30, 1953, 21.

488 "Check of Building Permit Before Issuance," *Sacramento Bee*, April 8, 1966, 17.

489 "Hearing on Moving Dance Hall Is Set," *Sacramento Bee*, May 17, 1968, 25.

490 "Bill Conlin's Column," *Sacramento Union*, November 4, 1973, 33.

491 "Olive Branch Election," *Evening Bee* (Sacramento), December 11, 1896, 4.

492 "Red Men Celebrate Washington's Birthday," *Sacramento Bee*, February 23, 1898, 2; "Last Night's Installations," *Sacramento Daily Record-Union*, January 14, 1898, 4.

493 "Fire Destroys Famous Resort," *Evening Bee* (Sacramento), June 6, 1898, 5.

494 "The Last of the Romantic Line of Knightly Gamblers," *Sacramento Bee*, November 27, 1914, 5.

495 "Wolgast Wins Lightweight Championship," *Oakland Tribune*, February 23, 1910, 12

496 "Wolgast Wins Lightweight Championship against Nelson in 40 Rounds," *Chicago Daily Tribune*, February 23, 1910, 14.

[497] "Lightweight Championship Results," *Los Angeles Daily Times,* July 5, 1912, 24.

[498] "Ad Wolgast Dies," *Los Angeles Times,* Fri, April 15, 1955, 1.

[499] "A Real Deal Called Mexican Joe Rivers," *Los Angeles Times,* June 25, 1999, 161.

[500] "Charley Doyle New Secretary," *Sacramento Union,* January 10, 1920, 7.

[501] "Beating About Bushers," *Sacramento Union,* October 22, 1933, 13; "Better Baseball Budding," *Sacramento Union,* January 6, 1934, 8; "Benefit Game Shaping Up," *Sacramento Union,* June 5, 1935, 6.

[502] "News and Comment of the World of Sports," *Sacramento Union,* April 11, 1920, 10.

[503] "Charlie Doyle Night Must Wait Another Year," *Sacramento Union,* July 19, 1948, 4.

[504] "Newton Kripp Rites Friday," *Sacramento Bee,* March 11, 1943, 5.

[505] "Kripp Cleared of Extortion," *Sacramento Bee,* February 20, 1917, 2.

[506] "Fred Kripp Fined $150 by Van Fleet," *Sacramento Bee,* May 11, 1920, 1.

[507] "Fred Kripp, Ex-Police Officer, Dies in Hospital," *Sacramento Bee,* September 27, 1934, 5.

[508] "'49 Pioneers at Reunion," *Sacramento Bee,* May 25, 1922, 1.

[509] "Woman Here in 1849 Observes 90th Birthday," *Sacramento Bee,* December 10, 1932, 5.

[510] "Oldest Capital Resident Dies at Age of 94," *Sacramento Bee,* February 15, 1937, 4.

[511] "Hair Studio Notice," *Evening Bee* (Sacramento), March 21, 1905, 8.

[512] "Personal Notes," *Sacramento Bee,* September 2, 1907, 5.

[513] "Summons," *The Recorder* (San Francisco), February 24, 1911, 23.

[514] "Closed by Creditors," *San Francisco Chronicle,* July 5, 1903, 27.

[515] "Marathon In New Home," *San Francisco Chronicle,* January 14, 1913, 9.

[516] "Groundbreaking is Set for Ball Park Site Store," Sacramento Bee, May 10, 1964, 76.

[517] R. E. Graswich, "Buried Treasure: Target Parking Lot Hides a Golden Past," *Inside Sacramento,* May 2023, https://insidesacramento.com/buried-treasure/.

518 Dennis Snelling, *The Greatest Minor League: A History of the Pacific Coast League, 1903–1957* (Jefferson, NC: McFarland, 2019), 58, 80, 83.
519 Paul J. Zingg, *Runs, Hits, and an Era: The Pacific Coast League, 1903–1958* (Urbana: University of Illinois Press, 1990); Michael Shapiro, *The Last Good Season: Brooklyn, the Dodgers, and Their Final Pennant Race Together* (New York: Doubleday, 2003).
520 Richard Ben Cramer, *Joe DiMaggio: The Hero's Life* (New York: Simon & Schuster, 2000), 94–105; Leigh Montville, *Ted Williams: The Biography of an American Hero* (New York: Doubleday, 2004), 48–55.
521 "Here is What Moreing Field Looks Like, When She's All Lit Up," *Sacramento Union*, June 5, 1930, 1.
522 "Senators Blank Oakland in First Night Game, 8-0," *Sacramento Bee*, June 11, 1930.
523 Dennis Snelling, *The Greatest Minor League: A History of the Pacific Coast League, 1903–1957* (Jefferson, NC: McFarland, 2019), 134.
524 "Steve's Sports Shelf – I Hope I'm Wrong," *Sacramento Union*, May 5, 1934, 9.
525 "Lewis Moreing, Former Solons Owner, Expires," *Sacramento Bee*, May 27, 1935, 1.
526 "Cardinal Field New Name of Ballpark," *Sacramento Union*, March 9, 1936, 6.
527 "Baseball Season Will Start Here Tomorrow—For Brand New Solons." *Sacramento Bee*, March 27, 1936, 28.
528 1937 Pacific Coast League Standings, *StatsCrew*, accessed February 19, 2026. https://www.statscrew.com/minorbaseball/standings/l-PCL/y-1937; "Sacramento Solons," *Baseball-Reference Bullpen*, accessed February 19, 2026. https://www.baseball-reference.com/bullpen/Sacramento_Solons
529 "Solons Come from Behind to Win First Pennant," *Sacramento Bee*, September 21, 1942, 10.
530 Dennis Snelling, *The Greatest Minor League: A History of the Pacific Coast League, 1903–1957* (Jefferson, NC: McFarland, 2019), 200; "Sport: Sacramento's Saviors." *Time*, March 1944.
531 "Solonville – Seattle, Sacramento Begin Series at Doubleday Park," *Sacramento Union*, May 16, 1944, 4.

[532] "Edmonds Field Drive Started by Local Club," *Sacramento Union*, August 9, 1945, 4; On the successive names and redevelopment of the Sacramento ballpark site—Buffalo Park, Moreing Field, Cardinal Field, Doubleday Field, and Edmonds Field—and its destruction by fire in 1948, see *Sacramento Bee*, June 11, 1930; March 9, 1936; March 15, 1944; September 10, 1945; July 24, 1948.

[533] "Edmonds Field Destroyed by Fire," *Sacramento Union*, July 12, 1948, 1; "Fire Levels Edmonds Field; Homes Damaged," *Sacramento Bee*, July 12, 1948, 1.

[534] "Spectacular Fire Levels Edmonds Field," *Sacramento Bee*, July 12, 1948, 1; "Edmonds Field Destroyed in Raging Ocean of Flame," *Sacramento Union*, July 12, 1948, 1.

[535] Paul J. Zingg, *Runs, Hits, and an Era: The Pacific Coast League, 1903–1958* (Urbana: University of Illinois Press, 1990).

[536] "Between the Lines," *Sacramento Bee*, April 9, 1964, 67; "Gemco Store will Open Tomorrow," *Sacramento Bee*, October 28, 1964, 52.

[537] "Solons Pay Rent for Hughes Use," *Sacramento Union*, October 22, 1975, 27.

[538] Sullivan, Neil J. *The Dodgers Move West*. New York: Oxford University Press, 1987.

[539] Murphy, Robert. After Many a Summer: The Passing of the Giants and Dodgers and a Golden Age in New York Baseball. New York: Sterling, 2009.

[540] Michael Shapiro, *The Last Good Season: Brooklyn, the Dodgers, and Their Final Pennant Race Together* (New York: Doubleday, 2003); *The Boom and Bust of Hope: The Pacific Coast League and What Might Have Been* (Society for American Baseball Research, 2025).

[541] "Did the Bee Give the River Cats Sufficient Coverage?," *Sacramento Bee*, September 24, 2000, 166.

[542] "Oakland A's," *Sacramento Bee*, April 5, 2024, A6.

[543] "Art Savage is the Quiet Force Behind the Success of His River Cats," *Sacramento Bee*, Sept. 19, 2000, L1; "Cats: Stadium Changes on the Way," *Sacramento Bee*, April 11, 2004, 20.

Index

About the Author

LISA JONSSON is a writer and independent researcher whose work explores the early history of professional baseball on the Pacific Coast. Through extensive archival research in newspapers, photographs, and public records, she reconstructs the stories of California's early baseball era and the entrepreneurs who shaped it.

She is a member of the Society for American Baseball Research and contributes to its *Nineteenth Century Notes* and BioProject initiatives.

Ed Kripp—whose life forms the center of this book—was her great-great-grandfather.

We would love to hear from you! If this story restonated with you, please visit the author at: www.giltedgeofambition.com.

www.ingramcontent.com/pod-product-compliance
Lightning Source LLC
Chambersburg PA
CBHW030020260726
48782CB00025B/244

9798994842614